Pure Bunkum

Reporting on the life and crimes of Buncombe County Sheriff Bobby Lee Medford

by Cecil Bothwell

Brave Ulysses Books
2008

Pure Bunkum
EAN-13: 978-0-615-26030-3
Copyright © 2008 by Cecil Bothwell
All rights reserved
cover art/design by the author

Brave Ulysses Books
POB 1877
Asheville, North Carolina 28802
braveulysses.com

also by the author
•*Gorillas in the Myth: A Duck Soup Reader*
2000/second edition 2008
•*The Icarus Glitch: Another Duck Soup Reader*
2001
•*Finding Your Way in Asheville*
2005/2009
•*The Prince of War: Billy Graham's Crusade for
a Wholly Christian Empire*
2007
•*Garden My Heart: Organic Strategies for
Backyard Sustainability*
2008
•*Can we have archaic and idiot? A collection of
fictitious tropes*
2009

Pure Bunkum

The Cast

Bobby Lee Medford-Sheriff ➡$☺,

Family/Friends
Judi McMahan Bell☹➡$
James Bell☆
Robert Bell☆
Jerry Biddix◀ⁱ
David Brown ꞁ ◀ⁱ
Bob Carter
Betty Donoho☹◀ⁱ
Charles Hazelett
Ron Honeycutt◀ⁱ
Larry McMahan☆◀ⁱ
Phillip McMahan☆
Jeff Medford
Brian Medford☺
Frank Orr✷!!➡$ꞁ◀ⁱ
Cynthia Roberts◀ⁱ

Officials who knew?
Roy Cooper, Attorney General
Kate Dreher, Asst. D.A.
David Gantt, County Commission
Wanda Greene, County Mgr.
Bill Hogan, Asheville Police Chief
Ron Kaylor, ALE ♥
Charles Moody, SBI ♥
Ron Moore, D.A.
Carol Peterson, County Commission
Nathan Ramsey, Commission Chair◀ⁱ
Bill Stanley, County Commission
David Young, County Commission

Famous actors
James Garner✷!!
Jack Lemon✷!!

BCSD Employees
Tracy Bridges ☆◀ⁱ☺,
Lester Bullock◀ⁱ
Kay Carter☹
Harry Clay ✪➡$
"Butch" Davis☆➡$ꞁ☺,◀ⁱ
Brenda Fraser☆
Don Fraser☆
James Grant☆◀ⁱ
Johnny Harrison☆➡$ꞁ☺,
Pat Hefner☆◀ⁱ
Rhonda House☹
Julie Kepple
Charles Long ✪
Jerry Miller ♥ ☆ꞁ◀ⁱ
Cody Muse ♥ ☆
Guy Penland✷!!➡$☺,
Walt Robertson ✷!!✪◀ⁱ
George Stewart☆◀ⁱ➡$ꞁ◀ⁱ
Sharon Stewart☹◀ⁱ
Mike Ruby ✪
Robert Robinson☆
Bill Stafford☆
Brian Styles☆
Buck Lyda ✪➡$
Mike Bustle ✪
Lee Farnsworth☆◀ⁱ
Homer Honeycutt ☹✪➡$◀ⁱ

Woodfin Police Dept.
Rob Austin☆
Pete Bradley, Chief ♥✪

Federal Judges
Thomas Selby Ellis, III
Dennis Howell

Machine owners/employees

Anna Deaton
James Henderson $☞
Barry Henderson $☞
Jim Lindsey $☞
Charles McBennett, Jr.
Charles McBennett, Sr. $☞
Jerry Pennington✶!!$☞
Jackie Shepherd☹✶!!📢$☞
Demetre Theodossis✶!!$☞
Dennis Theodossis $☞
Kaye Shepherd☹
Denver Shepherd

Hosted machines

Imran Alam✶!!$☞
Nick Anagnostopoulos✶!!$☞
Alvin Ledford✪$☞
Jack O'Leary$☞

Defense attorneys

Paul Bidwell
Sean Devereaux
M. Victoria Jayne
Stephen Lindsay
Bob Long

U.S. Attorneys

Richard Edwards, Asst.
Corey Ellis, Asst.
Gretchen Shappert, U.S.A.

FBI

Van Gill 🛡 ⛳
Andrew Grafton🛡
Kevin B. Kendrick🛡
Patrick Kirby🛡
Michael Kniffen 🛡
Michael McNeely 🛡
Rick Schwein 🛡

IRS

Eric Veater

Victims

Marvis Gail Davidson, denied prescription medication, died in jail
Carlos Payne, denied critical medication, prison time on false charges
Joey Max Rogers, died of broken neck "alone" in jail cell
Nisha Sherlin, allegedly beaten by sheriff's son, covered up

Key

Buncombe Deputy ☆
"Special" Deputy ✶!!
Former law officer ✪
Federal/state officer 🛡
Gambled with Medford ☹
Campaign worker/contributor 📢
Received illegal funds ☚$
Paid illegal funds to Medford $☞
Played golf ⛳
Convicted 🕐,

to Brian Sarzynski
who got there first

Table of Contents

"Bunkum, like lyin', is plaguy [disagreeably] apt to make a man believe his own bams [lies] at last. From telling 'em so often, he forgets whether he grow'd 'em or dreamt 'em, and so he stands' right up on end, kisses the book, and swears to 'em, as positive as the Irishman did to the gun, which he said he know'd ever since it was a pistol.

"Now, —that's Bunkum."

—Thomas Chandler Haliburton
The Attache; or, Sam Slick in England, 1843

Introduction

In 1820, Representative Felix Walker, a Waynesville, North Carolina, native whose congressional district included Buncombe County, unintentionally contributed a word to the English language. The U.S. Congress had engaged in a lengthy debate on the Missouri Compromise and members of the House called for an immediate vote on that important question. But Walker rose to deliver a rambling and completely irrelevant speech, refusing to yield the floor and insisting that his constituents expected him to make a speech "for Buncombe."

A colleague later remarked that Walker's untimely oration was not just for Buncombe--it "was Buncombe." The word morphed into "bunkum" and then "bunk," and quickly entered popular usage in England as seen in the Haliburton quote on the facing page.

It would seem that few people are immune to belief in their own lies, a tendency that fueled Abraham Lincoln's famous observation that, "No man has a good enough memory to make a successful liar." After many years following the rise and fall of Buncombe County's most famously crooked lawman, I have concluded that he was completely convinced of his own righteousness, and that the all too human failure of memory was part of his undoing.

Linguistic and legal ties between England and her former colonies were and are thoroughgoing. During the federal trial of Bobby Lee Medford, sheriff of Buncombe County from 1994 to 2006, the first government witness was Eddie Caldwell, Executive Vice President and General Counsel of the North Carolina Sheriff's Association. Caldwell testified that the office of Sheriff is the oldest elective position in North Carolina. He explained that it originated in English Common Law and remains today as the most powerful and independent office in the state. No one oversees a sheriff, and all department employees are enlisted or dismissed at the sheriff's pleasure.

What Caldwell did not mention is that the office we are familiar with today has swelled far beyond the position originally outlined in the state's constitution and general statutes. Under the authorizing law, a North Carolina sheriff is required to receive and serve process, serve summons, and manage the county jail. In the absence of a coroner, the sheriff was required to fill that role as well. Period.

All of the patrol and enforcement powers we generally associate with a sheriff's department have been gradually tacked on by state and municipal governments. While the sheriff's overall budget is provided by a county's board of commissioners, as a practical matter much of the spending and more of the actual function of the department is widely discretionary. There is plenty of room for mischief, and North Carolina's sheriffs have a colorful history of crime and corruption. Medford is one of the unlucky few who got caught.

Bobby Lee Medford often claimed that his best friend in the world was an old, one-eyed green parrot named Miss Meredith. If so, the fate of his dear bird during his prison term must be one of the sadder thoughts weighing on his mind today. Then too, he leaves behind an extended family which includes an ex-wife, two sons and four grandchildren as well as a long-time girlfriend and her children. Former employees have told me that he was a doting grandfather.

No matter how you look at it, Bobby Medford was what you'd have to call a scofflaw. He held himself above the rules. Even as his trial wound down, his ultimate conviction looming as all but certain to any reasonable observer, he insisted that he had a right to collect and distribute cash to those he deemed deserving: Tax law be damned.

Most visible, perhaps, was the cigarette habit which he continuously indulged in his office despite a municipal government ban on smoking inside county buildings. The staining and stench were so bad that incoming Sheriff Van Duncan had to have the place scoured and painted before he could stomach moving in.

Meanwhile Medford used his county car as his personal vehicle and drove it where and when he liked. Operating a Buncombe County vehicle outside of the municipality on other than county business is a crime under local law. Medford routinely drove it to Harrah's Cherokee Casino to gamble, to South Carolina to visit his hairdresser, to pick up his grandchildren wherever they happened to be, and, by two accounts, to Mississippi to gamble at another of Harrah's establishments. During his trial he stated that he interpreted his job to be 24/7 because he could always be reached by phone. That apparently made the Mississippi jaunt a business trip.

Furthermore, Medford drove his county car under the influence of powerful painkillers, another explicit violation of county law.

Then too, he lived with his girlfriend, in contravention of the state law banning cohabitation—not that the rule is much enforced in the modern era. However, at least one of Medford's deputies took wide exception to his living arrangement, and quit because of it. She had been assigned as a school resource officer and later told me, "How could I tell these young girls that sleeping around was a bad idea, or talk about the importance of obeying the rules, when the sheriff was shacking up, explicitly violating the law?"

But such abuses, while flagrant, fall in the realm of personal behavior, and it could be argued that they are therefore of a somewhat different order than those that impacted the public weal.

When Bobby Lee Medford went down, he went down hard. There is still no accurate accounting for hundreds of thousands of dollars that changed hands in back rooms and parking lots or disappeared from the county evidence locker. The federal prosecution only went as far as necessary to secure a conviction: there were no charges filed concerning illegal card games, sports betting, or, for that matter, a healthy chunk of the video poker industry that proved his undoing. Then there are the drugs missing from evidence kits of upward of 1,000 criminal investigations, and, too, the guns— hundreds of handguns, shotguns, rifles and automatic weapons that mysteriously evaporated while in his care.

The final chapters of this book present a detailed look at the federal trial of Bobby Lee Medford and Guy Kenneth Penland. I found the proceedings fascinating for the perspective offered on how the government stitched together its case. The FBI didn't stop with the bank slip or the poker machine receipt, but tracked down the wait-ress who served coffee to conspirators in a Waffle House often enough to identify them in court. They didn't leave much to chance.

By most accounts, Medford is intensely loyal and generous with his family and friends. He gained a reputation for public generosity during his twelve years in office as well, doling out money to beggars and arranging delivery of heating oil to needy elders in the community. His sons and their ex-wives reportedly lined up on Med-ford's paydays to receive their share of his largess.

To the end, Bobby Lee Medford held himself out as a sort of latter-day Robin Hood. His tax return for 2006 listed $45,000 in charitable donations. But the victims he left in his wake were commoners, not kings, and included the county's taxpayers, shopkeepers and families impoverished by addictive gambling—given that video poker may be the most addictive form of wagering. Far from playing Robin of the Wood, Medford was a real-life Sheriff of Nottingham.

1: Nothing happened

The patrol car kicked up loose gravel as it climbed the steep driveway that led to a smoke blue mobile home. When the engine died, a deputy sheriff climbed out and walked toward an ambulance crew already on the scene. The two EMS workers were conversing with a young woman whose small daughter clung to her leg. As the officer approached the group, another male figure started up the drive on foot.

"Nobody home," one of the medical crew members reported.

"Did you go in?" the deputy queried.

"Locked tight. And we figured there could be trouble," came the reply. "She told us the victim drove away." He gestured toward the woman. "And the boy-friend, too. But we figured we should wait for you."

The fellow coming uphill called out, "I own this place! Some kind of trouble?"

The deputy was noncommital. "Maybe so."

"She was hurt pretty bad," the woman offered. "She ran down to my house. She was bleeding."

Two more cruisers came up the road. One circled and the two parked belly to belly, blocking the drive. The drivers' windows were open. Neither deputy emerged.

The landlord had joined the group. "Some kind of trouble?" he repeated.

Offering little, the deputy demurred. "Could be."

The woman spoke again. "She drove off in her car. He went off with some men in a truck."

"Locked up tight," added the EMS driver.

The deputy accepted a key offered by the landlord and assured the group, "I'll take care of it from here." He spoke into a radio clipped on his shoulder and ambled to a weathered set of wooden steps. climbing to the landing. He knocked a rapid staccato on the door and waited. Again. No response. He turned the key and opened the door a few inches.

"Anybody here?"

Glancing down at the interior knob he noted brownish smeared stains, and called again, "Anybody home?" He pulled on a pair of surgical rubber gloves, swung the door open and stepped inside.

A smashed mirror hung askew on the opposite wall and thick shards of glass protruded from the paneling. The shards matched what remained of a coffee table top that bore the same red-brown smudges as the doorknob. Lamp shades were smashed flat, and the fluted glass globe of an overhead light lay broken in a dozen pieces. A dark hand print on the front wall caught his attention and, as his gaze swept the room, he saw a tee-shirt, shorts, a brassiere, a couple of towels and curtains pulled halfway from the rod, all with similar stains.

He followed a bloody swipe down the hall, four fingers had trailed across pale paneling to the bedroom door. Inside that room the bed was canted with its lower legs broken to the floor. Torn sheets were tied to the bedstead, head and foot, and shared the same telltale smears. The bedside table was piled with prescription pill bottles which had spilled onto the floor. Others were visible beneath the bed. A closer look showed that the bottles bore the names of four different patients all ordered up by the same doctor.

Oxycontin.

In the bathroom, the toilet tank lid had been smashed across the base. Brown spots on the dry porcelain faded into pinkish water in the bowl. The mirror above the sink was shattered in a starburst. A few stray hairs stuck to the glass suggested that the battering ram had been a human head.

Walking back up the hall the deputy noted brown spots on the vinyl flooring and more pill bottles in the kitchen where he picked up a purse and cell phone. He left by way of the door where he'd entered, pushing the button so the door locked when he clicked it shut. He stripped off his gloves, and returned to the waiting EMS crew.

"You're right. Nobody home," he said. "This purse must belong to Sherlin, will you give it to her?" He handed it off to the landlord and spoke to the emergency crew. "Nothing happening here."

The ambulance and the other sheriff's cars headed off as the deputy returned to the cruiser to fetch a roll of crime-scene tape. He tied yellow "Police Line" streamers across the trailer's front and back porches and then returned to his regular patrol, reporting completion of his assignment to the Buncombe County Sheriff's Department dispatcher as he pulled out onto Old Leicester Highway.

The transcript of that call is dated 10-01-02, 1:16 p.m.

"RESIDENCE WAS VACANT//LANDLORD MET WITH US TO ALLOW ENTRY. SPOKE TO FEMALE ON PHONE AND SHE REFUSED TO GIVE HER LOCATION TO MYSELF OR EMS. FEMALE SOUNDED INTOXICATED ON THE PHONE. NO SIGNS OF ASSAULT IN RESIDENCE RE INJURIES THOUGH NEIGHBORS STATE SHE RAN TO HER HOUSE WITH VISIBLE INJURIES. NO STATEMENT MADE TO ASSAULT."

It's unclear from the transcript exactly who made "no statement," presumably the missing victim. The transcript of another communication with the dispatcher, an hour *earlier*, stated:

"UNIT 1 OFFICE HAS BEEN ADVISED THE SHERIFF SON THE COMPLT WAS ASHELY WILLIAMS AT 8 MINK FARM ROAD SHE ADVISE THE FEMALE WAS BLEEDING FROM THE HEAD BUT SHE DID NOT KNOW HER NAME SHE ADVISE THAT THE MALE WAS THE SHERIFF SON."

Minutes later a call came in from another car:

"THIS WAS JEFF MEDFORD THE SHERIFF SON AFTER CALLING COMPLT BACK THE NUMBER IS 7 MINK FARM RD EMS COULD FIND THE PATIENT."

The radio transcript notwithstanding, when Buncombe County Emergency Services had arrived at the trailer, at 12:23 p.m., there was nobody home. They *could not* find the "patient." EMS had responded to Williams' phone call in which she reported that her neighbor had burst into her home bleeding and bruised, claiming that her boyfriend, Jeff Medford, had beaten her. She told the operator, "She has blood coming from her head, her throat and stuff is cut, and she's got bruises all over."

Williams later told me that she had heard her young daughter screaming. She hurried up the hall to find a woman standing in her living room. She told me the stranger was bleeding from her head and neck, and was bruised and battered. The stranger pulled up her clothing to reveal more injuries and said, "He's been beating me for three days."

Although the transcript is date-stamped at 1:16, other BCSD documents indicate that no deputy arrived before 1:53 p.m. Meanwhile a *second* incident involving the "patient," Nisha Gail Sherlin, was clocked in by the Woodfin Police department at exactly 1:53. That accident scene, in Woodfin, is a twenty minute drive from Mink Farm Road, even for a woman in a hurry.

Sherlin was in a hurry.

Leaving Williams' home, Sherlin had run back up the hill to her trailer. Addled from days of drugging and beating, she had escaped her bonds while Jeff was away, but now she was desperate to leave the scene before he returned. She jumped into her Volkswagen Rabbit and sped away, careening along back country roads and New and Old Leicester Highways. I would later learn she had picked up a friend, returned to the trailer, gone to her mother's home, dropped off the friend—somewhere—and raced on to the intersection of Elkwood Avenue and Lake-shore Drive where she shot past a red light and rear-ended a Hummer.

The Rabbit was totaled.

According to the official accident report, Sherlin leaped from her vehicle and pounded on the door of another car stopped at the light. Sherlin would later explain to me that she was desperate to get away. Given the close relationship between her boyfriend's father, Sheriff Bobby Medford, and the Woodfin police, that police department didn't represent anything that looked like help to her. Whereas the driver of the car she had approached regarded her behavior as assaultive, Sherlin said she was begging for a ride.

The Woodfin accident report noted, "No injuries to either party." However, an ambulance was summoned, and Sherlin was packed off to St. Joseph's Hospital, just south of downtown Asheville.

The odd coincidence of time on the two reports might or might not suggest collusion, as might the police report of "no injuries," whereas Sherlin had left her neighbor's home with blood running from her head.

But the record was about to become stranger still.

Soon Sherlin lay in bed surrounded by a medical team. They had treated her wounds, some of which were fresh, and had taken careful note of her condition, all while attempting to calm her down. A deputy had been dispatched to the hospital and a report of the officer's first interview with Sherlin indicates that the patient was extremely confused and probably drugged. In the space on the form labeled, "How Attacked or Committed," the deputy wrote, "suspect kicked females legs."

In the body of the report one reads, "Victim advises she was assaulted by suspect last night or the night before when she got into an argument with suspect. Victim believes it to be possibly Sunday [it was Tuesday] and advises she slept for 2 days on the bed without the frame; victim advises the frame was there before. Victim believes suspect drugged her but did not see him give her anything. Victim advises at some point suspect kicked her legs with steel toe boots and hit her in the head, she also believes suspect cut her neck and hand with a piece of glass but she doesn't know where the glass came from."

The deputy also noted, "Victim was transported to St. Joseph's after being involved in a motor vehicle accident," and reported that she took photos of the injuries.

Then the reporting officer requested the assignment of Deputy Brenda Fraser to the case.

The request made sense because Fraser was the domestic violence Victim's Assistance Coordinator at the Buncombe County Sheriff's Department. But the request was strange in another way. Medical records would later come to light that indicated Deputy Fraser had arrived at the hospital *before* Sherlin and that *Fraser* had actually conducted the initial interview. The report was, at best, inaccurate.

"Inaccurate" would come to feel like a very generous interpretation. "Fraudulent" seemed more apt.

As I would come to understand in ensuing months, the law enforcement agency paperwork was an after-the-fact addition bearing no certain correlation to events in the real world.

2: A very short phone call

My office phone rang a little past noon, October 3, 2002. "I'm calling from a phone booth," the caller said. "There's something you need to know. A woman named Nisha Sherlin was admitted to St. Joseph's yesterday. She claims she was beaten for a week by Jeff Medford, the sheriff's son. They're covering it up. Yesterday they took her to Broughton. The beating took place on Mink Farm Road in Leicester."

"How do you know this?" I asked, and was answered with a click.

I was then managing editor of Asheville's weekly newspaper, *Mountain Xpress*, and though I had only assumed the position six weeks earlier, I had reported for the paper since the late 80s and had received my share of phone tips and rumors of bad behavior on the part of Sheriff Medford, who was first elected in 1994. Brian Sarzynski, a reporter at the paper and my office-mate, had written at least two stories about the sheriff's bizarre conduct before I became editor. Sarz had even been personally threatened by the lawman after he reported on Medford's over-the-top behavior at a public protest, an "honor" I wouldn't share for another two weeks.

The tips typically involved gambling, guns, drugs and money. This call was different, however, because of its specificity. Instead of a vague rumor, this was something I could presumably verify.

I phoned the hospital and struck out. Sherlin wasn't a current patient and they couldn't tell me if she ever had been. Then I phoned the sheriff's office, where I was informed that nothing had happened.

I sat back and asked myself, "Why Broughton?"

Broughton Hospital is a state mental health facility located in Morganton, North Carolina, some sixty miles distant from Asheville. My immediate surmise was that it would be a fine place to keep someone out of sight and out of reach of the media.

I called that hospital to learn when they permitted visitors and in the early evening on Sunday, October 6, I stepped up to the desk at Broughton, asked to see Nisha Sherlin and handed over my I.D.

"Are you a family member or a friend?"

"A friend," I replied, feeling friendly-disposed, at least, toward any victim of an alleged violent crime.

I was permitted to enter through a locked door and rode an elevator to the designated floor. Going through another locked door into a sterile, cheaply furnished and well-worn waiting area, I was asked my business by an attendant and Sherlin was summoned. The double doors to the ward were wide open and I could see the 25-year-old approaching, peering expectantly, looking for a familiar face. She looked a little confused when she arrived and found that a stranger was the only visitor. Her neck and arms were mottled with bruises and there was a raw looking slash across her throat.

"Nisha?" I asked, and she nodded, "My name is Cecil Bothwell. I write for the *Mountain Xpress* news ..."

Before I finished my sentence she turned and fled back into the ward, shrieking, "He's a reporter! Get rid of him! He's a reporter!"

A stern-faced aide unlocked the door and stood aside while I exited. I hastened to retrace my way out of the building, wondering all the while if I had broken some law and half expecting to be accosted by armed, uniformed guards. However, I made my retreat without incident and I knew two things for certain. Something unpleasant had befallen Nisha Sherlin and my mystery informant wasn't simply a crank caller.

The next morning I contacted Buncombe County Emergency Services and requested a transcript of a 911 call to Mink Farm Road on October first. Forty-five minutes later I had copies of both the call and the written report in hand. What's more, I picked up another tip. The operator who handed over the transcript asked, "You know about the other call? In Woodfin?"

Soon I had a second report as well as tape recordings. Meanwhile I left a phone message at the sheriff's department asking for transcripts of their radio transmissions for October first. That call was never returned.

However, the EMS transcripts and tapes gave me what I needed to move forward.

911 call center: "911. Fire, police or medical?"
Williams: "Um, I don't really know who I have to talk to, police or medical assistance. The lady who lives above me just came down to my house and her husband's beat her really bad."
911 call center: "OK. Does she need an ambulance?"
Williams: "Um, yeah. She's bleeding from her head."
911 call center: "She is bleeding from her head?"
Williams: "Yeah."
911 call center: "OK, what's your address?"
Williams: "Eight Mink Farm Road."
911 call center: "What's your telephone number there?"
[Gives phone number.]
Williams: "If the police could hurry, I'm kind of nervous, being I've got my daughter here, and that man's still up at her house."
911 call center: "How old is she?"
Williams: "How old is she? She looks to be maybe about 30."

911 call center:"30?"

Williams: "Yes."

911 call center: "She is conscious and breathing?"

Williams: "Yes, she ran down here. I believe she has other medical conditions. That she is on other medications."

911 call center:"OK."

Williams: "He's right up above us and I'm afraid he's gonna come down here."

911 call center:"OK, I'm going to get an ambulance started to you, but stay on the line with me while I transfer you to the sheriff's department. OK?"

Williams: "OK." [Phone rings as call is transferred to Buncombe County Sheriff's Department.]

Sheriff's department: "Sheriff's office, 911. You have an emergency?"

Williams: "Uh, yes. This lady that lives above me, she's just come down here, and her husband's beat her really bad, or her boyfriend, I don't know one, which one. But I'm afraid he's gonna come down here and I think something else is wrong with her. She has blood coming from her head, her throat and stuff is cut, and she's got bruises all over."

Sheriff's department: "OK, this is on Mink Farm Road? [Silence—an unexplained blank spot on tape— then the voices resume at a different sound level.]

Sheriff's department: "What number do you think it is?"

Williams: "Seven Mink Farm Road "She lives up above us."

Sheriff's department: "What's the girl that's been assaulted? Do you know her name?"

Williams: "No, I've never met 'em."

Sheriff's department: "OK, we'll get someone on the way."

Now I had the address, so I headed out to Mink Farm Road, located in Leicester, an unincorporated rural area northwest of Asheville. As I approached the trailer, my stomach was churning. Confronting a potentially violent criminal isn't in my comfort zone. But there were no vehicles on the property, the weathered blue mobile was locked tight and no one answered when I knocked. Curtains or blinds obscured the only windows I could reach.

The Williams address was on the paperwork as well, though it wouldn't have been hard to guess, since the one-story ranch was the only home nearby. I knocked and Ms. Williams answered somewhat hesitantly but seemed relieved when she learned who I was and what I was about.

Williams told me that Sherlin had pulled up her clothing to display wounds and bruising on her legs and torso and reiterated that she had been bleeding from her head and neck. "She was really upset, I told her she could wait at my house for the ambulance, but she said she wanted to go back for cigarettes. Then I saw her drive away in a white car."

Williams affirmed that Sherlin had been alone and added, "The sheriff's department called me back and asked which son it was, I told them she had said 'Jeff.' A while later the ambulance arrived and I sent them up the hill."

The EMS incident report indicated that "a witness" reported seeing a truck with four people in it leave the premises and that the responders had found the premises deserted. Shortly thereafter, according to the ambulance crew's report, an unnamed male deputy sheriff arrived on the scene and searched the home. According to the ambulance crew's supervisor, the deputy found Nisha's purse and a cell phone on a table. Williams told me that she had seen those items given to the landlord. She also gave me the landlords' names and pointed to their home, the next driveway up.

Just before I concluded the interview, Williams added, "She came back."

"When?"

"Just after the deputy left, she came back. There was a man in the car with her. She went into the trailer for a few minutes. He waited in the car. She came out with a few things in hand, and they drove away again."

When I eventually assembled all of the paperwork in this case, Williams' concluding statement would tease me. The time on the Mink Road incident report precisely matched the time on the Woodfin accident report, but between the two events Sherlin had returned to her trailer. It just didn't add up. Someone was lying.

There was nobody home at the landlord's place and when I reached them by phone, several days later, neither of the owners was willing to say much. They did tell me that there had been no sign of Jeff Medford since the day of the incident, that they had cleaned up the mess at the trailer and were looking for new tenants.

3: No injuries?

The trail looked cold in Leicester, but what about Woodfin? The second EMS report indicated that Sherlin had been picked up in Woodfin following a traffic accident and transported to St. Joseph's Hospital.

The Woodfin Police Department was happy to give me a copy of an accident report filed by Sgt. Rob Austin. According to the report, Sherlin had rear-ended another car shortly before 2 p.m. (roughly ninety minutes after the initial 911 call). Her car was "totaled" in the opinion of Cutshaw's Towing owner Ron Cutshaw, who hauled the vehicle to his lot, while the other vehicle, a Humvee, sustained damage estimated at $50 by the reporting officer. The paperwork, which Austin hadn't filed until six days after the wreck, cites the "time" as 1:53 p.m.—the exact same time found on the sheriff's report of the incident on Mink Farm Road in Leicester. The Woodfin report lists "no injury to either party."

Why did you summon an ambulance, I asked Austin, if there weren't any injuries? "That's not something I can get into," he replied. "I can't answer that question, I'm sorry. "Fortunately, nobody was hurt," he added. "That was the main thing."

I found Sherlin's car in Cutshaw's storage lot and the front end was severely crumpled. There was a TV set in the passenger seat. Had Sherlin and a male companion returned to the trailer for her TV?

Weeks later I tracked down the owner of the Hummer which was registered to a corporation in Maggie Valley, an hour west of Asheville. The company had no listed phone number, so locating the owner required a long drive to the address which turned out to be a pizza joint where an employee identified his boss as the owner of a black Humvee. Reached by phone, that man told me his wife had been driving his car, that she was rear-ended, and that he had repaired the resulting scratched bumper with a few shots of black spray paint.

Chalk one up for Hummers.

The ambulance ride from Woodfin explained how Sherlin had landed in the hospital, but little else. What was the "something" Austin couldn't get into?

Getting no cooperation from the sheriff's office, I filed a written request for the paperwork. Under the North Carolina public records law, most documents other than personnel records are deemed public—including video and audio recordings. Julie Kepple, then department attorney, contacted me immediately upon receipt of my letter and soon I had copies of the incident report and the radio transcripts. The recording itself was still withheld.

"Questionable Conduct?" my first story about the incident, was published October 23. Sarzynski shared the byline because he provided invaluable help in pulling the pieces together—based on his earlier experience reporting on Medford's extreme behavior and the sheriff's wild excess of auxiliary deputies. At the time, the sheriff had nearly as many "special" deputies as Los Angeles and seemed to hand out the photo I.D.s like playing cards. Six years later those special deputies would be prominently featured in Medford's federal trial.

Sarz had it first. Nobody listened.

We wrote, "The incident report filed on Oct. 1-2 by Buncombe County Sheriff's Department Deputy Helen T. Hall and authorized by Lt. C. Frisbee lists the "time reported" as 1:53 p.m.—approximately one-and-a-half hours after the ambulance crew and other witnesses place three Sheriff's Department vehicles at the scene."

Also, "The incident report makes no mention of events reported by the ambulance crew and witnesses, nor of the deputy's search of a home, nor the fact that the victim was missing. The report does state that there is a suspect, but provides no name. The incident report begins with information obtained by a deputy from the alleged victim at Mission St. Joseph's Health System, where Jane [we changed Sherlin's name for the story, since her identity was not yet public] had been delivered by a different ambulance—not for the injuries that allegedly prompted the 911 call, but following a reported traffic accident, that occurred later in the day, in Woodfin."

Hall's incident report was written over a period of at least two, and perhaps three days, and Capt. Lee Farnsworth could not confirm or deny whether Hall had actually worked the case or had simply written it in her office. Hall wouldn't return calls.

The first question from a retired officer who examined the report was "Who was arrested?" He insisted that with a bleeding victim claiming domestic violence, there would have to be an arrest. "That doesn't mean the party is guilty, but in the case of a violent crime, when injuries are present and a suspect has been named, you make an arrest. That's the way the law works."

But not in this case.

I phoned Medford and he returned my call (it would prove to be both my first and last conversation with the man.).

Bothwell: "Thank you for calling back. The reason I called you is that we're putting together a story that involves an incident that occurred on October first."

Medford: "I'm familiar with it, yes."

Bothwell: "Right. And we have witnesses and con-firmation by the SBI [State Bureau of Investigation] that it involved your son."

Medford: "Sheriffs want to do an investigation—if there's an investigation to do."

Bothwell: "Has there been an arrest in the case?"

Medford: "For what?"

Bothwell: "There was an allegation of domestic violence."

Medford: "Well, that would be up to the SBI, now, right?"

Bothwell: "I believe ..."

Medford: "Now, don't pick on my son, OK?"

Bothwell: "I'm not attempting to pick on your son."

Medford: "Now listen to me, all right? Now, do your story, okay? But now, you're gonna have enough problems coming out of Morganton [the site of Broughton State Hospital] that I don't have to cause you any, okay? Now, I'll talk to you later, son." (Hangs up.)

Whew.

Medford knew I'd been to Broughton. Not that I'd tried to cover my tracks there, using my legal I.D. and stating my name aloud in the ward, but what ram-ifications would that entail? Had I broken some law after all?

And I had to ask myself why Medford insisted it "would be up to the SBI." With a bleeding victim making charges of assault, there *had to be* an arrest under state law.

We printed that conversation as a sidebar to the story in the paper. At the same time, I contacted the SBI again and asked if that department planned to look into the matter. Agent Charles Moody told me, "We are not conducting an investigation."

With the election two weeks away, the appearance of corruption was a hot potato. Medford claimed our story was politically motivated and the local daily paper, the *Asheville Citizen-Times,* assigned the wife of one of Medford's deputies to write its coverage. That reporter insinuated that my paper was grandstanding and attempting to make journalistic hay out of a non-issue. The daily then endorsed Medford, repeating similar endorsements in 1994 and 1998.

Medford's opponent, former Buncombe Deputy Mike Ruby, had made charges of corruption throughout his campaign, and had blasted the sheriff for failure to adequately address domestic violence issues. But Medford sailed to an easy victory.

He had won the first round, but I wasn't giving up, and all unknown to me, other events that fall would prove to be of far greater consequence to Medford and his department than the torture and beating of a bruised and battered young woman named Nisha Sherlin.

4: Accident or intent?

I renewed my contact with Sherlin by the middle of January. She started our interview with an apology for her reaction at Broughton Hospital. "They warned me not to talk to the press," she said. "They threatened to hurt me if I did."

"Who threatened you?" I asked.

"Bobby and Jeff," was the reply. She told me that after her release from the hospital she had been briefly jailed on assault charges, then released with the charges dropped. Then, up until the election, "Bobby was so nice to me. He'd pick up my meds, and give me rides in his sheriff's car. He gave me one hundred dollars every time he saw me." Sherlin's face took on an exasperated look, "That was hush money. That's what that was! After the election he dropped me like a hot rock!" At the end of the interview I obtained written permission to access all of her medical records.

Sherlin's intake report from the E.R. listed bruises of multiple ages among her injuries. As we all know from personal experience, bruises change over time. On fair-skinned people they go from the initial dark blue-black to yellow and brown, fading into yellowish until they are healed. Medical professionals sometimes use more specific terms to describe such contusions and healing patterns, but the important bottom line is that the appearance of bruises changes as they heal.

Doctors I consulted assured me that the only way a body exhibits multiple-age bruising is to sustain bruises over time.

On the other hand, the E.R. physician, Dr. Joe Frazer, had noted that Sherlin's injuries were related to an auto accident. Was that note based on his professional observation or the simple fact that she had been transported via ambulance from the scene of a vehicle wreck?

From the medical report I learned that, during her hospital stay, Sherlin had made frequent requests to talk to her mother, Judy Mathis. Deputy Brenda Fraser had relied on the mother's support in shunting Sherlin off to Broughton. Would Mathis help me out?

I discovered that Mathis wanted no part of an investigation into the sheriff's department, and evinced some fear about possible repercussions from that quarter, but she did give me the name of Sherlin's uncle who had helped clean up the scene of the alleged beatings and also recovered a few of her daughter's personal effects.

Some of Sherlin's bloody clothing, I learned, was stashed in a box in the uncle's basement, but Mathis had instructed him not to make it available for examination. The uncle did tell me that he had cleaned the trailer with the landlord. "There was nothing breakable that wasn't broken," he said. "There was bloody clothing all around and the bed was broken to the floor at one end. I've never seen so many pill bottles, and the prescriptions were to different names."

"Everything broken?" I asked.

"Even the glass-topped coffee table. There were shards sticking out of the wall, stuck in the paneling."

"Where were the prescriptions from?" I asked.

"CVS [pharmacy], made out to different names but all from the same doctor. I've never seen so many pill bottles," he repeated. "Did she tell you about the credit card?"

When I answered in the negative, the uncle said, "They got Judy's card, and he was charging all those pills on her card. She's afraid to press charges because she's afraid of the sheriff."

"You said, 'he,'" I replied. "Who was that?"

"Jeff Medford."

"And bloody clothing all around?"

"Yes. Underwear and tee shirts. Blood on the walls. On the curtains, too," he continued. "I've never seen such a mess."

I phoned the landlord again. He wouldn't talk on the record, but allowed, "It was a real mess." He also confirmed the presence of "lots of pill bottles."

I knew the State Bureau of Investigation had initiated its probe of the sheriff's handling of the case *after* I contacted them, though Medford soon claimed that *he* had initiated their involvement. In October, Moody of the SBI told me, "We are not conducting an investigation." After we published our first story, however, the bureau did decide to get involved. Later, Assistant District Attorney Kate Dreher told me that our news reports were included in the SBI investigative file turned over to the DA's office.

Two years would elapse before a source informed me that that local SBI employees included former Buncombe deputies who were friendly with Medford and that their investigation had been cursory at best. A deputy present during the "investigation" told me, "It was a joke. They just asked the administrative staff if anything had happened and everybody said 'No.'" At the time, however, I assumed the State Bureau agents were honest watchdogs.

Under state law, an SBI investigation results in a report which is turned over to the district attorney in the relevant jurisdiction. The D.A. then decides whether or not to file charges. I made frequent calls to the SBI and the D.A.'s office in the weeks following the election. No comment.

Finally, in early February, I called the state Attorney General's office to see what I could learn and was told that the SBI investigation had been turned over to the D.A. some weeks earlier. When I called his office armed with the new information, D.A. Ron Moore was suddenly more forthcoming.

Yes, he had received the report. (What a surprise! Just a few days earlier he had not.) No, he saw no reason to prefer charges.

"Why?" I asked. "There is an injured party involved who made charges of assault."

"Well, I'm extremely hamstrung about what I can say because it obviously contains a lot of medical records about the lady, some things I'm sure she wouldn't want me to be broadcasting. That I don't feel comfortable broadcasting. I don't see where anybody did anything wrong in terms of investigating or how they handled it. Based on the SBI investigation, medical records and other folks we talked to, I don't see where there's anybody that can be prosecuted for whatever may have happened out there. As I sit here right now, I'm not sure anything did happen."

I pressed Moore. "Do you feel that the report reconciles the stark differences between eyewitness accounts which said there was blood in every room of the trailer and the deputy's radio report that said there was no sign of violence in the trailer?"

He replied: "Well I think that the medical evidence which I am, again, hamstrung to talk to, did not indicate that there were any injuries that happened at the time of the reported or alleged incident. The medical folks didn't find anything that would support anything having just occurred in terms of recent injuries."

"What about the 911 caller who said that she was bleeding profusely when she ran into her house?"

Moore answered: "Well, at some point, and I don't remember who, but it didn't appear that there was a lot of fresh bleeding going on, there may have been dried blood that may have been there for several days, but again, I am very hamstrung about getting into what Ms. Sherlin has told other people about some of her activities."

Then I asked Moore about the SBI investigation. "I was puzzled that the last time I talked to the 911 caller and the landlady, that the SBI had not talked to them. Is that the case?"

He told me that the SBI claimed to have interviewed Ashley Williams in November. Williams flatly contradicted this statement both before and after my conversation with Moore. Someone in the SBI was lying.

At the end of our conversation I asked Moore, "If this does exonerate the sheriff's department, do you plan to make a public statement about it?"

"No," he answered. "I'm not of the opinion that the sheriff's department needs to be exonerated. You raised the question about their handling of it. We've had it investigated by the State Bureau of Investigation to see if anybody should be charged criminally in the case. I don't find anything that would allow us to charge anyone. They didn't do anything wrong."

Sherlin insisted she had been tied and beaten over a period of three to seven days. There was an intake medical report that appeared to support her allegations, nevertheless the D.A. found no correlation between the two. Either the records on Moore's desk were different from those on mine, or he was lying. That left open the possibility that the SBI had delivered incomplete—or false—medical information to Moore.

Now I had a deputy's radio transmission claiming no sign of violence, Sheriff Medford's claim that nothing had transpired, D.A. Moore's denial of medical evidence, the clean-up crew's confirmation of a disastrous scene of the crime including what might have been illegally-obtained prescription drugs, a medical report of extensive injuries and my own first-hand witness of an injured woman in the hospital.

Somebody had to be hiding something.

I looked back over the chain of evidence. Dr. Frazer had noted "MVA" on the hospital form under "Nature of Accident." Okay, that's clear enough. She was delivered from the scene of a motor vehicle accident. I phoned him to inquire whether Sherlin's injuries appeared to corroborate that cause, but received the standard answer that he couldn't discuss such matters due to the proscriptions of medical ethics.

Then, I wondered, what about the accident itself? Why Woodfin, for instance? Medford had very close ties to Woodfin, owned a home there and maintained connections to the mayor and cops. In fact, the police force in the municipality operated as a sub-agency under the sheriff's department. Had the accident been faked as a cover story for Sherlin's injuries? How likely was it that Sherlin had rear-ended an essentially indestructible Hummer? Was the owner connected to Medford in some way? Was all of that somehow tied to Sgt. Austin's demurral concerning an ambulance summoned to transport someone from an accident with "no injuries"?

Days spent on background checks yielded nothing. In those first months of my editorship my tipsters frequently mentioned video poker machines and allegations that Medford was involved in a protection racket. I wondered if the Hummer owner figured in gambling somehow. I returned to his pizza parlor in Maggie Valley. There were no poker machines in sight, which proved little. But the two-hour round trip gave me time to think.

Maybe I needed to talk to the ambulance crews.

The EMS team that responded to the first call from Mink Farm Road couldn't add anything to their report, but the Woodfin responders added a fascinating detail. They *weren't* the first officials on the scene, and neither was the Woodfin cop. A security team from the University of North Carolina, Asheville, had called in the first report.

I contacted UNCA security and was routed through the school's public information office, played phone tag and explained and re-explained what I wanted to find out. Days later I finally connected with one of the school officers who had just happened to stumble onto the scene shortly after Sherlin's wreck. Off the record, he confirmed that, as far as he could see, she had, in fact, rear-ended the Hummer. He also told me that the driver of the second car wanted to press charges against Sherlin for assault.

"What did she do?" I asked.

"She was flipped out, trying to get into his car, and banging on the hood, begging for help," he said.

"Help for what?" I countered.

"She really wanted to get away from there, bad. Real bad."

I talked to the second UNCA officer who told me, "She jumped into his car. She was desperate to get away."

"Did she assault him?" I asked?

"Nah. She just wanted a ride."

It was months before I would come to understand that Sherlin was well aware of the Medfords' connections in Woodfin, and Woodfin was one of the last places she would turn for official help to escape her troubles.

I decided to track down the other driver.

5: Reading the record

Thanks to the UNCA security guards I was able to locate the driver who had preferred assault charges against Sherlin. Though I assured him that I would preserve his anonymity, he refused to talk about anything that had occurred other than stating that he definitely felt assaulted.

Did she jump into his vehicle? No comment. Did she appear to be frightened? No comment. What did she do as he drove away? No comment. Did he really feel threatened by a young woman standing beside his car and yelling? No comment. Was she bleeding or bruised? No comment. "Please don't call me again," he said. "Ever." He hung up the phone.

What was that all about? Somebody who felt assaulted by a frightened woman, and felt strongly enough about it that he filed charges, but had nothing to say about the incident? I wondered if Medford's department had something on the young man, some sort of law enforcement lever with which to coerce participation— but an extensive background check revealed nothing.

Then what about the deputy whose name was all over the report from the hospital? Deputy Brenda Fraser apparently arrived at the ER *before* Sherlin got there, and appeared to have been present through most of Sherlin's short stay at St. Joseph's. While the psychiatric nurses seemed to believe that Sherlin was doing fine, Fraser kept stressing the idea that she might harm herself and pushing for commitment to Broughton. I contacted Fraser in October and again in April. Both times she refused to comment and directed me to the department's public information officer.

But according to hospital records, Fraser phoned Sherlin's mother shortly after her daughter's arrival at the ER and told her that Nisha had been involved in a traffic accident. Fraser also told emergency-room personnel that Sherlin had "threatened suicide—wanted to cut throat."

I re-read the documents. Sherlin was received at the St. Joseph's Hospital emergency room on October first at 3:43 p.m. and told the triage nurse that she'd been beaten by her boyfriend. The nurse's notes state: "Multiple scratches on patient's arms, neck, chest and legs— note different stages of bruising on arms and legs— patient states 'he hurt me a lot—hit me in the head— scratched me.'"

During examinations by psychiatric nurses on October first and second, the records indicate that Sherlin repeatedly denied any attempt to harm herself and consistently maintained that she'd been abused. One nurse noted, "She is concerned that nothing will be done about Jeff's assault on her because his father is sheriff." The medical records also contain the following entry about the traffic accident: "Patient states she was trying to get away from boyfriend Jeff Medford and her brakes failed."

On Sherlin's "Emergency Department Psychiatric Assessment/Presenting Problem" form, nurse Barbara McCampbell, noted on October first that, "pt. has multiple lacerations inc. a slash on her neck. she blames b.f. for cutting her neck with a piece of a glass table he broke. She denies attempting to harm herself. Reports that MVA was due to brakes failing on car. pt. tried to take another car following the MVA, trying to assault the driver: per police to ER."

From this form, under "DANGER TO SELF" I also learned that Sherlin had been to Broughton once before, after taking an unloaded gun to a baseball game where she had put the weapon to her head and pulled the trigger. Under "DANGER TO OTHERS" the nurse had described the alleged assault on the other driver. Those two categories constitute legal cause for commitment. But again, later in the day, McCampbell noted, "Pt. continues to deny any attempt to harm self. States boyfriend drugged her and beat her up."

As to Sherlin's assertions concerning drug intake, whether voluntary or involuntary, her blood work confirmed "patient is positive for phenobarbital, benzodiazepines and cocaine."

Two pages further on, McCampbell recorded, "Pt. spoke only briefly to this psw [psychiatric social worker] apparently due to sedation and distress. She indicated that she wants to go home to her Mx [mother] & wants to stay away from Jeff Medford. She concluded the conversation by saying that 'Bobby Medford is running for reelection and I'm fucked.' and pulled the blankets over her head."

On the following page, the "Emergency Department Psychiatric Assessment Disposition" form, under "FINAL DISPOSITION," in different hand-writing and not dated, "Involuntary commitment to BSH to Dr. Mohivddeir."

But there was more paperwork, a Progress Record filed by McCampbell that began that first night at 7:40 p.m. with a note that Sherlin's "Mx and step Fx were in the lobby, that pt. was sedated & that BCSD Brenda Fraser had information re this pt." The parents told McCampbell that Sherlin had lived with Jeff Medford since July, first with friends and more recently in their own place. They also said that they provided principal financial support for the couple, neither of whom worked, and that Sherlin had recently asked for money to repair her brakes. When they refused, she allegedly threatened suicide.

Next McCampbell recorded a phone conversation with Fraser. "Brenda states that pt. was in BSH & has seizures. Also states: pt. has threatened to kill herself. pt. broke glass over the weekend & scratched her throat & wrist. pt. wrecked a car today & then tried to beat up a bystander & steal his car. When asked how she knows this info, Brenda said that pt's boyfriend told her. She states that there was a 'scuffle' between pt & b.f. B.friend told Brenda that pt. tried to cut him w/ a steak knife & that B.friend also has bruises. B.friend said he was trying to keep her from killing herself." McCampbell asked if the boy friend had received medical treatment and Fraser said she had advised him to do so. The nurse also noted, "Brenda never offered b.fr's name. Brenda reported that in her capacity c/ victims of violent domestic crime, she interviewed pt. here in the ER. She asked if pt. will be going to BSH & is told that it hasn't been decided."

So Fraser had been in touch with Jeff Medford who placed the blame on Sherlin, and the deputy was also concerned to know if Sherlin was being routed to Broughton.

The following day, a little after noon, a second psych nurse, Eleanor Jones, noted that "Barbara Frazier calls to say she just 'reassessed' pt. & is 'very, very worried' about pt. because pt. told her she is suicidal. Pt's RN confirmed that female law enforcement officer was at pt's bedside about 30 minutes ago." Jones must have been referring to "Brenda Fraser," and, again, Fraser had stressed the suicide threat. Twenty-five minutes later Jones noted, "pt. ~~Aunt~~ cousin called earlier today stating she is worried about pt. who has hx [history]of MVA p/ [illegible] & cocaine abuse. pt. has had 'hard life' & her Mother is 'not the best role model.' Aunt is concerned that pt may hurt self or others."

Curiously, an unidentified "cousin" or "aunt" had called to make the case for the same *specific legal causes* for involuntary commitment.

The only nurse I was able to locate and contact was McCampbell. She declined to comment due to the customary medical ethics restrictions, despite the records release I had obtained from Sherlin.

I went over the medical records repeatedly and then I noticed something strange. At 3:15 p.m., the emergency-room physician made initial arrangements for Sherlin's involuntary commitment to Broughton. Hold it. Roll the tape back.

This is twenty-eight minutes *before* Sherlin was officially admitted to the emergency room, according to Emergency Department records. This is several hours *before* Sherlin's first evaluation by the St. Joseph's Psychiatric Department. They were already arranging for Sherlin's commitment *before* she was examined by medical staff.

However, those arrangements appeared to come *after* contact with Deputy Fraser, who alleged (according to the ER nurse's notes) that Sherlin "threatened suicide —wanted to cut throat. Tried to beat up another driver."

I called the hospital. St. Joseph's spokesperson Merrell Gregory told me hospital policy allows an attending physician to initiate contact with Broughton—to explore the possibility of committing a patient—without a psychiatric exam, based on information received from a law-enforcement officer involved in the case. Typically, said Gregory, this would involve someone who appeared to be a threat to self or others.

The first nurse to examine Sherlin, K. Jackson, noted, "mult. scratches on pts. arms, neck, chest & legs – note different stages of bruising on arms & legs, pt. states 'he hurt me a lot, hit me in the head, scratched me' pt. is not oriented to date."

The attending physician, Emergency Department head Dr. Joe Frazer, completed his ER report at 9:12 p.m. on October first. In it, he paraphrased statements attributed to Fraser and/or the EMS crew that delivered Sherlin to the hospital. There's no mention of the alleged beating noted by both the triage nurse and another nurse in the ER, or of Sherlin's repeated references to the beating in her psychiatric interviews. Frazer did note, however, "The patient has multiple old bruises involving all four extremities." So he matter-of-factly noted that the victim of the "auto accident" had been previously bruised up.

I reread notes from psychiatric nurses that suggested the patient was frightened but rational, and repeated notes from Fraser that Sherlin was bent on self-destruction. Who was calling the shots in the hospital? Who was pushing for commitment? To all appearances it was Fraser and someone claiming to be a cousin.

The scenario that seemed most likely to me was that the deputy, acting at the behest of the sheriff, had begun the process of hiding the victim in a state mental hospital as soon as the incident was reported. On October second, just after four o'clock in the afternoon, barely twenty-four hours after Sherlin was admitted to St. Joe's, deputies from the Henderson County Sheriff's Department arrived to transport her to Broughton.

It seemed that justice had been cleanly and quickly obstructed.

6: Losses and wins

I reconnected with Sherlin at the end of April. She reaffirmed her story in its entirety and added a few fascinating details. At the end of her ten-day stay in Broughton, Bobby Medford himself had arranged for her ride back to Buncombe County.

I repeated an earlier question, "You said that when you were taken to Broughton State Hospital and later when you were placed in the Buncombe County jail, "they" told you not to talk to anyone. Who were "they?"

Sherlin replied, "Bob and Jeff."

"Bob and Jeff Medford? Not any other sheriff's deputies or medical personnel?"

She answered, "Just Bob and Jeff. And you know the funny thing is, when I got out of Broughton, Bob sent a woman in his car to pick me up and she took me to his office and I sat in his office for about an hour before he told me he was going to have to put me in jail. But he told me he would get me out the next day. Later on, after my Mom came and got me out, I had to go find Bob because all of my clothes from Broughton were still in the trunk of his car. And he said to me, "What are you doing out?" I said, I wasn't going to wait for you, my Mom came and got me."

It was clear that Medford had a special interest in this woman to whom nothing had supposedly happened.

At this point I had enough to go forward with a story, which I wrote and submitted to the news editor at the paper. The editing process took a while, between fact-checking and careful scrutiny by an attorney. There were potential libel land mines and everything had to be nailed tight.

Finally, in June, more than eight months after the incident, my report went to press as a cover story. "Buncombe Justice On Trial," laid out the case that Nisha Sherlin had been beaten by someone, allegedly the sheriff's son, that there had been no arrest as required by law, that the sheriff had lied, that the D.A. was either lied to by the SBI or had lied himself, and that nothing had come of the whole affair. It included Sherlin's allegations of hush money from Medford. I expected public outrage.

Outside of a couple of letters to the editor, nothing happened. At least, nothing local. The following summer the story would rate an award for investigative journalism from the Association of Alternative Newsweeklies. The award was satisfying in its way (at least *somebody* was paying attention), but in the meantime the sheriff remained in office and the phone tips about wrongdoing continued.

My video poker file continued to grow, but there was very little in the way of concrete evidence to go on. South Carolina had experienced a rash of electronic gaming in the 1990s. A poorly worded gambling law had permitted the establishment of hundreds of mini-casinos in strip malls and convenience stores. Public opposition gradually gained traction and in 2000 the state legislature finally, albeit inadvertently, banned the machines.

Although South Carolina law long prohibited gambling on machines with cash payouts, video poker owners squeezed through a loophole in the law by using machines that issued tickets to winners instead of paying off in cash. Winning tickets could then be redeemed for cash. At the high point there were 33,000 machines in use, or one for every 100 state residents.

Gambling opponents raised the issue to a fever pitch in 1999 and the legislature deftly sidestepped the issue by passing a law that banned the machines *unless* voters approved them in a state-wide referendum. However, the South Carolina Supreme Court stepped in and prohibited the vote because there is no provision for state-wide referenda in the state's constitution. Thus the legislative ban automatically took effect.

Machine owners who had occasionally ventured across the state line began to move their equipment north in earnest. At the same time they began to pour money into the campaign coffers of Tar Heel politicians. During its 2000 session the North Carolina General Assembly passed a law explicitly legalizing video poker. Daily individual winnings were capped at ten dollars worth of merchandise and no more than three machines were permitted in any one place of business. County sheriffs were saddled with mandatory machine registration. Sheriffs were required to evaluate and approve applications, issue free registration stickers for permitted machines and report registrations to the county tax collectors. And, of course, it was their job to enforce the law by investigating suspected violations of gambling laws.

During the 2002 legislative session, a bill banning the machines was introduced in the General Assembly. The North Carolina Sheriff's Association voted to support the legislation. Their support for the ban on video poker arose both because legalization had imposed an unfunded mandate for additional work and due to concerns about the creation of a new gambling industry. All one hundred sheriffs in the state, including Bobby Medford, signed a letter of support for the bill which was delivered to the General Assembly.

Democracy NC, a nonprofit watchdog group, examined campaign contributions in 2002 and traced thousands of dollars to video poker sources. The total would exceed $100,000 in the 2004 legislative races. The biggest recipient of the operators' largesse was House Speaker Jim Black, who used his office and influence to block the legislation at every opportunity.

Meanwhile the machines seemed to proliferate in Buncombe County—in convenience stores and beauty parlors, furniture outlets and service stations. Although the law required that such machines be in plain view of anyone entering an establishment, the rule wasn't routinely enforced. I stepped through an unmarked back door in a Hot Dog King restaurant in Fairview to enter a smoky chamber with three players feeding money into three machines, punching control buttons in rapid succession. In the Payless convenience store in Forks of Ivy another unmarked door led into a similar mini-casino.

My file grew, but other matters grappled for my time and attention. An inmate had died in the Buncombe County Detention Center and no one was being held to account.

7: Sudden cell death

In between phone calls about gambling issues in the county there came sporadic tips about bad treatment of inmates at the Buncombe County Detention Center. Informants said they were roughed up or beaten in the jail elevators (where there were no security cameras to record the incidents), that they were kept in holding cells for weeks without toiletries, mattresses or blankets, and that they had been denied prescription medications. Spokespersons for the sheriff's department denied that there were any problems. Complaints were chalked up to the predictable disgruntlement of criminals who'd been caught and incarcerated and there seemed to be no way to confirm such allegations.

But one caller told me to look again at the case of Joey Max Rogers who had died in the county jail in September, 2001. By all appearances the death was just one more among the many local stories given short shrift in the tumult following the attack on the World Trade Center and the Pentagon on 9/11. I remembered, vaguely, having heard about Rogers' demise, but by the time of the phone call it was almost two years in the past.

My anonymous informant, who claimed to be a jail employee, said, "We all know that boy killed him."

"What boy?" was my obvious question.

"One of the guards threw Rogers against the wall. Everyone at the jail knows."

"Does the boy have a name?" I asked.

Click.

I phoned a friend with contacts inside the sheriff's department. He told me he'd heard that Rogers was arrested for operating his lawn mower while drunk and booked into the county jail where he died about a half hour later under mysterious circumstances. I wondered aloud, "Can you be arrested for DUI on a lawn mower?"

"I guess you can."

The sheriff's office was no help. If there were questions about the death, there might be an ongoing investigation, but in any case they wouldn't be able to comment. So much time had passed since Rogers' death that it seemed doubtful to me that any investigation was ongoing but a paper trail surely remained.

I obtained the state medical examiner's report which was pretty bare-bones: "Arrested by B.C. Sheriff's Dept. for drunk & disorderly—apparently was combative —placed in locked room at approximately 2100 hrs. ... Checked at 2130 & found dead on floor." His neck was broken. Neither the medical authorities nor the sheriff's department had explained how a highly intoxicated man who was also found to have a high level of phenobarbital in his blood (a legally prescribed medication, according to the medical report) had managed to break his own neck while alone in a locked room.

Two years further on, another jail employee, then recently retired, sat in my office for an off-the-record interview. He told me the same story, and once again said, "That boy killed Rogers." And once again my informant wouldn't state the name.

I pressed him, "You obviously trust me to keep your identity confidential, or you wouldn't be here today. What's keeping you from naming the guard?"

"Bobby Medford," was his terse reply.

Another puzzling story concerning Medford's department crossed my desk during 2003. An off-duty deputy, Brian Styles, traveling in his patrol car, had elected to tag along on a high-speed chase when the report came in on his radio. Deputy Styles and an unnamed reserve deputy were headed west on Patton Avenue at a high rate of speed when an accident occurred involving at least three other cars which were stopped at a traffic light at the intersection with Leicester Highway. The driver of another car which wasn't directly involved in the accident, a Hispanic man, was charged with responsibility for the wreck. Exactly how an uninvolved car could have caused a high-speed wreck was unclear from official reports. I tucked that away in my growing Buncombe County Sheriff's Department file.

Another year would pass before I gained any useful insight into that wreck. In the summer of 2004, former Buncombe Capt. Don Fraser told me his version of that event. (How I came to interview Fraser and his wife, Brenda, is better told a little further on in this narrative.)

Don was in a grocery store at the intersection when a customer came in and told him that the accident had occurred. He had gone directly to the scene and described to me what he had found:

"Styles wound up facing eastbound in the westbound lane of Patton just above the Leicester Highway intersection. I had some great pictures at one time, but they were taken on the sheriff's office digital camera and I don't have them now. You could look at the accident scene and tell it wasn't like they said happened. Brian was clearly at fault. He was *not* running his lights or siren at the time. Brian and the reserve were working off duty in the housing projects and had responded to whatever call it was without telling anyone. If I remember correctly the call was a chase, out on old Haywood Road where the chasee was doing all of 15 mph. He simply wouldn't stop."

Don Fraser's account suggested that the accident reporting was flawed, but Deputy Brenda Fraser offered even more damning testimony. Brenda worked in the administrative section of the BCSD at the time of the accident and she told me she was present when the Styles accident was discussed by Medford and other administrative officers. "They decided to blame the Mexican," Fraser told me. "And one of them said, 'That's my story and I'm sticking to it."

That amounted to criminal conspiracy—apparently a successful one. It would be another three years before I was able to collect more substantive information about the wreck.

Don had one detail wrong. There were actually *two* chases underway in that neighborhood that afternoon. The slow-speed pursuit was on Haywood Road, and involved someone who simply refused to pull over. The other was focused on a DUI driver who was racing west on Patton Avenue, careening into the oncoming lane at times. She was pursued by a half dozen deputies who by all accounts had emergency lights running but no sirens.

Styles was at the rear of the law enforcement pack and ran a red light at the intersection with Leicester Highway. A man who I have only been able to identify as "Jose" was making a legal right turn from that road onto Patton. The sirens and lights had passed him by and it was raining and, by some accounts, icy. He allegedly proceeded. Styles apparently reacted and lost control of his car. He careened across the intersection into the oncoming left turn lane where he slammed into the first stopped car. The momentum of the patrol car caused the two vehicles to ricochet down the line of traffic, damaging a series of other vehicles in the process.

The young woman whose car was t-boned by Styles suffered a broken ankle which required surgery and insertion of a steel pin. Five years after the accident, she still faces further surgery for removal of the pin. Her uninsured motorist insurance paid for her car, which was totaled. After three years of legal wrangling, she is said to have received five thousand dollars in compensation from the county for the nuisance of being crippled, losing months of work and enduring the pain and trauma of the accident.

Jamie Coulson, whose car was also totaled, never received a penny of compensation.

An apparently innocent Hispanic man was charged with the accident and except for the nominal payment to the young woman, the county washed its hands of the case.

8: Missed meds

The voice on the phone was deep and strong with a barely definable sense of threat beneath the surface.

"This is Mister Payne," he informed me. "I want you to meet me at the Sycamore Temple. In one of the classrooms downstairs."

"What does this concern?"

"You'll want to know. It's about the sheriff and the D.A."

"Can you tell me about it now?"

"I can't talk on the phone," his rich tone became a conspiratorial stage-whisper. "They tape phone calls and I've got the D.A. on tape."

"My office is right downtown," I countered, "Just a few blocks from the church."

"I don't know I can trust you. Meet me at the Temple," he fairly growled. "Tomorrow at 2 p.m. My uncle will let you in." Mister Payne hung up.

I turned to my office-mate, Sarz. "Don't think I want to go there. Some kind of scary shit going on." I described the call.

Sarzynski reminded me of the rule he'd picked up at the Medill School of Journalism, from writer David Carr. "Don't ignore the nut-jobs. They know things." Obsessive/compulsives, paranoiacs, neurotics, manics, depressives, all manner of slightly or greatly delusional people often notice, remember and report details that average folks miss. And while Mister Payne would prove to be obsessed with the injustice he suffered, he was hardly a "nut-job." Furthermore, my reporting on his case would lead to exposure of extensive abuse in the county's detention center and a wrongful death law suit that could eventually have significant repercussions in North Carolina law.

But at that moment I was confronted with the prospect of going to meet a scary-sounding stranger in a basement to get my kernel of news. I didn't think so.

Sarz added: "Don't go alone. I'm going with you."

The next afternoon we walked over to the Sycamore Temple. We introduced ourselves to a few people in the front yard of the church and indicated we had an appointment with a "Mister Payne." All of them denied any knowledge of the name at first, then one of them stepped forward and said, "Follow me." I knew the voice. We followed Mister Payne into the basement of the Sycamore Temple. He proved to be a tall, muscular African-American man named Carlos.

We listened to a taped conversation he'd had with District Attorney Ron Moore.

"See, he's lying." Payne observed.

I didn't quite get how or what was being misrepresented, but I nodded agreeably.

Then Payne launched into a complicated description of his legal problems. His narrative was hampered by a maddening inclination to digress, to repeatedly focus on details rather than the story line, with references to allegedly misstated dates and forged signatures on an endless stream of documents plucked from his briefcase. He had blazed across many of the documents with a highlighter and had kept copious notes. Payne proffered a detailed list of hundreds of complaints he had filed while an inmate in the Buncombe jail and claimed that his complaints had led to a prison term, a term during which he also kept copious, elaborate lists of correspondences and complaints.

It was a little overwhelming, but two hours later he had apparently decided he could trust me, and promised to provide me with copies of his documents. Walking back to the office I asked Sarz, "Whaddya think?"

"There's a story there," he said, then grinned and added, "I'm glad it's yours."

It would take me well over a year to unravel Payne's story, to fully understand what he had been through, and to frame it in a way that would make sense to newspaper readers. In the meantime, another prisoner would die in a county cell, and Payne's story would offer clues and eventually turn up a witness to that death.

I looked into Payne's criminal history. He'd done time for "death by motor vehicle," but there was no transcript of his hearing because he'd pleaded guilty. Transcripts are normally prepared only when a conviction is appealed, and guilty pleas are rarely appealed.

Payne delivered a thick stack of documents and we went over them in detail. The most obvious problems seemed to be clerical. By intent or inattention, the man's legal records were full of inaccuracies. According to the official police and court paperwork he was convicted the same day he was arrested, he was sentenced before he was convicted, and he was found guilty of parole violation before he was paroled.

As I would learn over ensuing years, such paper-work errors are extremely common in state and local court records in Buncombe County. I have yet to examine *any* case records which don't contain glaring errors. Maybe this doesn't much affect the system of justice in the big picture, but it makes the whole affair appear to be extremely slipshod. The lack of concern for accuracy in matters of life and liberty, even life and death, is inexcusable and appalling. The slovenly record keeping lends an appearance of injustice and can hardly help convince those found guilty that they received judicious treatment.

I told Payne I would study it and get back to him. Over the ensuing months, his impatient phone calls became familiar. "I don't see anything in the paper," he would start out. "This is Mister Payne." And I'd explain that I was doing what I could and hoped to have a story soon.

I tried to obtain Payne's court records, but learned that they were being held in the D.A.'s office and were unavailable. When would they be available? The D.A.'s secretary couldn't say. Why are two-year old court records of a closed case still in the D.A.'s office? Same reply.

Between the documents and Payne's idiosyncratic verbal account I pieced together his story. Payne told me he had given a ride to a girl who, unbeknownst to him, had just ripped off two men in a drug deal. As he came around a corner, the two men ran out of an alley toward his car, one brandishing a gun, the other wielding a trash can which he slammed into Payne's windshield. Payne stepped on the gas to escape and unintentionally ran over one of the assailants. He later learned that the man had died and he turned himself in to the sheriff's office that same evening. He was charged with second-degree murder and pleaded down to death by vehicle. He was sentenced to twenty-two months in state prison, but would only be required to actively serve ninety days in the county jail, after which he would be paroled.

It seems that Mister Payne was not a compliant inmate. He referred me to the hand-written list of complaints he had filed and letters he had sent to local and state agencies alleging mistreatment. Every complaint concerned his health and failure of authorities to deliver medication. He showed me his pre-incarceration medical records which indicated seriously high blood pressure and an associated prescription, and claimed that the jail had withheld his meds. Payne noted that the doctor who had initially prescribed the medication at a county clinic was the same doctor who oversaw the jail clinic and examined him in jail, which made it seem even more bizarre that he was denied his meds.

After my story about Payne was published, the doctor wrote my paper asserting that my information was false and that no inmate under his care had ever been denied medication. However his signature appeared on both Payne's prescription and Payne's jail records, so he must have known about the scrip.

The sheriff's department flatly denied that any prisoner was ever denied prescription drugs.

With Payne's authorization and after a prolonged series of phone calls I finally obtained his jail medical record, and, sure enough, the blood pressure readings recorded by the nursing staff ranged from high to dangerously high. Finally, radiating pain in his head and neck coupled with a very high blood-pressure reading landed Payne in the emergency room at Mission Hospitals on July 25, 2001. A doctor there ordered that Payne's medication be resumed, and he was returned to the Detention Center to complete his sentence. The jail apparently complied, though they punished him by keeping him in solitary and forcing him to sleep on concrete.

The written record was clear. Payne had received his medication after, but not before, his hospitalization.

Payne obtained help from a guard in the jail several months into my investigation. The guard printed out a computer transcript of Payne's incarceration record which explicitly confirmed his version of events. At the same time, one of Payne's court records reappeared in the courthouse file room. I was also able to obtain a transcript of the probation violation trial because he had appealed that ruling. The court records also corroborated Payne's account.

A few days before Payne was to be released on probation, he was charged with violation of his probation. Soon a court found him guilty and he was sent to prison to complete his full sentence. How could he have violated his probation *before* he was accorded that status?

One condition of probation is that the inmate must follow all of the rules while serving his active time. Payne had complained bitterly and vocally, even cursing guards for failure to provide him with his blood pressure medication. Cursing guards is against the rules.

All told, the documents make clear that Payne was denied the medication for more than 60 days of his 90-day active sentence. During that time, according to the record, Payne shouted about it, demanded it, demanded to see a doctor, threatened staff, blacked out and suffered broken teeth and other injuries, and yelled some more. During Payne's trial on the probation charge, however, a Detention Center administrator made statements under oath that are contradicted by the jail records.

Payne's attorney, Todd Lentz, asked Administrative Lieutenant Tony Gould, "Specifically, are you aware that he receives treatment and is currently on medication for high blood pressure?"

Gould replied, "No, he didn't state high-blood-pressure medication."

Lentz then showed Gould an inmate-request form, signed by Gould on the 20th day of Payne's incarceration (June 14, 2001), stating that he had high blood pressure and was requesting medication. "Is that your signature at the bottom?" queried Lentz.

Gould: "Yes, sir, it is."

Later, Judge Michael E. Helms asked Gould, "Has this defendant ever complained to you that the reason he's conducting himself [in proscribed ways] is because he's being denied any medication?"

Gould: "No, your Honor."

Yet both Payne's medical records and his incident reports show him repeatedly expressing his need for medication and becoming outraged when his requests were denied.

In sharp contrast to earlier portions of Payne's record, the medical entry for July 26 reads, "explained to [inmate] BP med would begin today, but we had to order & receive from pharmacy. I.M. was *cooperative & calm*." (Italics added.) From that date forward, Payne's incident reports contain no mention of cursing or threats.

Yet when Judge Helms asked Gould how many threats Payne had made after he'd resumed taking medication, Gould replied, "Ten."

This came as a complete surprise to Payne, who later in the trial asked to be shown the incident record (which had not been admitted as evidence). He said: "Can I see that? Because I wasn't never disciplined or never told about it."

Judge Helms responded, "You were present in court and you heard him [Gould] testify about it."

As Payne told me, "After I came back from the hospital, I had three weeks left in my sentence. They kept me in the holding cell or in solitary for the whole time, and I slept on the concrete."

During the trial, Gould confirmed the first part of this, when he reported, "After the 26th, Inmate Payne was housed in Booking."

The judge asked, "It's like solitary?"

"Well, it's a single cell."

"And have there been any incidents while he's been in Booking of him just talking to officers and ..."

Interrupting Helms, Gould replied,"No, sir."

Yet when Helms delivered his judgment, he said:

"I have no reason at all to believe the testimony of Mr. Payne. He has every reason to not be truthful, whereas I can find no reason whatsoever to question the veracity or credibility of the officer who testified in this case."

Payne testified during the trial that he was informed at the end of his jail time that he would be charged with probation violation. "Mr. Gould said, 'Well look here, we can change that if you sign this statement.' Mr. Gould had a statement written, and it said that I received proper and adequate medical attention." Payne told the court he had refused to sign.

Payne later told me that Gould's response was, "If you don't sign it, you're going to prison."

"A half-hour later," reported Payne, "he came back with Major Stafford and said, 'You're going to prison on a probation violation.'"

My questions to Capt. Glen Matayabas, the jail administrator, about Payne's case, were forwarded to Sheriff's Department Attorney Julie Kepple, who told me: "There's no such release. It would make no sense—it would be worth less than the paper it was written on, because you can't waive that kind of right."

Mister Payne was found guilty and served seventeen months in a series of state prisons.

As a further legal kick in the teeth, Payne has since been denied his application for reinstatement of his commercial truck driving license. The N.C. State Drivers License office insists that he was convicted of death by vehicle involving a DUI, which automatically results in permanent revocation of a commercial license.

Payne has never been accused or convicted of DUI in this or any other context, but my repeated letters and phone calls to the state office have made no difference whatsoever. Once more the documentary record is flawed and a man who has served his sentence is being prevented from returning to his profession by a system that simply doesn't give a damn.

In recent years I've interviewed numerous other inmates and former inmates of the Buncombe County Detention Center, and while overall treatment of the prisoners seems to have improved, the systemic indifference and ineptitude remain entrenched.

9: Sudden insight

Bele Chere is an annual street festival in Asheville that means different things to different people. Some love the music, some hate the crowds, others turn a tidy profit, and many revel in the auto-free pedestrian novelty of the scene. The name itself was made up by a P.R. flack who aimed to give the event a bit of panache. The words meaningfully correspond to no known language (though the flack claimed its provenance as an obscure Celtic dialect). If it were French it would mean "moan food." That may be applicable to those who overindulge in funnel cake or beer, the two principal staples of festival-goers.

Chere, Bele?

For me, Bele Chere 2004 was and will remain singular because that's when my ongoing investigation of the sheriff's department opened like a lotus.

As usual, my newspaper had a booth at the festival, and we staffers worked the table, offering free refrigerator magnets, key chains and other tacky commercial memorabilia to attendees. I was in my office just around the corner when one of my co-workers stepped in and handed me a card. "Some woman stopped by the booth and asked me to give you her number. She'd like you to call."

The card sported a hand-written phone number and a name. B. Fraser. My pulse ratcheted. Brenda Fraser wanted to talk?

I waited a couple of hours, barely able to do other work, but figuring that anyone wandering around with a hundred thousand or so other fair-goers wouldn't be home yet—or be able to hear a cell phone ring. Finally I called. Fraser told me that she'd like to meet for coffee, that she had a lot to tell me. A whole lot. And that I'd only gotten one thing wrong in my story about Nisha Sherlin.

"What was that?"

"I didn't put Nisha in Broughton to hide her from the press. I did it to save her life. I was afraid Jeff would kill her. See you Tuesday."

Whew. I couldn't believe she had decided to come forward, and couldn't help but wonder why. And why now? I reread my reporting of the Sherlin events, pored over my notes and started a list of questions.

We met at a largish coffee shop in mid-morning. The place was all but deserted. I was keenly aware of not wanting to give Brenda any cause for alarm. I carried only a blank notebook, a typed list of questions and a pen. I assured her that I wasn't wearing a wire and told her that I would be happy to interview her on or off the record. She chose anonymity at the outset, and I guessed (correctly, it would turn out) that she was as nervous about the contact as I was. Soon enough we both deduced that we could trust each other and by the second interview we were both more relaxed.

The conversation launched from her comment on the phone about my getting most of the Sherlin story right. "There's no question that Jeff beat her half to death," Brenda told me. "She was out of her mind on drugs when she went into the E.R. She did talk about suicide—part of the time. Other times she denied it. I knew I had to get her someplace safe."

I learned that Brenda had been fired by Medford a couple of months before she had contacted me. By her account, later corroborated by Charu Kumaria, a reporter for WLOS TV-13 in Asheville, Brenda had been on duty in her role as the department's victim's advocate, working at the Family Resource Center, a facility set up to permit unhappily divorced couples to hand off child custody without meeting face to face. Medford called her and ordered her to do an interview with Kumaria. Brenda told me she told the sheriff that she was then interviewing a young girl who claimed to have been sexually molested by a parent and that she had deemed that task to be far more urgent than doing a sound-bite for TV news.

Kumaria, on deadline, had called Brenda's cell phone repeatedly, and when Brenda finally answered she "bit my head off," according to the reporter. Kumaria contacted the sheriff's office, attempting to find another talking head, and Medford was furious. Brenda was fired immediately.

The overview Brenda offered in that first interview was that the department under Medford was very corrupt. She said: "Most department employees, presumably all of them, know what's going on, but they're all afraid they'll lose their jobs if they talk. Some of them want Bobby's job and don't want to rock the boat. At the same time, many believe they can do a good job personally, in spite of what's going on."

Brenda also gave me my first glimpse of the sheriff's personal gambling habit. "He goes to Cherokee many nights. If his car isn't at his Weaverville apartment or the department, he's almost always off gambling. He's reliably at Cherokee on payday, every other Thursday. He shows up at the office to collect his paycheck then heads over there. Then he doesn't show up at work many mornings—supposedly because of his back—but it's because he gambles all night. He usually travels in his official car and he's usually with Sharon Stewart."

"Who's that?" I asked.

"Bobby's secretary. Her husband is Chief Deputy George Stewart."

"That sounds like expensive entertainment," I ventured.

"People bring Bobby money all the time. It's explained as 'gifts' because people appreciate his work. Lots of money. Cash. But he's still heavily in debt due to the gambling. He mortgaged his family home and he rents it out and lives in an apartment."

"Another thing you should know," Brenda confided, "He's addicted to prescription pain killers. He gets his scrips from a sports medicine clinic south of town. Debby is who you talk to there. Department employees are regularly dispatched to pick up his meds. He sent me sometimes. Other people bring him drugs at work when he is out."

"Do the drugs slow him down?" I wondered out loud.

"They change him. He's mean and sometimes explosive, depending on his drug level. He has an incredible temper and throws things at employees. I saw him throw a phone once. And he's sexist toward department employees, he even calls female deputies 'my cunts.' But he sure is charming to the public."

Our conversation turned toward ranking officers and other characters in the department. She told me that one son, Brian Medford, worked for the department as a civilian. "He doesn't come to work many days, and he always leaves by 3 p.m. Department employees chauffeur Brian in official cars—to the liquor store, to purchase drugs, to the motel where he goes with his girlfriend ... That's the Nakon Motel on Smokey Park Highway. He lives with his mother. When Brian's girlfriend was in jail in Hendersonville, department employees were assigned to transport him to visit her there."

Brenda added a story that would soon be reiterated to me by other officers: "The Asheville Police Department recently found Brian drugged out of his head, and drunk, in uniform. They didn't report it: they phoned Bobby and he rounded Brian up."

I was well aware that I was interviewing someone who could be characterized as a disgruntled former employee, but in the years since those first interviews *everything* Brenda told me would be corroborated by other former deputies. Ultimately a good bit of the information related to me would end up in a bill of indictment and be affirmed by a federal jury.

Following our second meeting, Brenda told me her husband, Don, was willing to talk to me as well and that they had both decided they were comfortable going public with their stories. For a reporter long stymied by the fear-factor, the breakthrough was incalculable. Off-the-record sources are always inherently suspect. Is the source simply making up information? Is the putative source actually in a position to know the facts being put forward?

Furthermore, the combination of the Frasers' fearlessness and the trust they showed in me soon led others to speak out as well. I will always believe that Bobby Medford's eventual federal indictment would not have occurred absent their selfless act of courage. The Frasers had absolutely nothing to gain from going public and much to lose.

My first conversation with Don started with an extensive delineation of nepotism in county hiring practices. He told me that County Manager Wanda Greene had taken responsibility for sheriff's department bookkeeping away from the department and placed it within her domain, then hired her sister-in-law to do the work. Greene hired Don to write a grant proposal for the department, which proposal included Don as grant administrator.

When the county was awarded the $1.3 million grant, Greene appointed someone else, one Pat Freeman, to administer the money. While Don felt cheated by Greene's betrayal, he told me that Freeman did a good job in the post.

Don noted that Medford employed his girlfriend's sons and sister in the jail, and that he'd also hired both of his girlfriend's brothers. As we'll see in the next chapter, North Carolina's nepotism law doesn't account for hiring relatives of one's paramour, and actual enforcement of the nepotism rules is sketchy at best.

While such favoritism is, at least, questionable, the next thing Don told me would prove to be far more significant. "Brenda was placed in charge of registering poker machines when the law first went into effect. When Jackie Shepherd went into business with a man in South Carolina and tried to bring in machines, Brenda denied him permits. So the job was given to Johnny Harrison, who was promoted to Lieutenant."

Don went on: "Harrison suddenly obtained a home in Myrtle Beach [South Carolina] and the permits were granted. "

When I later compared property transfer records from Myrtle Beach with county payroll records, Don was proved precisely accurate.

Don went on to tell me that Harrison spent much of his time at the new home in South Carolina. "He doesn't work more than two days a week and never stays in the office past noon, except on pay days. I shared an office with Harrison, so I was intimately aware of Harrison's work habits."

The talk turned to Shepherd. Don told me, "Jackie was bragging to me about how much money he made on his machines. He showed me a printed receipt that he claimed represented the money from one machine for one week. It was $27,000."

Shepherd would deny that figure when I spoke to him in 2005, though he didn't deny having shown Fraser the slip. He told me, "It ain't true." Asked what a more accurate estimate would be, he replied, "The girl in my office does the paperwork on them and turns it in for the taxes, but that isn't nowhere close."

He also challenged the Sheriff's Department's record of how many machines he operated. "I've only got sixteen machines," he told me. Told that the Sheriff's Department credited him with thirty-nine machines, Shepherd said, "Thirty-nine is probably how many I've got, but I'd have to get with the boy that runs that to find out how many we have on location."

Shepherd's business was evidently growing. Three years after my interviews with the Frasers and two years after I talked to him the feds confiscated Shepherd's equipment. They rounded up more than fifty video poker machines. Jackie Shepherd, his company and his business partners became the subject of a federal indictment for gambling activities, as did his son, Denver, who came up next in our conversation.

"Within the last six months a patrol officer, Roger Webb, caught Denver Shepherd with some drugs," Don alleged. "Within ten minutes Jackie and Bobby showed up. The evidence and the case disappeared and Webb was transferred to the east end of the county." Denver's name would come up again during the Medford trial, when Jackie Shepherd testified concerning his son's drug use.

10: Nepotism

Bobby Medford hired his long-time girlfriend's brothers and sons, a move that clearly violated the spirit, if not the letter, of the state's anti-nepotism law. But then he hired his son, Brian K. Medford, and clearly crossed the line. The county board of commissioners, which had to approve the hiring, appears not to have been given either the applicant's name or key information about his criminal record. That failure can be chalked up to the county manager, Wanda Greene, who pushed the approval through the system.

Don Fraser told me that Brian Medford was accorded preferential treatment while serving a sentence in the Buncombe County jail for DUI level 2. Don and other former department employees allege that the sheriff's son continued to receive special treatment after his hiring. Various department staffers contacted in connection with my investigation—including both Medford and his son—failed to respond to repeated phone calls and written inquiries. Finally, Medford wrote me and told me to talk to his attorneys.

County Personnel Department records showed that Medford hired his son as an office assistant on January 18, 2000. According to the minutes of that day's Board of Commissioners meeting, the "consent agenda" (a listing of routine matters that are collectively rubber-stamped by the commissioners) included this item:

"Approval of employee under NCGS 153A-103(1)." Brian Medford isn't mentioned by name, either here or in the supporting material appended to the official meeting transcript.

As a safeguard against nepotism, North Carolina General Statute 153A-103(1) stipulates that each sheriff or register of deeds "has the exclusive right to hire, discharge, and supervise the employees in his office. However the board of commissioners must approve the appointment by such an officer of a relative by blood or marriage of nearer kinship than first cousin or of a person who has been convicted of a crime involving moral turpitude."

Tom Sobol was chairman of the Buncombe County Board of Commissioners at the time of Brian's hiring. He told me, "I have no memory of the mention of Brian Medford's name." Sobol said he wasn't trying to pass the buck, but he believed that only County Manager Wanda Greene could answer the question.

Commissioner Patsy Keever, on the other hand, remembered that approving the Medford hiring was on the consent agenda but said such matters are routine. "It wasn't a big deal," she explained.

Sounding a similar theme, Commissioner David Gantt said: "We don't micromanage the sheriff, because he doesn't report to us. Like us, he is an elected official, and we count on him to make good decisions." Asked about the missing name, Gantt told me, "Since the reason for the law is to regulate nepotism, we should have said the name."

Commissioner David Young, who made the motion to approve the consent agenda on that date, said he doesn't remember either the vote or Brian Medford's name being brought up in any context. "It should have been mentioned," conceded Young.

Commissioner Bill Stanley did not attend the meeting in question.

Asked about the failure to mention the applicant's name, Greene told me, "There was a cover letter accompanying the agenda that discussed what we were going to do." That letter doesn't give Brian Medford's name either; it merely grants the sheriff permission to hire a relative. The county manager was unavailable for further comment, but her office relayed a message saying, "Including the name is not required by law."

David Lawrence, a public-records expert at the N.C. School of Government, took a somewhat different view. "There isn't any established law concerning this matter, but I would have thought that the motion needed to mention the name," he told me. "Otherwise it is unclear who the Board of Commissioners had authorized the sheriff to hire. My advice would have been to put the name in the public record."

Apparently, neither Greene nor the Sheriff's Department informed the commissioners about Brian Medford's two DUI convictions. "I would certainly remember if there had been discussion of a criminal record in connection with hiring at the Sheriff's Department," Sobol told me. And both Keever and Gantt confirmed that there'd been no mention of the applicant's having a criminal record.

Asked if the board would have investigated the case, Sobol said: "No. That would be up to the department head."

County Attorney Joe Connolly told me that the law "does not specifically state that the individual being hired must be named in the approval. But clearly, the better practice would have been to have named the individual and make it part of the official minutes. I take responsibility for this oversight."

Concerning Brian Medford's criminal record, Connolly said, "I could not find a definitive answer regarding this issue, but I did check with other lawyers, who share the same opinion: that driving while impaired is not a crime involving moral turpitude."

Internet searches including Findlaw.com and MirrorofJustice.com proved inconclusive on this point. In some jurisdictions only aggravated DUI convictions qualify as moral turpitude, in others repeated offenses or specific blood alcohol levels may qualify, and in some states it seems to be left to judges to interpret the offense. Notwithstanding these variations, an impaired driving conviction is sufficient grounds for revocation of law enforcement certification in North Carolina, as would come to light during the Medford trial.

According to state records, Brian Medford was convicted of DUI level 5 on June 2, 1994, and of DUI level 2 (a class B misdemeanor) on November 11, 1995. He was sentenced to a seven-day term in the work-release program on November 28, 1995; Don Fraser confirmed that Medford had served time in the county jail system.

Don held various positions within the department between 1985 and 2004, including annex supervisor at the county work-release facility while Brian Medford was an inmate. "Our orders were, 'Don't worry about where he goes,' even if he came in at 1 a.m.," Fraser told me. Furthermore, "We were told, 'Don't worry about what's in his locker.'"

According to Deputy Patrocinio Valdez, who worked in the jail, "Work-release prisoners are only allowed time to get to their work shift and back to the [jail] annex. They are only permitted to have what they purchase here. When they come in, all they bring is just the clothes on their backs."

Capt. Glen Matayabas told me: "Jail records are public records. I can e-mail or fax them to you if you tell me what records you want."

But after being given Brian Medford's name and the approximate dates of his incarceration in an August 30, 2004 e-mail, Matayabas failed to respond to the request. Contacted again by phone in October of that year, Matayabas told me that he'd turned the question over to Attorney for the Sheriff Julie Kepple in early September.

In a subsequent phone conversation, however, Kepple denied having received information about my inquiries during the previous two months.

During the same conversation, Kepple told me, "I wouldn't trust that source if I were you"—even though no sources had been named or even mentioned in any communication with the department. Asked what source she was referring to, Kepple responded, "Brenda Fraser."

When I told Fraser about Kepple's warning, she told me about another, possibly more serious warning she had recently received. Brenda reported, "I was talking to Kaye Shepherd [Jack Shepherd's wife] recently and she told me, 'You better not be talking.' I said, 'They don't have anything over me.' The next day Kaye called back and said 'You know I don't really talk to Jack about this stuff, but I mentioned what you said and he got really mad. He said you shouldn't fight the sheriff's people because they will win. I repeated that they don't have anything over me and Kaye said "They'll kill you and eat you up. They are a mean crowd."

Brian Medford, meanwhile, continued to work for the Sheriff's Department, earning $26,500 per year. At various times, his responsibilities included overseeing the metal detector at the courthouse and escorting prisoners between the jail and courtrooms. According to Kepple, who was soon named personnel director at the Sheriff's Department in addition to her duties as the department's attorney, the sheriff's son answered phones at the front desk in the sheriff's office.

As of 2005, according to the N.C. Division of Motor Vehicles, Brian Medford had not reclaimed his driver's license (which was revoked in November 1995 in connection with his second DUI conviction) because he never completed the substance-abuse assessment requirement. Under North Carolina law, a person whose license is revoked in connection with a DUI conviction "must have a substance-abuse assessment and, depending on the results of the assessment, must complete either an alcohol- and drug-education traffic school or a substance-abuse treatment program." As a result of that failure, he was only permitted to hold a civilian job at the department.

Both the Frasers and other former deputies (who requested anonymity) alleged that Brian Medford was routinely chauffeured on personal errands by department employees using county vehicles. Brenda Fraser told me that she had repeatedly performed this task herself, under orders from the sheriff.

Letters to the sheriff dated August 31, September 6 and October 18, 2004, went unanswered, as did letters to Brian Medford dated August 31 and October 18. Kepple told me on November 4 that if no reply had been received to those letters, "it should be interpreted as refusal."

11: Missed meds—a reprise

During my investigation of Payne's woes a 42-year-old inmate, Marvis Gail Davidson, had died at the Buncombe County Detention Center in July, 2004, and other reports of mistreatment continued to accumulate. These came directly from former inmates and their families and through the local chapter of the American Civil Liberties Union. Karen VanEman, then-president of the WNC chapter, told me that she kept hearing the same allegations over and over again. Stories of prisoner abuse and unexplained deaths cropped up elsewhere in the state as well.

Nor were inmates the only ones reporting in-humane treatment at the Buncombe jail. The former guard who had reiterated the story about Rogers' homicide (and who requested anonymity, fearing reprisals from Medford and others) described having seen serious problems while working there. Two complaints, the former guard said, were filed "about [Marvis Davidson's] medical treatment, including failure to correctly administer insulin. And I was told by another guard that Davidson said she had severe stomach pains for four days before she died." The autopsy report, which I obtained from the state medical examiner, said she died due to an ischemia (decrease in blood supply) and resulting hemorrhage of her small intestine. Diabetes is a contributory cause of ischemia, according to *First*

Principles of Gastroenterology, an online textbook, but the examiner's report offered no proof of that diagnosis.

At an April 18, 2005 ACLU forum in Asheville, former Buncombe inmate Joshua McKinney said he'd been forced to sleep on a bare concrete floor while in a holding cell at the facility, adding that other inmates had been kept under such conditions for as many as fourteen days. Prisoners in the holding cells are not provided with personal-care products and are denied showers, McKinney reported, adding that toilet paper is in very short supply.

This was consistent with what Payne had told me. "When I said I wanted a shower, they told me I'd have to be in shackles—hand and foot, with a chain between them —for me to get a shower," said Payne. "I asked them how I was supposed to take a shower when I was in chains, and they said that was the way it would have to be."

Former inmate Edgar O. Teague Jr., who served ten days beginning March 28, 2005, told a similar story about the conditions in holding. "There were up to thirty-two people in my cell at one time, with no shower. I finally told them that another inmate had urinated on me, and they let me out to get a shower," said Teague. "Some of the other inmates saw what I did and claimed the same thing, so they got showers, too."

My story featuring Payne's treatment ran in May, 2005, and included mention of Davidson's and Rogers' deaths along with allegations from several other former inmates. I had no way to establish whether or not she had been, in fact, a diabetic until another former inmate contacted me, having read my story. The woman, an attorney who insisted she had been wrongly imprisoned for embezzlement and was then seeking expungement of her record and readmission to the bar, had been a cellmate of Davidson's at the North Carolina Correctional Institution for Women in Raleigh. She told me that

Davidson had been receiving regular insulin injections while at the Raleigh facility and had been remanded to Buncombe County to face a court proceeding shortly before she died.

Almost one year later, Davidson's daughter contacted me to ask what I knew about her right to file a wrongful death suit concerning her mother. In the course of our conversation, she confirmed that her mother had been a diabetic and told me that another inmate who had been incarcerated in the Buncombe jail at the time of Marvis' death had come forward to say that Marvis had been begging for her medication and complaining of stomach cramps for days before she died. I put the daughter in touch with a local attorney of my acquaintance, P.J. Roth, and a law suit was initiated just two days before a two-year statute of limitations deadline.

12: The letter of the law

While Medford was certainly legally responsible for prisoners in his charge and for the behavior of his guards, his legal and ethical shortcomings are shared by many of his peers and colleagues.

Concerning prisoner protection, here's the legal rub: Under North Carolina law, you can sue a municipality for damages only if it carries liability insurance or if there is a specific state statute which permits such a suit. Thanks to the political pull of insurance companies, most municipalities carry liability insurance. Even then, the legislature has granted local governments a five hundred thousand dollar deductible.

Deductible from claims, that is. Not actually a payable deductible like an individual might have on an auto or health policy. No one ever collects that money.

The municipality is permitted to assert "sovereign immunity" on the first half million, and the insurance carrier is responsible for the balance on larger set-tlements. This keeps the cost of insurance lower because such large settlements or judgments are rare. While it lends the appearance of fiscal responsibility, this tends to be more smoke and mirrors than compensatory justice.

The chance that a claim will exceed the five hundred thousand level is slim. Thus there is little financial incentive to reign-in abusive guards, as long as they indulge their violent impulses out of sight.

It's no surprise that some jailers feel they can act with impunity and that municipal administrations feel no pressure to improve conditions. The truth is that there is also a widespread public presumption of guilt on the part of inmates even if there is a legal presumption of innocence. Plus, there's a general feeling among many average citizens that jail isn't supposed to be a nice place and that rough treatment may help maintain order or discourage recidivism.

A single statute on the books in North Carolina addresses criminal mistreatment of prisoners by jailers and awards *triple damages* to successful litigants. The difficulty lies in proving criminal behavior or criminal negligence on the part of the guard(s). Roth moved ahead with Davidson's case based on this statute. On August 4, 2008, Roth filed a complaint alleging criminal negligence on the part of Buncombe County contributed to Davidson's death.

As with so much else in our legal system, this state of affairs favors the rich. A rich person is unlikely to be sitting in a cell in the first place, since she would be able to bail out pending her trial. The rich rarely do time for petty crimes. Besides, if a practicing forty-two-year-old doctor died in a cell, the jury might well assess her lost income at two hundred thousand dollars per year, or four million by age sixty-two.

But suppose you are a forty-two-year-old unemployed, divorced, black woman with a low-level criminal history and no dependents and you die in your cell. What will a jury think your life was worth? Maybe you'd have found and kept a job and made minimum wage to age 62 and then gone on Social Security. Your expected wages would only amount to about half the magic figure.

But let's suppose the jury feels some compassion for your adult children and grandchildren and awards them six hundred thousand in damages. After the five hundred thousand deduction they only actually receive one sixth the settlement amount and an attorney working on contingency claims up to half of that. For the loss of a mother and expenditure of a few years wrangling with the system, attending meetings with your lawyer and going to court, your heirs receive fifty thousand dollars. Nor is the attorney satisfied, because the years of work and staff expenses almost certainly represent a net loss. All of this because your family was lucky enough to *win* the case.

As I learned in my pursuit of Payne's story, the presumption of the courts seems to favor law enforcement officials. In Payne's case the judge chose to believe a guard who actually perjured himself *right in front of the judge* in the course of a short hearing, rather than believe a prisoner who was telling the truth which was fully supported by jail documents. According to the trial transcript, Payne's lawyer pointed out that discrepancy during the hearing, and the judge still ruled against Payne.

Roth took the case partly because he is outraged about Davidson's treatment, but even more so because there is the possibility that he could make "good law" to the effect that in cases of criminal misconduct or negligence by local government the state cannot claim sovereign immunity. He said: "At rock-bottom, a win at the appellate level means a chance to 'make' good law by which to empower lawyers and victims to seek redress for their injuries. Of course there's the more likely chance that my efforts will result in making 'bad' law through an unfavorable decision, but since the inmates' plight in North Carolina can't get much worse than it is already, I don't perceive the possibility of an unfavorable decisions as sufficient reason not to try."

His hope is that if he wins and enough lawyers use the statute to score big settlements, municipalities and the state will be forced to change their ways and ultimately result in better treatment of prisoners statewide.

Rogers' survivors reportedly considered filing a wrongful death suit but couldn't find a lawyer to take their case. The Statute of Limitations has long-since run out on the Rogers' case.

For all his woes, Mister Payne was a lucky one.

He got out alive.

13: Machine politics

The end of legal video poker in South Carolina launched a flood of machines across the state line. The North Carolina General Assembly sprang into action—legalizing and regulating the burgeoning trade. The state's sheriffs were saddled with machine registration and oversight and they reacted in two ways. While all one hundred of them signed a letter to the legislative body requesting that the machines be banned. Meanwhile, a subset of that group recognized a golden opportunity.

For some it may have simply been too tempting to ignore—finding themselves placed in charge of guarding the hen house *and* providing the only accounting of the hens. For others it was simply one more opportunity in a long history of racketeering. Crooked sheriffs have a long and storied history.

When the new law went into effect, Medford appointed Brenda Fraser as registrar of the machines. The North Carolina Sheriff's Association issued registration forms and identification stickers. It was Fraser's job to distribute forms, collect and file the completed paperwork and issue stickers which were to appear in plain view on the machines. The form included the owner's affirmation that the machine been in the state as of January 31, 2000, listed as business property with the county tax department and had been put into operation no later than June 30 of that year. Notarized signatures

were affixed to the forms and the department's responsibility under that law was limited to ascertaining that the
form was filled out correctly and filed. Owners were
expected to be honest and the registration and stickers
were provided free of charge.

Enter Jackie Shepherd.

Shepherd and Medford went back decades—both
men are north-Buncombe County natives, and back in the
day it was small enough that everybody knew everybody.
While Medford made his way in law enforcement, first
with the sheriff's department, later with the Asheville
Police Department and then back to being a sheriff's
deputy again, Shepherd became a shopkeeper, building a
small chain of convenience stores, laundromats and
groceries as well as the Cherokee Trading Post, a pawn
shop with an emphasis on tobacco and guns. On the side
he ran gambling operations which my sources indicate
included high-stakes card games and slot machines.

In 1990 Charlie Long was elected sheriff and fired
Medford, then a detective with the county. Medford
found a job as police chief in Rutledge, Georgia, a tiny
town about fifty miles east of Atlanta. By his account,
offered in federal court, Medford hated the position,
served out a one-year contract and returned home to take
jobs, as a car salesman or collection agent (perhaps both)
for a couple of car dealers. By 1993 he was working for
Shepherd, "collecting money from the washing
machines".

Meanwhile, Sheriff Long had cracked down on
illegal gambling in Buncombe, making Shepherd a very
unhappy man. As Shepherd testified at Medford's trial,
"We needed some changes in the county. We needed him
[Medford] to go in and clean up the county." In short, he
decided to buy himself a more accommodating sheriff.

Shepherd hired a tailor to make Medford a couple
of suits and later claimed he had hired a speech con-

sultant to teach his chosen law man how to speak in front of crowds. He told friends, "I made Bobby sheriff." (In court, Medford would confirm the tailoring, "He bought me three suits," but denied the speech lessons.)

Shepherd said he spent $20,000 to $30,000 getting Medford elected in 1994. Long no longer caused him headaches. Medford took a very different approach to gambling enforcement as was evident two years later when one of his detectives, Mike Bustle, organized a raid on an alleged gambling house owned by a prominent Asheville attorney, also a friend of Medford's. Bustle was fired. End of problem.

(I contacted Charlie Long in the course of researching this book, but he declined to make any statement whatsoever.)

Fast-forward to late 2000 when Shepherd appeared in Fraser's office seeking to register video poker machines. He had been in and out of the department offices with some regularity since Medford's 1994 election, so he was a familiar face to Deputy Brenda Fraser. Kay Carter, a part-time department employee with whom Fraser then had a congenial relationship, worked for Shepherd as well. Add to that the fact that the department community was close and gossip-filled, and it's easy to understand that Fraser was well aware that Shepherd had lately formed a partnership with a South Carolina gaming operator and that the gambling machines he sought to register were recent imports from south of the border. She denied Shepherd's registration request.

Medford took swift action to solve the problem. Fraser was immediately reassigned and Deputy Homer Honeycutt was put in charge of registration.

Honeycutt wore at least three hats in Medford's world. He worked in management for the Bi-Lo supermarket chain, was Mayor of Woodfin and was employed by the Buncombe County Sheriff's Department. He drove an unmarked sheriff's cruiser equipped with a radio and blue lights and was seen on many occasions driving the county-owned vehicle to campaign functions (before he was elected) and using it to conduct town business (after he was elected mayor).

Moreover, Honeycutt together with Medford and D.A. Ron Moore, was involved, albeit murkily, in the public humiliation of Woodfin Police Chief Pete Bradley who apparently knew too much about corruption in WNC law enforcement.

In 2000, Bradley informed the State Bureau of Investigation of alleged criminal activity concerning the Department of Motor Vehicles which he charged involved coerced political contributions, cash bribes and favors for Democratic politicians up to and including then-Governor Jim Hunt. He also made allegations of ticket fixing by DMV employees and fraudulent weight inspection of commercial vehicles owned by insider companies.

After leaving the DMV in 1999, Bradley had opened a law enforcement supply business. The next year he tried and failed to get his DMV job back. He told a reporter, "They wanted more money to come back. That's when I went to the SBI," he said.

He asserted he was asked to give Democratic candidates $5,000 to recover his position. "That's when I blew up and said, `I'm sick of this crap,' " he said. That's also when he went to federal and state investigators.

Just before he filed his charges, he received an anonymous blackmail letter. It alluded to parties he had attended with men who wore diapers and snapped pictures of one another.

According to Wikipedia, "Paraphilic infantilism is a paraphilia characterized by the desire to wear diapers and be treated as an infant or toddler. One who engages in infantilistic play is known as an adult baby (AB). About one in three adult babies is also a diaper lover (DL), so they are collectively known as AB/DLs. The majority of infantilists are heterosexual males." Other online sources suggest that diaper parties are more commonly the province of homosexual or bisexual behavior.

"No threats here," the letter read, "but I would suggest leaving well enough alone to preserve YOUR privacy or people may need to know the deal. The repercussions could be bad for any careers, yours and others. Let it go man."

Bradley later acknowledged participating in the consensual gatherings and publicly self-identified as a bisexual, which he called his personal business. On his attorney's advice, he gave SBI investigators the letter only after being assured it would remain confidential.

In February, the portion of the SBI report involving the diaper parties was leaked to the Asheville media and published in a couple of papers. Fliers containing it were distributed at a town meeting. The town board fired Bradley shortly afterward.

The source of the leak was never established, though District Attorney Ron Moore admitted he gave portions of the report to a law enforcement agency he wouldn't identify. Given the circumstances and the known friction between Bradley and Honeycutt, it was broadly speculated that the department in question was the Buncombe County Sheriff's Department. Bradley stopped talking pending his civil rights law suit and the substantial cash settlement he ultimately received was contingent on Bradley's silence, so his testimony never emerged and the DMV investigation quietly died, as did Bradley's wife.

In a truth-is-stranger-than-fiction coda to Bradley's travails, his sometimes too-talkative wife, Patsy, was found dead of a gunshot wound in a room locked from the inside. A suicide? Bradley was charged with murder, but was acquitted. My sources have suggested all kinds of scenarios including a purported sex-swapping-internet ring in Biltmore Forest and suggestions that she was ready to go public concerning either the DMV corruption or other matters.

On the other hand, Bradley was convicted of violence against a female for allegedly assaulting his wife months earlier. She had also obtained a restraining order at the time she filed charges. The trial and conviction, however, came after her untimely demise. Members of her family continue to press for further investigation of what they allege must have been a murder.

Whatever the accuracy of Bradley's corruption charges might have been, Governor Mike Easley ordered a reorganization of state law enforcement which removed weight inspection from DMV and handed it over to the North Carolina Highway Patrol.

In November, 2001, a Woodfin patrolman taped Honeycutt bragging about fixing tickets. "I fix more tickets than you probably write," Honeycutt boasted on the tape obtained and reported by the Asheville *Citizen-Times*. "You write 'em, I fix 'em." Ticket fixing would come up again during the Medford trial with the lead prosecutor noting that the government considered inclusion of that crime in its indictment, but decided that it constituted a relatively minor matter when compared to extortion, fraud, gambling and conspiracy.

Years later, Johnny Harrison's testimony during the Medford trial revealed that Honeycutt used his management position at Bi-Lo to facilitate money laundering in the multi-year golf-tournament/extortion/mail-fraud scheme for which the former sheriff and others are now doing time. Honeycutt cashed checks made out to the Medford re-election effort, an explicit violation of campaign finance law.

According to Fraser, Honeycutt was "hopeless" as a record keeper and her careful filing system was soon reduced to a shambles. But Shepherd's machines were stickered in short order, so Honeycutt was taking care of the business that mattered to Medford.

However, Honeycutt proved a little too parochial in his loyalties. Jerry Pennington testified that when he showed up to register machines for Henderson Amusement, "Mr. Honeycutt said they had plenty of machines in here and didn't want more. But Mr. Penland said that Honeycutt had no right to do that and that he would talk to Medford."

Sure enough, Honeycutt was out of that job in a heartbeat and Johnny Harrison was placed in charge of the video poker machine business. And Pennington got his stickers, too.

14: Same as it ever was

Medford's defense attorney, Stephen Lindsay, alluded to the history of gambling in Buncombe a couple of times in the course of his client's federal trial, but never succeeded in making much hay for the jury.

Lindsay noted that gambling machines had been in use in the county at least as far back as the administration of Sheriff Harry Clay. His co-counsel, Victoria Jayne, also elicited from Johnny Harrison the fact that Harrison is married to Clay's widow. For the rest of the trial, attentive listeners had to be wondering if Lindsay or Jayne would make some further connection in hopes of blaming Harrison for corruption ongoing since Clay's era, and thereby lightening the load on Medford. But the defense team never followed up.

Harrison seemed to understand what Honeycutt had missed, that there was plenty of money to be made in the video poker business—more than enough to satisfy Shepherd and Henderson and whoever else wanted to opt in—and that the pinch-point under the new law was located in the registration office. He was ready and willing to squeeze.

Under Harrison's management, poker machine operators quickly learned that repeated "contributions" to Medford were part of the game plan. They became supporters of the semi-annual "Bobby Medford Golf Classic" and allowed themselves to be extorted for more money between golf games. The term "bagman" is applied to all sorts of characters, ranging from helpful assistant to hired gun, but it can never be more literally applied than to Harrison. He testified that he kept a bank bag of cash in his patrol car trunk, ready to dole out to Medford as needed.

Almost simultaneous with Harrison's appointment to the registration detail was his acquisition of a beachside condominium in Myrtle Beach. None of the names associated with the past ownership of that unit or the overall condo development available in the Horry County, South Carolina Register of Deeds office have turned up in my fairly exhaustive background checks of video poker operators in both states. Perhaps his new-found income stream simply moved Harrison's retirement plans up a notch or two on his calendar. He retired in May, 2005, twenty months before he was indicted.

During Jayne's cross-examination she inquired of Harrison, "Your ability to enjoy the beach in your later years will be somewhat restricted if you are in jail."

"Ma'am, you've got that right," he replied. But evidently sensing that her intent was to impeach his testimony he added, "It's hard for me to sit up here and say what I've done. What Bobby has done. What Guy has done or to talk about Frank Orr [a civilian co-organizer of the golf tournaments who escaped indictment]. I pleaded guilty because I am guilty and I would appreciate any consideration I might receive."

Harrison had been an organizer of the semi-annual Medford Golf Classics since their inception in 1994, so he was well-practiced at shaking down donors interested in buying a piece of local law enforcement. That first year, the spring and fall tournaments were cast as campaign fundraisers and moneys collected were routed into the campaign account. Checks were written to the election campaign and cash payments were happily accepted. There was a fee for each team and sponsorship of holes and golf carts, which earned the donor a yard sign advertising his or her business.

After Medford won his four-year post, the golf tourneys still seemed like a good idea, and so they continued. In off-years the money was routed directly to Medford, then in election years it was directed to the campaign. As late as his trial, Medford insisted that he was entitled to the money and claimed that he used it for charitable causes. No one could ever accuse him of being ungenerous to his family and there were many stories about food and fuel and clothing purchased for the needy, particularly the elderly. How much he collected and how much he gave away is, of course, a matter of conjecture.

Cashing checks written to the committee to elect a politician is, however, indefensible. They are supposed to be deposited in the campaign account. So Harrison turned to Medford's friend Honeycutt and started cashing checks through Honeycutt's employer, the Bi-Lo super-market on Leicester Highway in Asheville. Apparently there are so many checks flowing through a large grocery that no one higher up in management ever questioned the practice. When Honeycutt transferred to the Weaverville Bi-Lo, the check cashing operation moved as well.

Later, when Honeycutt left his grocery job, Harrison found a willing cashier in the person of Nick Anagnostopoulos, a Greek national and owner of several convenience stores in WNC, each of which housed illegal video poker operations. He had every reason to accede to the sheriff's needs. Like Medford's benefactor Jackie Shepherd, Anagnostopoulos had built a chain of stores, and though he came late to the gambling business the lucrative crime and perhaps a good head for business allowed him to expand far faster than Shepherd. He had video poker machines in all of his stores starting in 2001. His demeanor is that of a well-heeled businessman with street-smarts and expensive tastes. At the time of the

Medford trial he was building himself a mega-mansion on Town Mountain, one of the "right" places to live in Asheville, and a fine place to land for the "community confinement" to which he was ultimately sentenced, assuming, of course, that his felony conviction doesn't cost him his Green Card.

Between Medford's first run for office and his final foray in 2006, North Carolina's election laws were tightened, a fact which caused increasing trouble for the illegal scheme. The maximum amount of anonymous cash donations was reduced to $100 then to under $50, and donor addresses, phone numbers, professions, employers and check numbers had to be submitted as well. Expenses required more detailed accounting and "petty cash" outlays were restricted.

But Harrison was able to manage his end of the job. He kept careful, if informal, records of all of the golf tournaments in notebooks which would come back to bite the sheriff when the federal government became interested. In election years he turned over the money, or some of it, to the campaign treasurer, who faced the increasingly daunting task of creating a plausible accounting.

In the summer of 2004, with the help of the Frasers, I was following several threads at once. The most immediately fruitful was a quick look at video poker machine registration. I began to drop in on poker locations, checking for stickers and on October 13 we went to press with a short news item, "Letter of the law?" The lead ran:

"Video-poker machines in Buncombe County appear to be out of compliance with state law. In recent visits to eight local establishments that have such machines, we did not find any that seemed to satisfy the letter of the law.

"The most frequently encountered violation was placing the machines out of sight. According to NCGS 14-

306.1.(f), "Any video gaming machine available for operation shall be in plain view of persons visiting the premises." On other machines, the required registration information wasn't visible."

The story went on to mention both Honeycutt and Harrison and reported the runaround I"d gotten from Alcohol Law Enforcement, the State Bureau of Investigation and the sheriff's department when I raised questions about the violations.

One response to that story was an anonymous tip from a woman who told me her son had won $5,000 at the Hot Dog King in Fairview.

During this period, I looked back at Medford's campaign finance records from the 2002 election. I was astonished. There were pages and pages listing $100 anonymous cash donations, plus aggregated and unattributed cash donations from fund raising events. Oddly, many of the $100 "aggregated individual" donations were listed as "checks," with no explanation of why checks couldn't be attributed to check-writers. Altogether these amounted to $17,024 of the $61,000 he raised that year. Numerous substantial donations were attributed to associates and administrators in the department and some of the names were, as one would expect, big names in local Republican party campaign circles.

However, beyond some incidental omissions of address information, the account fulfilled the requirements of applicable election laws at the time. I filed it away and turned my attention to a more easily documented violation of the law: payroll fraud.

15. Willful blindness

In addition to tipping me off about Harrison's purchase of a Myrtle Beach condo, Don Fraser had said, ""He doesn't work more than two days a week and never stays in the office past noon, except on pay days." He added, "And he drives his patrol car back and forth to the coast." I wondered about documenting such absences, but both Don and Brenda said they had been ordered to falsify payroll records for the administrative staff, and that others were ordered to do the same, so those records would be of little value.

On top of that, I soon learned from Director Ron Thornberry of the county personnel department, that payroll records were not public documents. He could and did provide me with a full list of sheriff's department employees, but nothing about their hours, absences, vacations and so forth.

Then I thought back over what Brenda had told me about Medford's gambling habits and his work hours spent at Harrah's casino. That, too, would involve travel outside the county.

What I really needed was documentation of some sort. I talked to Bob Hunter, head of the county fleet maintenance division, and learned that every county car came equipped with a specifically assigned credit card and that credit card records were deemed to be public documents since they reflected public spending. All I needed in order to file a request was a tag number. So I cruised through the sheriff's department parking lot a few times snapping photos of tags and cars and learned from the Frasers who drove which vehicles.

Medford's credit card record showed two gas fill-ups outside the county, one near Cherokee, one in South Carolina. Driving a county car outside the county on other than official business is a violation of the law. Kepple could provide no explanation for the sheriff's travel outside the county on those occasions, so once again I confirmed that Medford entertained no scruples when it came to the law.

Harrison's account revealed that he bought a lot of gas for a non-patrol officer, but maybe he just liked to cruise. I contemplated staking out the condo in Myrtle Beach, a six hour drive from home. But I decided a coastal venture seemed like far too expensive an endeavor in time and money.

I decided to approach the problem head-on and wrote letters to Medford, Harrison, Chief Deputy George Stewart, secretary Sharon Stewart and factotum Brian Medford, requesting access to their county payroll and attendance records.

I wrote:

My paper will soon go to press with allegations concerning payroll fraud in the Buncombe County Sheriff's Department.

My sources have implicated you in this matter, either as a beneficiary of falsified time-sheets or as being aware of the practice and failing to report it.

If you have any comments to make concerning this matter, you can phone me or reply by mail or e-mail. I am interested in your response, either on or off the record.

Several other current or former BCSD employees have spoken to me on condition of anonymity, as they are concerned about the possibility of professional repercussions. In fact, Sheriff Medford has dropped the certification of at least one former deputy, Marcia Dies, who had not spoken to me (see her letter to the paper, enclosed), so the threat is real, whether or not you choose to talk to the press.

For your information, if you choose to talk off the record, my compliance is absolute. In accord with the strictest standards of professional journalism, I will go to jail before I reveal the names of off-the-record sources.

None of them favored me with a reply.

Then Brenda had an inspired idea. "Sharon Stewart keeps phone logs. Sharon, or whoever is at her desk. Each call that comes in to Bobby is logged and initialed by whoever takes the call. You could easily figure out when Sharon was out of the office because someone else's initials will be there, mine, for instance, when I was answering." She added, "Those logs are in a closet off the hall near Bobby's office. They go all the way back to 1994. Can you get your hands on them?"

Through an inquiry to the N.C. School of Government, I learned there was just one hangup. Phone logs are not required paperwork and therefore are not deemed to be public records. There was no way to demand to see them. The only way to obtain them was through a court order, and that would likely require an official investigation.

In the past, when I had discussed sheriff's office matters with county commissioners, I had been informed that the only power they had over the sheriff's office was in funding and in employment of relatives. In late December, 2004, I e-mailed the five county commissioners informing them that I had on-the-record sources alleging payroll fraud, which involved both employment and funding, and asking if any of them were interested in doing something about it. Chairman Nathan Ramsey told me it sounded serious and that I should take it up with the county attorney, Joe Connolly. Commissioner David Gantt said it sounded serious and he wanted to look into it. Others didn't reply.

So I talked to Connolly, and at his urging, to D.A. Ron Moore. Connolly said he would look into it while Moore said he could do nothing unless someone swore out charges against Medford.

A month went by. Five weeks. Finally I phoned Gantt and asked him if he would be willing to walk in the front door of the sheriff's department with me and request—demand if necessary—to see the phone logs. I didn't see how the sheriff could refuse such a request from a commissioner, and I hoped I would be on safer legal ground because Gantt is also an attorney.

He demurred and said he thought he knew a back-door way to obtain those records, and having no good option in sight, I assented.

A week later I received a letter from Kepple denying my "request" for access to the phone logs, which, I could easily guess, no longer existed. I learned that Gantt had asked County Manager Wanda Greene for help in obtaining the logs.

Greene had obviously tipped off Medford.

I was feeling less and less certain who could be trusted, and received multiple warnings from friends that I should watch my back—more than one suggested that body armor wouldn't be inappropriate. Sarz pointed out that bad cops sometimes used false drug charges to waylay their opponents. I started getting regular urine tests to establish a clean track record and tried not to be nervous traversing dark streets downtown.

16: Wanna bet?

My payroll inquiry had been thwarted and my newspaper
editors refused to publish a story about alleged fraud,
despite my on-the-record sources and the documented
cooperation (collusion?) between the county administration and the sheriff's office. But my gambling
investigation moved forward. I compared the county tax
office records of gaming machines with a list of machines
I pried out of the sheriff's video poker registration office.
Medford initially refused to grant access to the records,
but I filed a formal request under the state's open records
law, and, following a long delay, Kepple finally handed
me a list and permitted inspection of a file drawer in the
registration office. The records themselves appeared
scrambled, some signed by operators, others simply filled
in, without signatures. There was no readily apparent
alphabetization or arrangement by date. But at least I had
the list.

I quickly discovered significant discrepancies, with
each agency listing some machine owners who didn't
appear in the other's records. They should have matched
exactly. State law required sheriff's departments to report
all such machines to the county tax office because they
are subject to *ad valorem* taxation as business equipment.

Adding in a dozen or so units I discovered on my
own which were not included on either list, I came up

with an estimate of 520 machines. These were housed in convenience stores, gas stations, body shops, furniture stores, tire stores, beauty parlors, restaurants, fraternal organizations and other venues throughout Buncombe County. An exact tally was impossible, given inaccuracies and omissions in Sheriff's Department records and the fact that many machines were hidden from view.

North Carolina general statute S14-306.1(f) read, "Plain View. - Any video gaming machine available for operation shall be in plain view of persons visiting the premises."

Evidence from other parts of the state suggested that such gaming was likely to be a multi-million-dollar business in the county. I read that gambling experts call such machines "video crack" because like crack cocaine, the cost per "hit" is low, but the effect can quickly become addictive. I staked out a handful of locations and learned that users typically played one-handed, keeping the other hand free to extract and light a steady stream of cigarettes. Butts mounded up in ashtrays as players fed fresh $20 bills into the automated slot when the credits on the screen drop to zero. "Winnings" ran up into hundreds or thousands of dollars on the display, only to melt again as the player delivers rapid-fire hits to the touch-screen or button control.

Asked about the discrepancies, Business Personal Property Appraiser Heather Lunsford of the Buncombe County Tax Office told me "If the Sheriff's Department has names of video-poker-machine owners that we don't have, then the sheriff hasn't been reporting the names to us."

The sheriff's department listed at least thirty-nine machines that didn't appear in county tax records, but it was difficult to estimate how much that cost the county, since the tax listing assigned widely varying values to different owners' machines. Robert D. Garren's thirty-six machines were pegged at $4,186 each, for example, whereas Charles McBennett's thirty-nine units were valued at a mere $64 apiece (which Lunsford said may have represented a depreciated value). At the higher figure, Buncombe County was losing about $1,000 per year in tax revenues from unreported machines. And if all of the machines in use were valued at the higher rate, the county would have collected more than $14,000 per year from their owners in property taxes. In any event, the missing thousand dollars amounted to about a third of actual collections which came to some $3,000 annually, according to the Tax Office. All of these figures amount to small potatoes compared to payoffs to the sheriff and the endless stream of twenties fed into machines by eager gamblers. (Machines located within the city limits are also subject to city taxes, but the missing taxes were still pretty paltry in the big scheme of illegal gambling.)

Kepple, who was charged with maintaining the video-poker files, or at least straightening them out, responded to questions about the records by observing that the video-gambling business was essentially self-regulating. "They report to us when they move a machine," she said. "We don't go out looking for them."

During Medford's trial Kepple testified that "an editor" had requested access to the records and that she had found them in wild disarray. She said she sorted the mess and contacted owners to update the listings before permitting the editor to see the files.

When I examined these documents they were still a jumble, but she did give me a collated and theoretically current list. The actual registration papers included sworn statements by the machine owners that they were in compliance. There was no evidence of any effort by the sheriff's department to corroborate the statements. Asked about this, Kepple said she felt certain that the owners would not misrepresent the information "because they could get in trouble with the FBI."

She was right about that.

Months earlier, when I had contacted the Alcohol Law Enforcement agency's Asheville office to ask about unregistered machines I had discovered I was referred to the Sheriff's Department. But after two subsequent calls, I was put through to Ron Kaylor, the director of the ALE's District IX office, who said: "The problem for our department is personnel. We have about eighty field agents to cover the state, and we tend to focus on underage drinking and sale to minors. But we do enforce the gambling laws, and there are two cases in process in the eastern part of the state which should prove to be precedent-setting."

One of those cases involved an Asheboro video-poker vendor named Clarence "Bucky" Jernigan, who was charged in a public-nuisance lawsuit. Jernigan settled out of court with Randolph County in April, 2005. agreeing to quit the business, surrender hundreds of poker machines, and pay a $500,000 penalty. The *Herald-Sun* of Durham reported that the investigation "showed Jernigan's 263 poker machines took in $4.3 million in the last four years at 126 convenience stores and other businesses in 18 counties." The Randolph County lawsuit was based on investigations by state and local law-enforcement agencies, which found that convenience stores and other businesses where Jernigan's machines were located routinely made cash payouts. Store owners were charged with misdemeanors and paid small fines. But in a virtually unregulated cash trade, even the $4.3 million figure amounted to an informed guess, at best.

In 1999, during the political battle that led to the South Carolina ban, a CNN report stated, "Each machine costs about $6,000 to buy but rakes in about four times that amount annually." That would put Jernigan's actual receipts at six to nine million per year and I calculated that rates of return comparable to either figure would place Buncombe's video-poker trade at somewhere between $2 million and $12 million a year.

In a follow-up conversation in May of that year, however, Kaylor backpedaled and noted that the ALE didn't have a lot of incentive to investigate video gambling, because the machines might soon be banned. "If the state institutes a lottery, it is hard to imagine that they will tolerate competition from video poker," he said. At the time, the state Senate was considering a lottery bill passed by the House and being pushed hard by Gov. Mike Easley. As Kaylor predicted, once the lottery was in place, the competition in the form of video poker was axed and all machine gaming was banned as of July 1, 2007.

Jackie Shepherd owned Western Amusement, then the fourth-largest video-poker-machine operation in the county. He later told the court he formed Western Amusement corporation to run the gaming in 2000, and brought in a partner from South Carolina named Irvin Keith Comer. Comer paid $75,000 for his half of the business ($50,000 cash and a $25,000 note to Shepherd repaid with machine profits.) In 2008, Keith Comer, Kerry Lee Comer and Joseph Wayne Vinesett, co-defendants in Shepherd's indictment, were all convicted of crimes associated with Western Amusement's illegal gambling operations.

In 2005, Western Amusement held permits for somewhere between thirty-two and thirty-nine machines, according to Sheriff's Department records. And though Shepherd told me that he didn't operate any machines outside of Buncombe, Haywood County Sheriff's Department records indicated that he also had machines in operation there. Shepherd told me his poker machines were "in convenience stores and commercial rental property, and that's not anything that I depend on." Could be, but it certainly provided him with a nice chunk of walking money.

At the rate of return reported in South Carolina, 30 machines would bring in as much as $720,000 per year—and it's important to remember that those estimates are almost certainly low. Retired Capt. Don Fraser, who knew Shepherd well, told me the game operator showed him a register tape to support a boast that he'd taken in $27,000 from one machine in a single week.

But Shepherd denied that when I talked with him. "It ain't true." Asked what a more accurate estimate would be, he replied, "The girl in my office does the paperwork on them and turns it in for the taxes, but that isn't nowhere close." Shepherd also challenged the Sheriff's Department's record of how many machines he operated. "I've only got sixteen machines," he told me. Told that the Sheriff's Department credited him with thirty-nine machines, Shepherd said, "Thirty-nine is probably how many I've got, but I'd have to get with the boy that runs that to find out how many we have on location."

Whether he had one dozen or three dozen at the time of our conversation, business seems to have been good. By the time he was busted two years later, on June 28, 2007, he had at least fifty-four machines in operation.

"Wanna Bet?", my story outlining the extent of gaming in the county and numerous enforcement failures on the part of the sheriff, went to press in July, 2005. As I had come to expect, nothing happened.

As a footnote to this chapter, it's worth noting that Shepherd may be cast as the most noble of the players in Buncombe's gambling drama. When he negotiated a plea bargain he only asked for one concession. He agreed to confess and testify for the prosecution if the government dropped charges against his son and step-son. "I said this is my responsibility. Take my sons off the list and I'll plead guilty." Whatever one might think about his crimes, his sons owe him an enormous debt of gratitude, particularly given the history related at the trial where

Shepherd testified that he got into the video poker business in 1999, when he took the business away from his son. "He was into drugs and wasn't tending to business, and he stole some money from me."

17: An interview and a letter

Between the refusal of my editors to take on the payroll issue and the apparent lack of interest by government officials or the general public in the corruption I and others had reported over several years, I was feeling pretty frustrated. What would it take to end the reign of criminality?

I resubmitted my payroll fraud story in August, 2005. That story started out:

Harrah's Cherokee Casino regulars say he is a familiar figure with his carefully coiffed reddish hair and wire rim glasses, hunched over a high stakes machine, cigarette dangling from his mouth, attention focused on the rapidly changing screen. His car is parked in the Diamond Membership parking area just outside the casino's VIP entrance. Coworkers report that he invariably heads to Cherokee every other Thursday, as soon as he cashes his pay check, and frequently drags into the office late on Fridays. But they also report that he spends many another night in Cherokee—when he isn't dealt in on high stakes poker games up on the Buncombe/Madison county line.

By most measures he is just one more regular gambler, the sort of aficionado who is a welcome customer at Harrah's and other gaming establishments across the country. Poker has lately become something of a national craze and, as reported in these pages, video poker is exceedingly common and apparently unregulated in Buncombe County. In another way he is unlike every other patron in the casino because he is the elected sheriff of the most populous county in Western North Carolina: Bobby Medford.

I went on to delineate the reports and allegations I had gathered and wrote:

According to multiple reputable sources, time sheets for various Sheriff's Department employees are routinely falsified—under orders from Medford. Employees whose work hours have been misrepresented are said to principally include administrative personnel.

"The time sheets are a joke," a former lieutenant told Xpress. "Medford is the worst of the lot. Bobby Medford spends ninety percent of his time in Cherokee, at Harrah's." (This former officer spoke on condition of anonymity, fearing reprisal.)

And Brenda Fraser told Xpress: "I can confirm, firsthand, the falsified time sheets. I was ordered to do that when I filled in those sheets." Fraser also said: "Bobby always comes to work late—he blames his bad back, but it's because he is out until all hours at Harrah's. That and the drugs. ... Bobby is on addictive prescription painkillers."

Don Fraser also alleges payroll fraud in the department. "At one point, it was my responsibility to fill in the time sheets for the administrative staff. I was under orders to fill in eight hours every day, five days per week, no matter what people actually worked. The staff cross-signed for each other to verify their time."

Specifically, said Fraser, "[Lt. John] Harrison doesn't work more than two days a week and never stays in the office past noon—except on paydays. I know because I shared an office with him."

I had reputable sources on the record, I wrote the story and laid out the case, but the newspaper once again refused to publish it.

Later that month, Haywood County Commission Chair Mark Swanger received an award for his work implementing open government practices and I was assigned to interview him. In the course of our conversation I learned that he had stepped into politics after retiring from the FBI and that his final post at the bureau had been as head of investigations of municipal government corruption.

Following the formal interview I asked Swanger if he was willing to listen in confidence to my story about municipal corruption in Buncombe County and perhaps offer some advice. When he assented I laid out the broad outlines of much of what I have written to this point in this book and told him of my frustration that reporting over several years had had no apparent effect.

Swanger said, "If I were you, I would put all of that in a concise letter and mail it to the U.S. Attorney for this region. I would send copies to the FBI station chief and the Asheville Chief of Police. If you only send it to the U.S. Attorney, it might get ignored, but if you send it to a few people, it's more likely to draw some attention."

Several weeks later, I mailed the following letter:

*Gretchen C. F. Shappert, USA**
227 West Trade Street, Suite 1650
Charlotte, NC 28202   *October 19, 2005*

Dear Ms. Shappert,
    I am an investigative reporter in Asheville, North Carolina. In the course of a three year investigation of the Buncombe County Sheriff's Department, I have heard dozens of allegations of misconduct on the part of

Sheriff Bobby Medford. These allegations have included on-the-record reports, as well as off-the-record allegations and anonymous tips. What has struck me is that independent sources repeatedly allege the same facts.

I have obtained documentary evidence of some of the charges and am aware of documentary evidence that could be obtained with a subpoena. The NC Attorney General's office recommended I contact the Board of Commissioners concerning some of the charges, which I did. They have done nothing over the past ten months. The Division of Alcohol Law Enforcement has told me it isn't their job, and say they are too busy. The State Bureau of Investigation actually conducted an unenthusiastic inquiry into one set of charges and managed to find nothing, even though I explicitly documented and reported outright lies on the part of the sheriff, deputies and District Attorney Ron Moore.

So, on the advice of Haywood County Board of Commissioners Chairman Mark Swanger, who was with the FBI from 1969 to 2001, including a post as principal investigator of corrupt public officials, I am writing you and the the Special Agent in Charge of the Charlotte bureau.

I am herewith stepping out of my role as a journalist and back into my more fundamental role as a citizen. Attached please find a list of charges that have been made, together with corroboratory allegations.

I believe, though I don't know, that some of my off-the-record sources would willingly testify in a legal investigation. They are not willing to risk their careers or their personal safety for the sake of a newspaper story. If you decide to pursue this matter, I would be happy to provide you with contact information for my on-the-record sources and for any others who are then willing to come forward. Most of the people involved are afraid to speak out.

Best regards,
Cecil Bothwell

cc: Special Agent in Charge: Kevin B. Kendrick
Chief William Hogan, Asheville Police Department

1. *Video poker*
   Multiple off-the-record and anonymous sources have alleged that video poker operators in Buncombe County make illegal cash payoffs to players. The sheriff's department is charged with enforcement of video poker in this state, and the laws are not being enforced. I have documented non-enforcement of registration and reporting laws. Retired Capt. Don Fraser told me on-the-record that machine owner Jackie Shepherd showed him a receipt for $27,000 on one machine in one week. I have obtained a printed ticket from another machine for one day's receipts that indicates $1,211 for one day's operation. This suggests the possibility of $300K per year, times 520 machines I have accounted for (and who knows how many others there are?), or a possible total of $156 million in cash trade each year. There would seem to be considerable room for illegal activity with that much cash floating around.
   Multiple off-the-record sources have alleged that the sheriff is paid off. Two or more off-the-record sources have told me that Johnny Harrison is the bag man (his assigned post is

registration and regulation of the video poker machines).

One off-the-record source has indicated that Pakistani convenience store owners in Buncombe County have been shaken down, pressured to install the machines for which they then pay the required protection money.

2. *Illegal gambling*

It has been reliably reported to me by off-the-record sources that Medford engages in illegal gambling on a regular basis and allegedly "won" $30,000 in a card game this summer. (Whether he won it or was allowed to win it as a form of payoff is unclear.) There are reports of regular locations where illegal card games go on and a house set up as a semi-private casino by the fourth largest video poker owner in the county, Jackie Shepherd (Western Amusement).

Shepherd has close ties to Medford and has bragged to more than one of my sources (on and off-the-record) that he "made" Medford Sheriff. Whatever his contributions to the campaigns might have been, they are not recorded in campaign finance reports.

3. *Payroll fraud*

Two former sheriff's deputies, Capt. Don Fraser and former Deputy Brenda Fraser, have told me on-the-record that they were each ordered by the Sheriff to falsify time sheets for administrative personnel in the sheriff's department.

Four other former sheriff's deputies have confirmed off-the-record that such fraud occurs.

The six have stated that one of Medford's Lieutenants, Johnny Harrison, only regularly reports to work on paydays, and spends much of his time out of state at a home he owns in Myrtle Beach, S.C.

An anonymous source within the department has made the same allegations about Harrison's out of state address and the time sheets.

I attempted to obtain phone records which would have corroborated these allegations and was denied them by the Sheriff's Dept. attorney. I assume those records no longer exist. Payroll records are private, but could be revelatory.

4. *Obstruction of Justice*

In October 2002, as I reported in the Mountain Xpress, Medford's son allegedly tied and beat his girlfriend for a week. She escaped and was hospitalized with multiple-age bruises and open wounds. (I was able to obtain her medical records later.)

The deputy who searched the trailer where the alleged beating took place recorded "no sign of violence" in his report. The owner of the trailer and another person who helped clean up told me on-the-record that there was nothing breakable in the trailer that was not broken, that there was blood on every wall, bloody clothing on the floor, that one end of the bed was broken to the floor. The Sheriff did not investigate.

After my story broke, the SBI investigated and turned over its report to the D.A. who told me he couldn't discuss the case because it involved the girl's medical records. He said nothing in the medical record indicated that her accusations of being beaten over time were true. Assuming that the SBI gave the DA the same medical records I obtained from the hospital, the DA lied to me. The Sheriff lied to me and to the public   .

The girl alleged that Medford paid her hush money to suppress the story until after the Nov. 2002 election.

5. *Insurance fraud*
   Concerning a multi-car accident caused by a deputy, it is alleged by Don Fraser (who was on the scene soon afterward) that the Sheriff and others misreported in order to fix blame on an uninsured Latino driver. Brenda Fraser, who worked in the administrative office at the time, overheard a conspiratorial discussion about framing the Latino in the administrative office, including the department attorney and the Sheriff.

6. *Distribution of weapons*
   One on-the-record source and one off-the-record have told me that Medford gives weapons from his evidence locker to friends, and records them as destroyed.

7. *Allegations of minor infractions*
   Medford has blocked enforcement of drug laws concerning his other son and enlisted deputies in that effort. He regularly drives his official car outside the county on personal trips, and drives under the influence of prescription pain killers to which he is reportedly addicted—both violations of county personnel regs. There are also repeated, independent allegations of fixing traffic tickets.

I received no reply, an outcome that didn't particularly surprise me, but I was satisfied that I had done everything in my power to address the pervasive governmental corruption.

18: The money laundry

Medford was aware of increased investigatory interest in illegal gambling as he considered a reelection bid in 2006. The previous May, "Captain" Guy Penland had "run" a license tag for gambling operative Jerry Pennington which proved to be that of an undercover federal officer. The car in question was a 1999 Chevy Tahoe parked outside of a store operating Henderson Amusement video poker machines in Cleveland County.

Pennington phoned Penland who radioed Deputy Robert Robinson, a communications officer with the Buncombe County Sheriff's Department to check N.C. tag number MSL 3610. It came up "unregistered" which meant it was either an undercover agent or a DMV mistake. Penland reportedly told Pennington, "It's probably a law officer."

It would later prove to be an FBI vehicle.

When Medford got wind of Penland's action he exploded. He ordered his communications staff to respond with "unregistered" to all future tag requests from Penland. At the same time he decided to force him out of his volunteer work for the county. He reportedly had a stormy confrontation with his wayward Captain.

Later Pennington recruited Penland to stake out the federal court house in Asheville, to watch the comings and goings of possible witnesses during grand jury hearings. In a Keystone Cops sort of bungle, it turned out that Pennington had the grand jury date wrong. But it seems unlikely that Medford was unaware of the circumstances because, despite Penland's exclusion from quasi-official functions, he had remained in close touch with his law enforcement buddies.

Medford was reluctant to run for reelection in 2006, according to his testimony in the trial. Whether this was true at the time or part of his effort to appear to the jury as pitiably infirm and tormented by chronic back pain is a matter open to conjecture. Once he made the decision to run for a fourth term, the sheriff decided to reign in some of the excesses of past campaign finance efforts. He hired a professional to keep the books and insisted that at least the letter, if not the spirit, of election law was to be followed.

At the same time he seems to have stepped up his extortion from gambling operators and increased his visits to Harrah's Cherokee Casino. The latter move could have helped obscure some of the illegal money flowing through his hands, or perhaps, just offered him escape.

During his trial Medford suggested that his gambling excursions were undertaken as a way to see a bit of the world before he died. During closing arguments Assistant U.S. Attorney Richard Edwards, the lead prosecutor, reminded the jury that "His idea of seeing the world was sitting on a stool at Harrah's, staring at a machine."

An equally plausible surmise is that he was so very sure of himself, so accustomed to being boss of the county, so fully covered by long-time friends in the State Bureau of Investigation and Alcohol Law Enforcement, as well as the D.A.'s office, not to mention the powerful influence of Congressman Charles Taylor's with whom he shared a personal attorney—Bob Long—that he felt invulnerable.

Harrison had retired the previous May and Lt. Ronnie "Butch" Davis had taken over both video poker registration and management of the Bobby Medford Golf Classics. As usual, golf tourneys were scheduled for spring and fall, with gaming companies routinely strong-armed into registering teams.

Captain Tracy Bridges had joined Medford's department as head of internal affairs in July, 2005, though he had known his boss for several years before his employment through his work with the Republican Party. A career enforcement officer with a law degree, he seemed well-suited for the post which involved investigation of alleged wrong-doing by officers and other "problems" within the force. Before long his political experience and computer skills were called on for the election effort and he was directed by Chief Deputy George Stewart to download information and forms from the N.C. Board of Elections Web site.

When Bridges was ordered to submit Medford's $1,055 filing fee for reelection, he learned from the Board of Elections that they would only accept a certified check. During the trial Bridges testified that Medford told him to obtain the guaranteed check from Premier Federal Credit Union and that Stewart had provided him with $1,070 in cash to purchase the instrument. "I showed him the check and the receipt for the cash and gave him back $15," explained Bridges.

In the initial filing for a campaign the BOE form includes an entry for "cash on hand," and the form filed by Medford's 2006 campaign reported that figure as zero despite the semi-annual Bobby Medford Golf Classic Tournaments

During the trial it would emerge that both Bridges and Capt. Lee Farnsworth asked Medford for a dollar figure. Bridges recalled, "Medford was very upset. He said

'No! It's none of your business!' So Farnsworth gave him the Summary Sheet for cash on hand and he said there was no cash." Bridges said he wasn't allowed to complete any more report forms after that point.

Medford was so angry with Bridges that he considered dismissing him, according to his trial testimony.

Soon it was announced that Certified Public Accountant Lester Bullock had been hired as campaign treasurer. Bullock ran his office by the book, insisting that donations were to arrive on his desk as checks or money orders.

Later, when Bridges was left holding the bag for the campaign in the form of "around $10,000" in tournament cash, Bullock refused to accept it. So Bridges went to the U.S. Post Office on Merrimon Avenue in Asheville to purchase money orders, but "the clerk giggled and said she couldn't do that." She explained that to purchase amounts above $3,000 he would need to fill out a form.

Bridges took that information back to Medford who ordered him to make purchases at multiple post offices. Davis gave Bridges a list of names to fill in on the money orders, attributing donations to "donors" who hadn't donated anything, and told him to purchase several in $500 denominations so they would correspond to putative entry fees for the tournaments.

Some of the names used were those of donors from previous campaigns as well as legitimate businesses which had participated in the golf outings. The money orders were then deposited into the campaign account. Though there is nothing inherently illegal about purchasing money orders, doing so in order to evade federal election law elevates the practice to a felony: money-laundering. Use of false names compounds the crime with fraud.

Bridges reported a meeting with Medford, campaign manager David Brown and Sharon Stewart at which he said Brown expressed concern about putting money orders into the campaign account. At the time Jim Black, former Speaker of the North Carolina House of representatives was on trial for accepting bribes and illegal campaign contributions. Black had been closely tied to gambling interests during his tenure and was the largest single recipient of gambling company money in 2002 and 2004. The high-profile trial had Brown worried.

Bridges later testified, "Medford jumped on me for doing that. He said I needed to stop. But after Brown left Medford said, 'Fuck him. We're going to continue to do it this way.'" Bridges added, "Later I bought more money orders at post offices."

While Bridges completed that work for the campaign, he was distressed about the apparent illegality and went to Van Duncan with his concerns in October, 2006. Duncan was the Democratic candidate for sheriff at the time. "I told him I was being made to do things I didn't want to do." The candidate advised him to hold on to any paperwork he had and to go to the FBI.

Bridges later turned over all receipts for the money orders and Davis' hand-written list of "donors" to FBI agent Michael McNeely and IRS agent Eric Veater. He also agreed to wear a "wire" and to continue his work for the campaign.

Soon his role underwent a subtle change. Medford knew Bridges was receiving cash from Davis for purchase of money orders, and began to intercede, demanding the money himself. "He would tell me to hold off on purchase of money orders. He told me not to tell Butch [Davis] that I was giving him cash." Bridges kept track of the requests which he said ranged up to $1,000, "So I wouldn't be accused of taking the money myself." Medford also asked him to cash a check from Sandhill Grocery—which operated poker machines—and demanded he make cash deposits to Medford's and his girlfriend's accounts at Premier Federal Credit Union. Bridge's provided Veater with paper records of those transactions as well.

When I obtained Medford's final campaign finance records in January, 2007, familiar names leapt out at me. Many of the "donors" had close ties to the gambling companies I had investigated in 2005. Included in the names were deputies and officers as well, and the amounts credited to them stretched my credulity.

I went back and reexamined the 2002 records mentioned in Chapter 14. By 2006, the amount of cash reported had dropped dramatically, thanks to Bullock's firm hand. I carefully corroborated the names and connections and within two weeks submitted a story to the *Mountain Xpress* which read in part:

In Buncombe County, contributors tied to video poker made generous donations to Medford's campaign in both 2002 and 2006. He took in $12,300 from machine owners or operators last fall and $2,400 for the previous election. In addition, the Medford campaign reported dozens of $100 anonymous cash donations, with cash receipts totaling $4,789 in 2006, and a whopping $17,024 in 2002.

To put this in some perspective, Medford reported receipts of $72,000 in 2006, so known video poker operators pitched in 17 percent of the total while seven percent of proceeds were cash. Van Duncan, who defeated Medford in November, took in $120,000—none of which came from anyone visibly linked to video poker —and collected $2,260.56 or two percent in cash. Anonymous cash donations up to $100 each were completely legal until Jan. 1, 2007. A new campaign finance law has reduced that figure to $50.

Looking back to 2002, Medford's challenger Mike

Ruby didn't record a single donation from a video poker interest while his cash donations totaled $9,074.

It should be noted here that connecting names to video poker operations is roughly akin to looking for Susan B. Anthony silver dollars in a mountain of quarters. In addition to the Sheriff's Department's sketchy registration log and the often conflicting county business equipment tax records, leads turned up in Asheville City business license records, Buncombe County property records, state corporation listings and Lexis-Nexis searches. Other campaign contributors may also be involved in the industry, but records of privately owned businesses are private.

Of the four people who donated $2,500 or more to Medford in 2006, at least two have video poker connections. Among the 19 contributing $1,000 - $2,499, three are linked. Of the 18 people who donated $500 - $999, six have video poker connections.

One $1,000 contributor is listed in Medford's campaign report as Tommy Webb, owner of F&J Auto, without a complete address (a violation of state election law). The only Thomas Webb listed in Buncombe County told me he is not a Medford contributor and the only F&J Auto this reporter could locate in N.C. is in Wilmington.

As a humorous aside intended for my editors rather than for publication I added:

(Another member of the $1,000 club is an Asheville waitress, which might offer some clue as to why all those folks with MFA degrees work in food service here.)

I purposefully did not include names of donors in the story because I knew the editors felt the risk of libel out-weighed the benefits of specificity. Nor did I include the fact that the waitress in question was living with a deputy. In the end, none of that mattered because the editors (or publisher) killed the story.

This was eleven months *before* Medford's arrest by federal officers on charges directly related to those campaign "donations"—or, in the language of the federal indictment, "extortion under color of office."

A further revelation of those campaign numbers was the odd connection between Medford's (Republican) machine and black Democrats. Two of the sheriff's top contributors were also the top funders for campaigns by African American candidates in the 2002 and 2006 Democratic races, James Grant and Walt Robertson. Scuttlebutt on the street had suggested that Medford hoped to suppress the black Democratic vote by funding those ill-fated primary efforts in hopes that disillusioned supporters would then skip the general election. An alternative theory was that the candidates would spread the word about Medford's backstage support and return the favor in November. The campaign records did nothing to refute those suggestions. Grant not only returned to work at the Buncombe County Sheriff's Department following his 2002 bid, but received a promotion.

In any event, I had documentary evidence that the gambling industry had underwritten Medford's 2006 run for office and strong circumstantial evidence that the same had held true in 2002.

19: An absence of evidence

Bobby Medford lost his bid for reelection in 2006 to a former employee named Van Duncan. Medford had fired Duncan for insubordination and stories diverge about the precise nature of that offense. By some accounts it was Duncan's inclination to enforce gambling law that raised Medford's hackles. In other versions it was Duncan's rumored intention to compete for the top slot that cost him his job. Whatever the cause, Duncan had taken a post teaching law enforcement at the North Carolina Justice Academy in Edneyville while biding his time and organizing a campaign.

In the weeks following the November seventh election, Medford's heretofore impregnable fortress began to collapse. Seven days after the election N.C. Alcohol Law Enforcement alleged that Demetre Theodossis had violated gambling laws. ALE conducted multiple raids, confiscated more than $2 million in cash from his home and seized machines from about fifty locations. Theodossis owns Hot Dog King, Inc., which was a video poker and sandwich business. In 2005 I could identify twenty-two locations operating Hot Dog King equipment, but as I reported at the time, record-keeping at the Sheriff's Department and the county tax office was haphazard at best. Regional A.L.E. chief Ron Kaylor called in agents from across the state to conduct the sweep of Hot Dog King's gambling locations.

As I recounted earlier, county sheriffs had been specifically charged with video poker enforcement since 2000 so I asked Kaylor why the sheriff's department wasn't involved in the bust. Kaylor had no comment and referred further questions to the state A.L.E. office. A spokesperson for the state office said the case had been referred to the U.S. Attorney's office in Charlotte. The spokesperson for that office told me they could not comment on an ongoing investigation.

Theodossis quickly hired one of the best criminal defense attorneys in the region, Sean Devereaux. (The Asheville attorney had garnered national attention when he was appointed to defend the Olympic bomber, Eric Rudolph. The feds clearly wanted to forestall any possible appeal due to incompetence of counsel.) Devereaux's office quickly returned my call with "no comment." In short order Devereaux negotiated a plea bargain and, as would emerge during Medford's trial, Theodossis became a cooperative witness.

Medford's office had responded even more quickly to the bust. On the day of the raid, November fourteenth, numerous calls went out from the sheriff's administrative offices to gambling operators throughout the county including Jackie Shepherd. It would be difficult to arrive at any conclusion other than the obvious: the sheriff, his chief deputy, his secretary or someone close to them was spreading an alarm. While the phone *logs* kept by the sheriff are not public records, phone *bills* paid by the county are. Other calls were made from Lt. Butch Davis' phone. Soon enough, federal agents picked up copies of the billing records and had an easy-to-follow score card of all those who had been warned.

The timing of the Hot Dog King bust was interesting in itself, coming shortly after twin Republican defeats. In addition to Medford's drubbing, eight-term Congressman Charles Taylor (who shared a personal attorney with the sheriff) had lost to his Democratic challenger as well. A suspicious reporter couldn't help but wonder if Taylor's powerful seniority had somehow staved off law enforcement action that was cut loose by his downfall. A year later, during Medford's custody hearing, I wondered aloud to Assistant U.S. Attorney Richard Edwards if that had been the situation. I noted that if the government had an indictment in hand a week after the election they presumably had a strong case the week before the election as well and that voters might seem to have a right to that information before they cast ballots.

Edwards said that elections do make some difference to FBI investigators and federal prosecutors but not in the way I imagined. "We don't want to be accused of politicizing enforcement, so, if anything, we *might* delay action during the run-up to an election."

A second more quiet investigation went forward in November as well. Under state law, county auditors are required to examine the records and contents of a department's evidence locker between administrations. The intent is to assure an incoming sheriff that all is in order.

When Buncombe auditors did a spot check on Medford's locker it was immediately obvious that all was *not* in order.

Following their standard procedure, auditors selected a thirty-item sample from the Evidence Inventory Database. The result of that examination revealed major problems. Fifty percent of the sample was no longer in the evidence inventory. Twenty-seven percent of the sample could not be located and fourteen percent of the items that could be located had been compromised. With a ninety-one percent error rate, the audit was expanded to a complete inventory.

In characteristic bureaucratic understatement, Buncombe County released a sheriff's evidence-room

audit report citing "poor management, poor organ-
izational skills and failure to maintain a clear chain of
custody" during the administration of former Sheriff
Bobby Medford.

The full audit revealed "poor inventory management" and "evidence bags found open with contents
missing," and noted that "the lack of controls and
management in the evidence room created an envi-
ronment that could lead to previous court convictions
being overturned or future cases being compromised."

Only an auditor could frame the situation with
such understated calm.

Items that could not be accounted for included
$217,769 in cash, 233 hand guns, 114 shotguns/rifles, and
drugs noted on 1,318 evidence-reporting sheets. In addition, the report says, "Numerous evidence items were
found with no case identification markings including
drugs, guns and rape kits."

The audit seemed to confirm allegations made to
me by Brenda Fraser who asserted, "Bobby gives guns
from the evidence locker to his friends."

More recently a former BCSD detective now
working in another state told me he offered evidence to
the FBI that Medford sold at least some of the guns to
Shepherd, and at least one of the guns to a private
individual who still owns the weapon. According to the
detective, that individual, who also asserts he was present
when Medford conveyed multiple guns to Shepherd, has
also talked to the FBI.

Another source, with connections to the office of
District Attorney Ron Moore, told me that Moore was
questioning possible suspects in the robbery of guns from
Shepherd's Cherokee Trading Post—guns Moore is said to
believe came from the evidence locker. Moore did not
returned my phone call inquiring about his investigation.

But Public Information Officer Ross Dillingham, of
the Buncombe County Sheriffs Department, told me that

his agency was investigating two alleged robberies of Jackie Shepherd's Cherokee Trading Post.

In addition the missing weapons lent credence to the story a woman had offered me some years earlier. She said she had reported spousal abuse to Medford and told him she lived in fear, to which he allegedly responded with the offer of a gun from the locker. "Pick one," was his supposed proffer—a suggestion he later denied.

One year after the evidence audit, the City of Asheville conducted a don't ask/don't tell gun buy-back program at community centers around town. Some citizens had become alarmed about an apparent increase in gun crime—though whether it was an increase in crime or reporting of crime is difficult to parse. The city council authorized a city-wide gun "buy-back" program funded with $25,000 from city coffers and a hoped-for matching amount from private donors.

The buy-back was carried out at several community centers during December, 2007. Officer Germaine Weaver told me "We collected 314 guns and spent $15,100 dollars." The breakdown was 155 pistols, 77 rifles, 64 shotguns and eight assault rifles. Weaver said, "We didn't get any private donations, so that was all city funds. Because we have money left over, we'll probably do it again when we can schedule it." While the guns are accepted on a "no questions asked" basis, Weaver said, "We run the serial numbers to see if they're stolen, and if we can make contact with the owners, the guns are returned. Three of the 314 guns proved to be stolen." He indicated that most of the guns will be destroyed though some will be retained by the department for training purposes.

Asked whether his department had been provided with a list of the 337 guns discovered missing from the Buncombe County Sheriff's Department evidence locker when Medford left office, Weaver said, "No."

The information disconnect between enforcement agencies seems curious if authorities believe the guns may be on the streets, but Weaver offered no opinion on the matter. In any event, during the buy-back the city paid $50 for each hand gun, rifle and shotgun and $100 for assault weapons.

As I reported at the time of the buy-back, inmates interviewed at the Buncombe County Detention Center uniformly reported that they wouldn't sell working pistols for $50. "If it didn't work, yeah," was a typical answer, "and I'd use the money to buy another one."

Taking my work-life pleasures where I can, I have to admit amusement at the city's labeling of the purchase program as a "buy-back." The clear implication is that the city sold the guns in the first place, and in a collateral way, it might have. Asheville routinely rents its Civic Center for gun shows at which cash transactions between private owners and buyers are self-policed. All perfectly legal, mind you, but it does make the city a participant in the gun vending business. "Buy-back" makes linguistic sense.

Medford's guns were still missing as this book went to press, and Public Information Officer Noelle Talley of the N.C. Department of Justice told me the SBI was still on the case.

No charges had yet been filed.

20: Arrest and frustration

Bobby Lee Medford was arrested at 7:30 a.m., December 13, 2007. Heavily-armed federal officers fanned out to surround the Weaverville apartment building while a local police officer rapped on the door. Judi Bell, Medford's girlfriend of twenty years, climbed out of bed in response and answered the knock.

"Bobby Medford's car has been vandalized," the officer told her. Could Mr. Medford come outside to look at the damage? She knew her boyfriend was particular about his car and wouldn't be happy, but didn't deem it worthwhile getting him up and out of his morning routine, so Bell agreed to inspect the vehicle herself.

Clad in pajamas, bathrobe and sandals, she followed the cop to the rear of Medford's car where another man walked up, flashed a badge, and told her federal agents were in place to arrest Bobby. "For what?" Bell asked. "The charges have been sealed," the officer said.

A phalanx of black-clad agents wearing helmets and Kevlar vests, with guns drawn, marched into the apartment. Shortly thereafter the former sheriff was escorted from the building in a pale blue casual suit and shackles.

The sealed indictment which ran to nineteen pages included charges of extortion, mail fraud, obstruction of justice and conspiracy. (For the complete indictment see Appendix A.) It commenced:

1. *Beginning by on or about October 1, 2000, and continuing through on or about December 3, 2006, BOBBLY LEE MEDFORD, also known as Bobby Medford, JOHN DAVID HARRISON, also known as Johnny Harrison, RONNIE EUGENE DAVIS, also known as Butch Davis, GUY KENNETH PENLAND and others known and unknown to the Grand Jury conspired to enrich themselves unlawfully by extorting money from persons involved in the illegal video poker machines business in Buncombe County, within the Western District of North Carolina. They thereby deprived the citizens of Buncombe County of the right to their honest services performed free from deceit, favoritism, self-enrichment, self-dealing, concealment, and conflict of interest.*
2. *During the period of the conspiracy, BOBBY LEE MEDFORD was the elected sheriff of Buncombe County, North Carolina. JOHN DAVID HARRISON AND RONNIE EUGENE DAVIS worked as lieutenants for the Buncombe County Sheriff's Office. GUY KENNETH PENLAND was a Special Deputy and volunteer who held himself out as a Buncombe County Sheriff's Office captain, with the knowledge and consent of his co-defendants.*

The indictment went on to list the methods of extortion (organized golf tournaments and direct demands for cash); employment of defendants by poker operators; obstruction of justice; gambling at Harrah's while on the county clock; money laundering; conspiracy; mail fraud; and the specific roles of Harrison, Davis and Penland in the extortion scheme. Though the document used initials to identify parties to the crimes, most of the names fairly leapt from the page as soon as I obtained a copy of the document.

HAI: Henderson Amusement, Incorporated, the largest video poker machine operator in the region, perhaps the largest in the Southeast U.S., with operations in at least four states.

JP: Jerry Pennington, employed by Henderson as a salesman. He convinced store owners to place the company's equipment in their establishments.

IA: Imran Alam, a Pakistani convenience store owner

RW: Robert Warren, a machine operator

DT: Demetre Theodossis, owner of Hot Dog King, Incorporated, a sandwich shop chain and video poker company. Theodossis operated machines illegally in his hot dog shops and placed machines in a few dozen other businesses throughout the county.

CMJ & CMS: Charles McBennett, Jr., and Charles McBennett, Sr., owned Mountain Music, a video poker operating company.

AL: Alvin Ledford, known to many of my sources in the county for running sports betting, probably for decades. Ledford's inclusion showed that Medford's protection racket extended beyond video poker to other illegal gambling activity in the county.

TB: Tracy Bridges, a former Captain under Medford, mentioned by several of my sources in 2005 as having some connection to Medford's illegal activities (though it wasn't clear to me what his connection had been before the indictment was handed down.)

JS: Jackie Shepherd, principal owner of Western Amusement, Inc. (perhaps the second largest video poker operation company in the county), the Cherokee Trading Post and a few small grocery stores. Shepherd was Medford's former employer and frequently claimed to have "made Bobby sheriff."

The document provided a level of specificity far beyond the activities I had been able to report based on my handful of informants and documents—and no surprise there. But I was immensely gratified to see that the only pieces of the puzzle I had missed were internal to the sheriff's office.

Mail fraud was tangential to the racket. Medford's department had ordered video poker machine I.D. stickers from the North Carolina Sheriff's Association in Raleigh, in itself a completely legal activity, but used the stickers in furtherance of their conspiracy to extort, which rendered the use of an interstate carrier "mail fraud." (In this case the carrier was actually United Parcel Service, not the U.S. Postal Service.)

Penland's surveillance of the federal courthouse during Grand Jury hearings and phone-in of a vehicle tag represented obstructions of justice that were presumably known to very few in Medford's immediate cohort. And fraud involving Pennington's court-ordered public service stemming from an unrelated charge was similarly known to only a few players.

Having interjected my self-satisfied reaction to the indictment, I need to add a note about my immense frustration as well. *Mountain Xpress* had refused to publish most of what I had uncovered concerning Medford's criminal behavior since the summer of 2005. I had turned in story after story, doing the work on my own time while I continued to attend to my other reporting duties. I could not and cannot fathom why that publication's editors and publisher refused to go to press with well-documented allegations backed up by on-the-record sources.

In October, 2007, I was summarily fired by that paper, for reasons unknown. I had written, reported and edited for the company for seventeen years, won some national awards and had served on the national editorial board of the Association of Alternative Newsweeklies—as a representative of the company to that national trade group—for five years. I represented the paper at public forums and at national meetings and felt immeasurable loyalty to the paper and to my colleagues.

I was stunned.

North Carolina is a so-called "right-to-work" state, which means, in practice, that employers can fire you without explanation. More specifically, "right-to-work" states don't allow union shops in which all workers are required to pay union dues. The result is diminished union power and laws which favor employers, including the "work at will" bias in employment without contract. Under such rules employees can be fired for any or no reason. That's me.

My relationship with the editors was often strained, as should be the case between any investigative journalist and those who oversee such efforts. Someone has to push at the margins or nothing of note would ever make it into print. So I pushed: In my view the relationship was nonetheless collegial and productive.

As a kind of added kick in the teeth, I was handed my walking papers two days after the paper's annual "Best-of" issue hit the street. That issue reported that readers had, once again, voted me the best print reporter in Asheville.

In any event, another publisher contacted me a couple of weeks later. He said he had already created a dummy issue of *Asheville City Paper,* to use as an ad-sales tool, and intended to enter the local market starting in December. Would I come on board as News Editor?

Twist my arm.

The first issue of that publication was slated to hit the streets on December 12. My cover story was the long-delayed blockbuster about Medford: the gambling connection to his election campaign, payroll fraud, abuse of office and obstruction of justice ... and on and on. My new publisher had money trouble. The print run was delayed a week.

Medford went down on December 13.

Damn. Damn. Damn. In the news biz, timing is everything. I hastily rewrote the story as an after-the-fact report, feeling cheated by fate once again.

21: The trials begin

At the arraignment, December 17, 2007, Magistrate Judge Dennis L. Howell ordered Bobby Lee Medford, John David Harrison, Ronnie Eugene "Butch" Davis, and Guy Kenneth Penland held without bond and packed them off to four different county jails to forestall communication between them. Judge Thomas Selby (Tim) Ellis III was called in from the Eastern Virginia District to preside over the trial and a scramble for legal counsel commenced.

While Medford languished in the Caldwell county detention center he wrote his girlfriend a note which she later released to the press.

Hey, Judi,
"I want to thank you for everything you have done for me. Your one of the few people that know how bad the federals screwed me over. I miss just sitting around on my chair playing with Miss Meredith. "I miss that bird." She was always wanting her way. A lot like you huh.
I never thought i would come to dislike my own kind. I think it about it all the time, and thats not good for anybody. It appears they have put a lot of trust in Bridges and Sheila. After 38 yrs. in this shit, you would think my word would carry a little weight. [Sentence or two deleted here.]

*Enough of that, my court date will come.
Especially since they didn't even bother to talk to me
before taking warrants. I don't feel like writing any
more write now. Back hurts pretty bad right now.
    Love Bobby*

*P.S. When you write back, tell me about the good things
happening in life. How's Bobby?*
                                                        —BM

There were so many gambling cases linked to the Medford racket—due to a series of busts of business operators, clerks, machine owners and law enforcement officials—that the pool of available attorneys unaffected by attorney-client issues had become quite thin. Matters came to a head at the Medford co-defendants' bond hearing on December 27 when Howell discovered that Asheville attorney Bob Long was representing both Medford and Jackie Shepherd.

After considerable discussion Howell permitted Long to represent the sheriff on the question of pretrial release, but insisted that Long not continue into the trial itself. The reasoning was clear enough—either man could have been called to testify against the other and an attorney who had held confidential conferences with both would find his attorney-client privilege compromised. In fact Howell's concern was ratified when Shepherd pled guilty and took the stand during his erstwhile protégé's trial.

Asheville attorney Stephen Lindsay was called out of semi-retirement to take Medford's case. As a single father, Lindsay had pulled back from his practice to attend to child-rearing and indicated some reluctance to take on the task. However, he eventually assented and was appointed by Howell on January eighth. The trial date was initially set for March 25.

Medford's first hearing before Judge Ellis in Asheville's federal courtroom was conducted on January 15 when the issue of pretrial custody was considered. Ellis ruled that risk of flight and danger to the community from possible ongoing criminal activity were relatively low and remanded each of the defendants to custody of family members with electronic ankle bracelets, phone monitoring devices, and a ban on cell phones and weapons in each household. Departure from the homes was strictly limited to legal and medical appointments approved in advance by the court.

When Lindsay suggested to Ellis that Medford be permitted to return to his own apartment in the custody of his girlfriend, Judi Bell, Ellis dourly observed that Bell was on both Lindsay's and the government's witness lists, and that it seemed entirely possible that she might also be charged with related crimes given her close association with Medford. Those facts precluded her appointment as a custodian.

Lindsay then suggested to the judge that given the twenty year relationship between his client and Bell there was no reason why they couldn't get married immediately, in which case Bell would automatically be granted spousal exclusion from testimony concerning her husband. Ellis expressed amusement at Lindsay's creativity but made it clear that he wouldn't entertain either the custody or the granting of spousal protection at such a late date.

In late February, co-defendant Johnny Harrison cut a deal and entered a statement of facts with the court as part of a plea bargain. About a week later, Ronnie "Butch" Davis admitted his guilt in a similar deal. Penland, apparently loyal to the man who had given him his big break in law enforcement, held fast with his plea of innocence and his attorney, Paul Bidwell, began to prepare a defense.

Lindsay told the court he needed help given the extensive evidence offered by prosecutors, but his initial request for appointment of a second attorney was denied by Judge Howell on February 29. In mid-March, again citing the large roomful of evidence and the massive number of documents to be examined, Lindsay requested and received an extension of the trial date to April 29. In early April he again requested appointment of a second counsel and on April 15, Hickory (NC) attorney M. Victoria Jayne was added as second counsel by Judge Ellis. The late appointment meant she only had two weeks before the trial to get up to speed on the case.

Prosecutors issued their witness list on April 27 and the defense attorneys proffered theirs the following day.

On April 29 jury selection began with the main players and the defendants seated at tables facing the judge. To Ellis' right, for the prosecution: Assistant U.S. Attorney Richard Lee Edwards, Assistant U.S. Attorney Corey F. Ellis, Federal Bureau of Investigation Agent Michael McNeely, and Internal Revenue Service Agent Eric Veater. (Judge Ellis made it clear that he and Corey Ellis were not related.) To Ellis' left, for the defense: Attorneys Stephen Lindsay, M. Victoria Jayne, and Paul Bidwell.

Ellis thanked the sixty-nine members of the jury pool for their participation and added, "I had the opportunity to observe the legal system in South America where I grew up, and in Europe. I am convinced that no system is better than ours, but it can only work with the participation of citizens like you." He then introduced the principal actors in the trial to the jurors.

The judge then sent the pool members out with questionnaires geared toward revealing potential conflicts, knowledge about the case, or hardships that might reasonably affect jurors' ability to serve or weigh the evidence impartially.

Following that step, two were promptly dismissed due to having immediate family members who were terminally ill. Another was dismissed due to a recent severe head injury. The questionnaires were collected and distributed to the prosecution and defense counsels. An hour later they had agreed on ten more dismissals.

The remaining pool members were then examined one-by-one in *voir dire* (direct questioning) that continued into a second day. By late afternoon, following challenges and counter challenges, the jury was empaneled. (See Appendix B: The Jurors)

Evincing impatience over the month-long delay in the trial itself and the two-day effort to select jurors, Ellis insisted that the trial commence immediately. So the prosecution soon presented its opening statement.

22: The prosecution opens

Assistant U.S. Attorney Richard Lee Edwards introduced his prosecution team to the jury and began to lay out the government's case at 4:30 p.m. The two defendants adopted poses they would assume through-out the ensuing trial: Medford stared straight ahead, chin in hand with one finger extended alongside his cheek; Penland bobbled, looking dazed and confused. For the duration of the proceedings it seemed that the former sheriff was purposefully avoiding eye contact with his all too hapless "Captain."

"This is a case about public corruption, the abuse of power and an effort to enrich Bobby Medford," he began. "Mr. Medford used his position to extort money from people, both his associates and others in the video poker industry. It was a pay-to-play system. People were paying money to the sheriff and his deputies because of the position he held here."

Edwards then offered a brief history of the law concerning video poker machines, machine registration and the sheriff's mandatory role in that process. "In 2000, Medford's department reported that there were 365 machines in operation in Buncombe County," Edwards paused, then added, "He ordered 1,385 stickers."

The prosecution had come equipped with two large diagrams, the first of which was a flow chart depicting how the machine registration process was supposed to work. County sheriffs would order the free stickers from the North Carolina Sheriff's Association. Machine operators were to fill out registration forms and submit them to the local sheriff. The department was then to issue the stickers to the owners. Edwards made it explicit: no fee was involved at any point in the process.

Next came a flow chart depicting how the government alleged Medford's registration system worked in practice. The stickers from the state office were usually free, but operators paid money directly to the sheriff or his lieutenants, both "voluntarily" and via explicit extortion. On at least one occasion an operator paid $100 apiece for 100 stickers. "That's $10,000," the prosecutor noted, to emphasize the point. Edwards then traced the chart to illustrate how operators were also pressed to pay substantial entry fees to participate in the semi-annual Bobby Medford Golf Classic. "After 2000," he added, "Roughly three-quarters of the donors to the Golf Classics were video poker companies."

He said some cash from the pay-offs and golf fees went directly into Medford's pocket or his Premier Federal Credit Union account. During election years, Edwards alleged, checks from both legitimate donors and the veiled extortion went to Medford's campaign account. During non-election years, checks were cashed at grocery stores with compliant managers and all of the cash during those off-years ended up in the hands of Medford and his co-defendants. "Some of the checks were cashed at George's Deli. Nick Anagnostopoulos owned that store. They ran some checks through a BiLo Supermarket where Homer Honeycutt was a manager. In fact," Edwards continued, "Mr. Medford banked at Nick's store, writing himself checks at a little convenience store on Leicester Highway."

Next Edwards mentioned Demetre Theodossis, proprietor of the Hot Dog King restaurant chain and a video poker operator, who had in excess of $1.7 million in his home when he was busted in November, 2006. "This was an extremely lucrative business," he added.

Following that, the prosecutor explained the 2006 change in the election finance law which proscribed cash donations above $50 and laid out the money laundering operation in that year's campaign. He said cash was laundered by Capt. Tracy Bridges through purchase of postal money orders which were deposited in the campaign account using the names of fraudulent donors supplied by Lt. Butch Davis. And Edwards added the name of Sharon Stewart, Medford's secretary, alleging that she too had laundered cash.

Then Medford's gambling habit was introduced and Edwards pointed out that Medford, Judi Bell and Sharon Stewart had been frequent visitors to Harrah's Cherokee Casino where the sheriff and his girlfriend frequently created overdrafts on their Premier Federal accounts—overdrafts that were always covered in the nick of time with large cash deposits.

Edwards then reiterated how profitable the video poker businesses had been, noting that Henderson Amusement took in $14 million on an annual basis and repeating that Theodossis had been holding $1.7 million at the time he was raided. "Mr. Medford organized the video poker business on a non-competitive basis, and the operators got to run their machines illegally." Edwards added, "He also issued special deputy badges to people involved in the video poker trade."

"Imran Alam, whose convenience stores ran machines, had a special deputy badge. So did Jerry Pennington, an employee of Henderson Amusement. In addition, Pennington and defendant Guy Penland staked out this federal courthouse," Edwards gestured to make it clear that he was referring to the building in which the trial was taking place, "During a grand jury investigation into video poker. Furthermore, phone records indicate that on November 14, 2006, the day Demetre Theodossis was raided, many warning calls went out from the sheriff's office to video poker operators."

Having moved on to Penland's involvement, Edwards noted that Penland had posed as a Captain although he was not an officer, and had worn captain's insignia, driven a car which appeared to be a cruiser and otherwise presented himself as a deputized officer.

Edwards concluded by asserting that the facts to be presented by the government would prove all of the charges included in the bill of indictment. "This was a conspiracy to extort by using their positions. They deprived citizens of the county of honest service."

23: Rising to the defense

At 5:05 p.m., Attorney Stephen Lindsay rose to lay out his opening argument. U.S. Attorneys aren't much inclined to prosecute corruption cases unless they appear leak-proof. This one would prove to be tight as Tupperware.

With precious little to offer in the way of a factual defense, Lindsay focused on his client's reputation, recent poor health and the onerous nature of a sheriff's duties. More significantly, he tried to lay the blame for Medford's entanglements on his predecessors.

"Let me take you back to 1994," he began, "that was a significant election. Republicans were elected across the board. It was a tidal wave. That was the year Bobby Medford was elected. But video poker was a part of North Carolina before 1994. It went back to [former Buncombe sheriff] Harry Clay. It extended back a long way."

Lindsay was factually inaccurate in this statement because video poker machines are a relatively recent spin-off of desktop computing. They use the same technology which emerged as the touch-screens used by restaurant servers since the 1990s and more recently applied in self-checkout lanes at supermarkets. However, gambling, and more specifically, illegal gambling under protection of a Buncombe County sheriff goes back at least as far as Clay's administration and Clay himself remains the subject of widespread rumor concerning illegal activity. Moreover, Lt. Johnny Harrison, Medford's long-time bag-man, worked for Clay and is married to his widow. Lindsay was clearly onto something here—a line of defense that could have pinned Harrison with principal responsibility in the case. Unfortunately for Medford, Lindsay never managed to develop this as a plausible explanation for miscreance on his client's watch though he did return to the Clay connection more than once.

Lindsay explained that the law had been changed starting in 2000, due to concern that machines were coming into the state from South Carolina. He said, "The law said that a player could not win more than once piece of paper worth ten dollars in store merchandise. The only way these little Mom-and-Pop stores could stay in business was to make cash payoffs." This presented an unusual line of defense which Lindsay was probably wise to drop after a single mention, since arguing for the financial necessity of violating a law is rarely successful.

He continued, "The new law put one thing on the sheriff—registering the machines and owners also had to show they had been registered for tax purposes. The legislature said, 'We know it's going to cost you extra money and we will cover the extra costs.' The legislature never did that."

Next Lindsay turned to his client's history. "Now let's talk about Bobby Medford. He has been a resident here his whole life. He was born here. He went to school here and played sports. He became an officer with the Buncombe County Sheriff's Department and became one of the best investigators around. From 1990 to 1994, when Charlie Long was sheriff, he worked elsewhere.

"He rented a little apartment and wore the clothes on his back, even when he went from making $25,000 per year to making $125,000 as sheriff." Here, Lindsay was clearly making an effort to demonstrate that disposable income was sufficient to bankroll Medford's extraordinary gambling habit. "When he got that extra $100,000 he stayed in the same apartment and he had a car provided."

Then the attorney lofted a "too busy to take notice" argument. "The sheriff's office has 350 employees and is responsible for criminal investigation, civil process and the school resource officer program. There is an elder program which checks in on the elderly on a daily basis. The sheriff runs the Buncombe County Detention Center and Buncombe Courthouse security to make sure judges and prosecutors are safe every day.

"With no funding for video poker machine oversight, you have to make certain decisions about priorities and you'll hear that video poker was not the highest priority. Bobby Medford was on call 24/7. He and his officers were responsible for solving some of the most serious crimes in this county."

Then again, he insisted that Medford *did* pay attention to the poker business. "You'll hear that Medford sent two officers to training about registering machines. He appointed John Harrison to oversee the program, a man who had a history going back to Harry Clay. Then the sheriff called a meeting with machine owners and Harrison was introduced at the meeting by Medford."

In another somewhat odd approach to the law, Lindsay said, "Bobby Medford told people that if they had machines they needed to keep them where they were. He was not going to have businesses trying to underbid each other." This amounts, at minimum, to restraint of trade and seems to place his client in the position of organizing gambling in the county.

Organized gambling was, of course, at the heart of the government's allegations.

Looking for a little sympathy, Lindsay then iterated Medford's health problems. "You'll hear about how his health began to deteriorate. He had seizures, cancer and back surgery. You'll hear about what he endured each day and that he was prescribed painkillers. Later he had a device implanted to control pain."

Back again, then, to blaming the bagman. "John Harrison took over. He came into contact early with Jerry Pennington who worked for Henderson Amusement. And you'll hear about cash gifts that Harrison put in his own pocket."

Now Medford's co-defendant came in for a mixture of blame and sympathy. "Guy Penland wanted to be an officer. He went and earned his G.E.D. and got his certification and got a job with the Buncombe department. Then he got a D.U.I. and lost his certification, but he wanted to volunteer, so Bobby used him for unfunded mandates. And you'll hear evidence that there was supposedly power from Penland's office over machines and cash payouts."

Veering back toward Medford's ill health and work stress Lindsay said, "You'll hear that Bobby found relief at Harrah's and you'll hear that it was all legitimate money. Then people talked him into running for reelection in 2006 and he said, 'Only if you run the campaign. And I'll retire after six months."

Then the attorney made his first effort to impugn those who would take the stand for the prosecution. "The last thing I'll say is that you should closely examine the witnesses and their credibility. People are given power when they are charged with a crime. Prosecutors have the power to reduce their time. They have the power to say 'We will drop charges.' I ask you to consider what witnesses were offered for their testimony."

Judge Ellis interjected, "Do you intend to offer evidence to that effect?"

"Yes your honor," Lindsay responded, then concluded, "Bobby Medford did not take money from video poker. He was a better investigator than administrator and I ask that you find him innocent."

At 5:30 p.m. attorney Paul Bidwell rose to make opening remarks in defense of Guy Kenneth Penland. His task was only marginally less daunting than that facing Lindsay, and he would have to walk the balance beam between assigning blame for any possible misdeeds to the sheriff and, at the same time, denying that misdeeds had actually occurred. He elected to start with a measure of candor. "There have been things that were done that were wrongful," he admitted, "But the two people behind me are not those people." Then, having played the loyal Musketeer, he quickly added, "These people are two people, two separate people, and in this room there are just Guy and me as far as I'm concerned.

"Guy was a volunteer. Yes, he wanted to be an officer. He had a small business but for all intents and purposes he was retired." Back then to candor. "Law enforcement of video poker in Buncombe County was, at best, lax, and Guy Penland was in there helping. He was told that people would bring in paperwork and if it was properly filled out he was to give them a sticker. The law was not to require checking on machines, but to require registration. It was a registration process."

Bidwell laid out an argument that his client was drawn in by a sharp operator. "Henderson Amusement in particular, along with others, saw an opportunity in Guy's position. There's a whole lot of money in video poker and Henderson Amusement sent its top salesman up here. Jerry Pennington. Jerry Pennington, who is a prosecution witness; who is a criminal; and who is a heck of a salesman.

"Pennington paid $500 per location to anyone who found a location. He found a congenial gentleman who knew everyone, who could introduce him around. Guy Penland helped find locations. Jerry Pennington found himself a dupe. He used Penland and he used him in a number of ways."

Here Bidwell once again gambled on candor, admitting wrongdoing by his client, but offering an alternative interpretation of its significance. "He used Penland to run a tag. He asked him if he would do it and he said, 'Sure.' The tag came up as 'Not on file,' which could have meant a number of things. It might have belonged to a law enforcement vehicle. It might have been mistakenly filed. Or it might have been somewhere in the registration process."

Next Bidwell joined Lindsay's effort to debunk prospective testimony. "The star witnesses in this case for the government are all criminals. Beyond the criminals' information there is very little evidence at all. You will hear about contributors to an election campaign and some of those contributors were from the video poker industry. but the evidence is going to fail to show that there was any protection of that industry. The evidence will fail to show any connection between money that was given to the sheriff's department and any failure of enforcement.

"You will find that Guy Penland is innocent."

At 5:50 p.m. the jury was released for the day with strict instructions from Judge Ellis not to discuss the case with anyone, not to listen to or read news coverage of the case, and to show up on time the following morning.

Once the jurors had exited, Ellis turned his attention to the defense lawyers. Speaking in a very stern voice he said, "Mr. Lindsay, it appeared that you were saying that the prosecutors were suborning perjury."

Lindsay rose and apologized, explaining that he had only intended to raise the question of ulterior motives on the part of some witnesses.

Ellis turned to the prosecution, "Did it strike you the same way?"

Assistant U.S. Attorney Corey Ellis rose to agree that he had heard Lindsay make that suggestion.

"That is a very serious charge, and it is why I asked if you intend to introduce evidence to that effect. Do you intend to do so?"

"No sir. I overstated my case."

"Don't let it happen again. The court stands in recess until 9 a.m. tomorrow morning."

24: First turns at the stand

The first day of testimony started with consideration of dismissal of a juror. Lead prosecutor Richard Edwards pointed out that juror #30 had mentioned playing cards with Wayne Garren, one of the probable witnesses and owner of Cues & Spirits, one of the video poker locations busted in the course of the state and federal crackdown. "He said he has played cards with Mr. Garren ten or fifteen times."

Judge Ellis called #30 in for questioning. After being told that the two were acquainted but not friends, Ellis said, "Will you be able to set aside any acquaintanceship with Wayne Garren who will be mentioned during the trial?"

The juror assured the judge that he could do so, and was sent back to the jury room.

Prosecutor Corey Ellis then rose to say, "I'm concerned about Mr. Lindsay's comments. I request that the jury be advised that he didn't mean what he said."

Judge Ellis said he had considered the matter overnight himself and had prepared a statement he wanted to read to the jury. He read a draft, elicited comment from counsel and once the jurors had been seated offered them a final iteration. "Mr. Lindsay inadvertently may have suggested to you that the prosecutors would undertake to have witnesses lie, but he didn't intend to do that. What he meant to do was to question the credibility of the witnesses which he is entitled to do."

At 9:35 a.m., Eddie Caldwell was sworn in as the first government witness. After describing his position as executive vice-president and general counsel for the North Carolina Sheriff's Association as well as his career history in the legal profession and law enforcement he explained the history of the office of sheriff in the state. Then he was asked to explain the history of the state's video poker laws, including the effort by his association to have the machines banned. Failing that, he said his group had prepared training materials, offered training courses and created registration forms and identification stickers. He said that while the General Assembly had specified that a uniform form would be used, it had not assigned any state office to the task.

Pictures of the stickers and forms were entered as evidence. Looking at laptop computer screens over the shoulders of the prosecutors, one could see the photographic evidence being displayed to jurors on video monitors mounted at the front of the jury box. (Binoculars would have helped.)

The stickers, Caldwell explained, were meant to help law enforcement officers easily determine if any machine in operation had been registered with the county and re-registration was mandatory if a machine was moved to a new location.

Caldwell noted that registration was to be free and that no fees can be collected by any government agency without approval from the legislature. He said that his organization shipped the stickers via United Parcel Service, initially per written request, and later taken via telephone. He testified that the Buncombe County Sheriff's Office had ordered a total of 1350 stickers between October 2000 and May 2005.

Caldwell explained that the legislature had required sheriffs to report to it on the number of machines they registered and that the Sheriff's Association had also provided a form for those reports. Buncombe County had registered 365 machines in 2000, he stated, and no new machines were permitted to come into North Carolina after that year. He testified that when machines were moved within a county, the sticker was typically left on the machine with the new form bearing the same sticker number.

Lindsay's cross-examination focused on establishing that registration was the responsibility of the machine owner, that the sheriff was assigned no special enforcement chores and that the legislature had failed to provide funding for the extra work required.

Finally Lindsay asked, "Is there any record of a request for stickers from Bobby Medford?"

"No," was Caldwell's reply.

During Bidwell's cross, he worked to establish that the Sheriff's Association had no statutory authority to issue stickers, suggesting that the stickers themselves were therefore in some fashion extra-legal. [Given that his client was accused of selling 100 stickers to Jerry Pennington for $10,000, his intent was apparently to establish the idea that Penland hadn't been selling legal documents.]

Next on the stand was FBI Agent Andrew Grafton who had executed a search warrant on the home of Ronnie "Butch" Davis on February 22, 2007. Grafton identified photos of foil wrapped bundles of hundred dollar bills his team had found stashed above ceiling tiles in the basement, with cash totaling $18,000. They also seized a Rolodex, a notepad detailing Golf Classic funding, a deposit slip for $25,000 in cash to Davis' account, a Cadillac, three sets of golf clubs, a video poker machine, and a sign that read "Don Chiles Auto Sales."

156 Cecil Bothwell

[The sign was typical of those used during the golf tourneys, when businesses sponsored holes.]

Grafton testified that the notebooks contained hand-written notes of receipts and disbursements for tournaments in April and September 2006.

Former Lieutenant John David Harrison was the next prosecution witness, one of the four men named in the Medford indictment. Harrison has strong, weathered features which make him look tough but he was soft spoken and extremely polite and his casual windbreaker and slacks gave him the look of a golfing retiree. He affirmed that he had worked for the Buncombe County Sheriff's Office under Harry Clay starting in 1965 and had come and gone from the agency over the years as incoming sheriffs fired and hired. He retired on May 31, 2005. He testified that he had pleaded guilty to several charges. He said he had been interviewed by federal authorities starting in late October 2007 concerning the golf tournaments and video poker and that he had cooperated with investigators.

Assistant U.S Attorney Richard Edwards asked, "Did you tell the truth during that October interview?"

"No." [Hence he was charged with giving false evidence, in addition to the alleged crimes he shared with the others.] He later pleaded guilty and agreed to testify.

Harrison detailed the history of video poker registration under Brenda Fraser and Homer Honeycutt before he took over in 2001, and said that Guy Penland had assisted him from the beginning. He described Penland's habitual garb—the shirt with captain's insignia — and said, "He represented that he was a captain and his phone answering machine message was, 'This is Captain Penland of the Buncombe County Sheriff's Department.' He carried an ankle gun and had a unit number."

Harrison said he had received money from both Demetre Theodossis and Jerry Pennington, "but not in the sheriff's office."

"I came up with the idea of the spring and fall golf tournaments," he explained. "In election years the money went to the campaign. In off-years I didn't have to report the income to anyone. Frank Orr and Homer Honeycutt helped me with the tournaments."

Harrison's testimony continued, "A lot of people who had video poker machines played in the tournaments starting in 2001. They brought cash to the office. At first the fee was $300, then $400 per team. Hole sponsorships were $100. The cash went into a bank bag I kept in the trunk of my car. It would stay there until we needed it." He said Orr usually purchased beverages and that Penland had often helped collect money.

Edwards handed Harrison a list of golf teams and he identified a large percentage who were connected to video poker. Then he was asked about how he handled fees that were paid by check.

"Bobby had asked that we cash checks without going to a bank. Nick [Anagnostopoulos, owner of George's Mini Mart] cashed checks. Also Bi-Lo [supermarket], when Homer Honeycutt was at the Leicester Highway store. Then he moved to the Weaverville Bi-Lo and we cashed checks there." Harrison then identified a $2,100 check written by Bobby Medford and a $400 check from Cowboy's Nite Life [a video machine location], both cashed at George's Mini-Mart. He also testified that both Orr and Penland had occasionally accompanied him when he cashed golf checks.

He said he had also been assigned to deposit money into Medford's Premier Federal Credit Union account on several occasions and that Jim Lindsey and Frank Orr had sometimes accompanied him on those errands. "Sometimes Bobby said he needed to cover checks so there was some urgency about getting the deposit to the bank." He said he had also made deposits to Judi Bell's account at Premier.

Asked about Medford's instructions concerning collections, Harrison said, "When Bobby needed money he would tell me and I would ask for money from the operators. Sometimes we'd go pick it up, sometimes cash was delivered to the lobby of the department."

During those years he said, Penland was getting $200 per new location from Jerry Pennington and he was giving half to Harrison. One Christmas, Harrison said, Pennington gave him $500 and a motorbike worth $600 for his step-grandchild. He explained that he had intervened when Pennington had been pulled over by a Hendersonville police officer who spotted a massive amount of cash and assumed it was drug money. "I told Officer Hill that it wasn't drug money, but was video poker money."

Harrison had also helped Pennington skip out on community service assigned by a court in Shelby. "He wanted to do his community service in Asheville, and got it transferred up here. I signed off on paperwork saying the work had been done. I didn't supervise him and I don't know that Pennington did any community service work at all."

The admitted bag-man said that Penland frequently loaned Medford money and then tried to collect from Harrison. "One day Penland wanted several hundred dollars, it was $1,200 or $1,500, and Bobby approved it. He used it to buy a Crown Victoria that looked like a cruiser.

"Penland had a radio that could transmit on the Buncombe County frequency. It was a radio that is only available to officers. Guy used his radio to run a tag for Pennington, which revealed that it was an undercover officer." Harrison continued, "Bobby was very upset. He said he was going to run Guy off."

The prosecutor asked about the Hot Dog King, Demetre "Jimmy the Greek" Theodossis, and Harrison said, "Theodossis owned the machines at George's Mini Mart and he paid cash and played at every golf tournament. I made direct requests to Theodossis for cash when Bobby needed money. He would give me $1,000 and Bobby $1,000."

Asked if he had ever met Theodossis' son he said, "Yes, at the Hot Dog King in Fairview while I was waiting for Jimmy to deliver money." [The son would prove to be an important link in the evidence chain because of a long distance phone call he placed to Italy.]

"Do you know Jackie Shepherd?" Edwards asked.

"I've known Jackie Shepherd for twenty-five years. He is a machine operator and I've asked him for money. I carried cash from Jackie to Bobby.

"Jackie was unhappy about other video poker operators moving him out. He wanted it stopped and Bobby didn't want machines moving around." Harrison said.

Next he was asked about Imran Alam, a convenience store owner. "Alam had video poker machines in a few locations. I solicited him for cash for golf tournaments. One time he sent $500 to Bobby. Alam wanted to change from Henderson Amusement to another operator. Henderson wasn't making payments for payouts or servicing the machines. I told him he couldn't switch and he asked me to talk to Bobby." Harrison said, "I told Bobby Imran wanted to switch to Mountain Music [owned by Jim Lindsey]." Harrison confirmed that a registration certificate for Mountain Music dated April 11, 2005 was a record of the switch that then occurred.

"Bobby told me to get $6,000 from Imran after the switch was made. I picked up Alam at one of his gas stations and drove him to Westgate Shopping Center. I called Bobby to meet us there and we pulled up window to window. Imran handed me an envelope and I handed it to Bobby, then he handed me another envelope. It was an even split. Three thousand to Bobby, three thousand to me."

Harrison said he had known Lindsey for more than twenty-five years and had solicited him for the golf tourney. "I asked Lindsey for money for Bobby now and then and he went to the bank with me one time. He had illegal machines and I signed off on them and got paid. Lindsey told me he was 'taking care of Bobby.'"

Harrison testified that he'd known Jack O'Leary and Ledford for thirty years and had known they were bookies. "Jack always gave Bobby a Christmas present and he sent money to me through Bobby." He said he'd known both Charles McBennetts, senior and junior, for a few years. "I knew junior first, when he came in to register machines. Later I solicited money from McBennett. He'd either come to my office or I'd meet him. Once I took McBennett Jr. to Bobby's house in Weaverville, his apartment. No money changed hands on that occasion."

Next the former lieutenant said he had solicited money from Theodossis, at Medford's request, for Deputy James Grant who ran for sheriff in the Democratic primary in 2006. "I took Grant to see Theodossis and Jackie Shepherd and I saw both men hand Grant money.

"Bobby knew Grant was running and he had no objection to that." [This was first-hand confirmation of Medford's meddling in the Democratic race.]

Harrison then testified that after he retired in May 2005, his role in video poker registration and the golf tournaments had been assumed by Lt. Ronnie "Butch" Davis. "Bobby appointed him."

Finally, asked about enforcement, Harrison said, "We closed down two places where we had too many complaints. They were running machines from South Carolina. We never closed down the ones that paid."

After the jury exited, Judge Ellis announced that he was considering further *voir dire* with juror #30 concerning his friendship with Warren. In the end, he decided to dismiss that juror and alternate juror, #13, moved into the box.

25: Following the money

Victoria Jayne's initial questions for former Lt. Johnny Harrison seemed aimed at justifying Medford's collection and distribution of cash. This appeared to pick up on attorney Stephen Lindsay's opening suggestion concerning Mom and Pop stores that needed to break the law in order to survive.

Jayne first confirmed that Harrison had overseen the sheriff's department's senior program. "Was that program Bobby Medford's idea?"

"Ma'am, I can't say."

"Do you know if the sheriff's department funded the senior program?"

"Ma'am I can't say."

"Do you know if money from golf tournaments in off-years was kept in the department for people who needed it?"

Harrison allowed that Medford was known to give money to the needy.

Jayne then elicited confirmation that Davis had taken over the tournaments after Harrison's retirement and asked, "Did you tell Davis about the tournaments?"

"No ma'am. he was always at the tournaments. He knew all about them."

The attorney next asked how the golf club was paid for tournaments. "We always paid the club in cash," he replied. She then asked how he handled checks and

Harrison answered, "I cashed checks when Bobby wanted money."

On May 2, Jayne began where she'd left off the previous evening. "You said you kept the golf tournament money in the trunk of your county car. How did you keep it?"

"In a bank bag," Harrison replied.

She then elicited the information that Harrison and others had routinely signed Medford's name and that he had given cash to Penland and Orr for gas and food in conjunction with the tournaments.

Had he ever threatened people to get them to join the tournaments? "No, ma'am," was his response.

Jayne confirmed Harrison's longstanding friendships with Shepherd and Lindsey, and then apparently hoped to make the Clay mud stick. "You married Sheriff Clay's widow?"

"Yes, in 2000."

But she dropped that ball immediately and asked who he reported to in the department. "Chief Deputy Stewart and Bobby," was the reply. Jayne then went over his October FBI interview and refreshed his confession that he hadn't told the whole truth at that time. She also elicited information about his serious medical problems.

"How many charges did you plead guilty to?" she asked.

"Eleven charges." Then, evidently sensing where she was going with her questions, he added, "Ma'am, I pled guilty because I am guilty and I would appreciate any consideration I might receive." [In fact, he was charged with eleven counts but pleaded guilty to one.]

"You completed a financial statement as part of your plea agreement. Do you recall?"

He responded directly, "I own a beach house in North Myrtle Beach, I don't own any property in Asheville. I paid $77,000 for it in January 2002. I kept it for

28 months and sold it in June 2006 and bought a home in North Myrtle Beach the same day."

Jayne said, "Your ability to enjoy the beach in your later years will be somewhat restricted if you are in jail."

"Ma'am you've got that right. It's hard for me to sit up here and say what I've done, what Bobby has done, what Guy has done, and to talk about Frank Orr. But, ma'am, I'm guilty. This is what we did."

Paul Bidwell started his cross just before 10 a.m. by asking, "Do you understand what you are charged with?"

"I think it was threat of force and corruption."

"How did you threaten force," the attorney asked.

"I didn't threaten. I think it was part of my position as an officer."

"Did they say things would go easier on you if you talked?" Bidwell suggested.

"No. But they did tell me that there were going to be indictments and I should consult counsel."

Bidwell then identified and Harrison confirmed a list of golf tournament donors who were *not* connected to video poker. He managed to get Harrison to confirm that Bobby had authorized him and Penland and Orr to sign checks written to Bobby. Harrison also confirmed that Penland was a part time worker, had helped with the video poker registration and the elder program.

The attorney elicited Harrison's statement that no stickers were given out from his office without paperwork being filed and that "no money changed hands in my office."

Bidwell then opened a line of questions about special deputy and honorary deputy cards. Harrison said there were numerous special deputies and that the cards were not given to political donors to his knowledge. He said that Sharon Stewart had been in charge of processing special deputy applications.

In his re-direct, Edwards focused on the money. "Do you know of Mr. Medford giving money to his family members?"

"Yes. His sons. His grandkids. They were in there often."

"You've said he went to Harrah's. How often?"

"Very often," Harrison replied.

"Did he go by himself or with others?

"By himself, and with others."

"Do you know who?"

"Homer Honeycutt is one. Homer would tell me about it the next day."

"You were asked in great detail about a piece of evidence. A notebook. Was it your practice to keep track of money from the golf tournaments?"

"Yes. I wrote it all down," Harrison said.

"Now, about your plea agreement. You pled guilty to count one of the indictment. 'Conspiracy to commit extortion under color of office.' The maximum penalty is a $250,000 fine and twenty years in prison. Do you understand what would happen if you testify falsely?"

"Yes sir. The agreement is void and I would face all of the charges."

Harrison was dismissed and George's Mini Mart owner Nick Anagnostopoulos was called to the stand. As might be inferred from his name, the business owner has the dark hair and olive complexion of his native Greece. He was very expensively dressed. His shirt looked more like Park Avenue, New York than Pack Square, Asheville. He testified that he had owned the store from 1983 to 2007 and had operated Hot Dog King video poker machines from 2000 forward. He said his split of receipts with Demetre Theodossis was 60-40.

Anagnostopoulos said he had attended the first sheriff's department information meeting concerning video poker machines and that Medford had told the owners, "If you don't cause problems for me, I won't cause problems for you."

Asked by the prosecutor if he had ever delivered money to Harrison, he replied, "I have paid him out on occasion. I also made donations for golf tournaments."

Anagnostopoulos testified that he had started cashing checks for Medford and identified a list of bank deposits to his account that included checks written to Bobby Medford. "I stopped cashing checks in 2006 because my banker called to tell me it was illegal to cash election checks."

"Have you ever cashed checks for Mr. Medford?"

"I have, though he didn't come in. A lady with Medford would come in with checks to cash."

"Was there ever trouble with any of those checks?"

"Two or three were returned NSF. I told Harrison about the problem and Harrison or Sharon Stewart or George Stewart would bring in cash to cover them."

At noon Lindsay started his cross-examination and Anagnostopoulos allowed that there were a small group of people who played his machines who he knew and could trust to whom he would give cash payouts for winnings. He said he cashed pay checks for some of them as well and that he always had a lot of cash around because it was a high volume store.

Anagnostopoulos said he was originally told that cash from the checks written to Medford was needed for the political campaign and said that Guy Penland, Butch Davis, Frank Orr and Johnny Harrison had cashed them. "It was always one of them who brought in the checks, never Bobby Medford."

Lindsay showed Anagnostopoulos a check for $800 written on August 20,2004, from Betty Donoho [one of Medford's two biggest contributors] to John Harrison. [$800 would have been the fee for two teams at that fall's Medford Golf Classic.] Lindsay's point seemed to be that it was a check from a non-gambling source.

Donoho is a major donor to Republican campaigns and owner of Asheville Electric, a large contracting firm which has been involved in development of Wal-Mart stores including the East Asheville Wal-Mart in which former congressman Charles Taylor held a significant interest. She has reportedly held repeated extravagant fundraising events for various candidates including Taylor and Medford. A relative of hers reported to me that she accompanied Medford to Harrah's on at least one occasion, but Donoho has no evident connection to gambling in Buncombe County.

Lindsay now turned to Anagnostopoulos' Grand Jury testimony on November 28, 2007 at 10 a.m.

"You were asked if you knew Mr. Medford and you said, "Medford came to cash checks but he would stay in the car. He would call first to find out if I was able to cash a check.'" The witness confirmed that he had so testified.

Lindsay: "Was it always after 6 p.m.?"

"Yes, to the best of my knowledge."

"You told the Grand Jury that Medford was never with the others cashing checks."

Anagnostopoulos explained that Medford wasn't with the others cashing golf tournament checks but came to cash his personal checks.

Paul Bidwell's questions for Anagnostopoulos were limited to asking if he had ever seen Guy Penland in uniform. "Not that I remember." And he was asked if Johnny Harrison had ever played the machines in his store "Once in a blue moon."

The witness was dismissed and the trial adjourned for lunch.

26: Tag, you're what?

Following the midday break, Buncombe Deputy Robert Robinson, a communications specialist, took the stand and testified that he had taken a radio call from Guy Penland requesting information about a license tag. He had recorded the call as a matter of routine and corroborated that a transcript and recording submitted as evidence by the prosecution were records of that call.

The jury, counsel, defendants and judge were provided with wireless headsets to facilitate their listening to the audio tape. We in the audience sat in silence.

Robinson said the vehicle tag in question turned up as unregistered which meant that it was either that of an undercover officer, or that there had been a mistake. An error could have occurred in registration or the officer could have made an error in the call, he explained.

He said that Medford had issued "a couple of memos after that incident pertaining to running tags for Mr. Penland." One memo ordered the Buncombe communications staff to tell Penland that any tag he ran was unregistered, another to stop running tags for Penland altogether.

The defense attorneys had no questions and at 2:13 p.m. a dapper businessman, Jackie Willis Shepherd, took the stand.

Under questioning Shepherd said he had taken over a video game operation from his son in 1999. "He was into drugs and wasn't tending to business, and he stole some money from me," Shepherd explained.

"In 2001 I started Western Amusement, with Comer from Spartanburg, South Carolina. We incorporated in 2004," he said, explaining that "Comer bought in for $75,000. Fifty thousand in cash and a note for $25,000 to be repaid out of profits. We ran the machines until June 28, 2007, when we were raided and the machines and records were seized."

"Did you make illegal payouts?"

"I did. If we knew the person that was playing, we paid them."

"Have you pled guilty to a crime?"

"I pled guilty to operating a business for illegal gambling. I said 'This is my responsibility. Take my sons off the list and I'll plead guilty." [Shepherd's son and step-son were initially included in his indictment.]

Asked about his history with Medford's department, he said, "Bobby was working for Black Mountain Chevrolet and I hired him in 1992. In 1993 I heard that [Sheriff] Charlie Long was watching my son's gambling operation. I decided we needed some changes in the county. We needed Bobby to go in and clean up the county."

Shepherd said he spent $20,000 to $30,000 on Medford's 1994 election campaign. "I had a tailor make clothes for him and I hired a speech lady to help him speak to crowds. I paid for a barbecue and helped with fundraising.

"I didn't help with the 1998 campaign because we had a falling out. But six years later he wanted to apologize and we made up in 2003."

In response to another question he said, "Kay Carter worked for the Buncombe County Sheriff's Department and for me at one of my stores. She was responsible for video poker and made payouts at the store."

Asked about payoffs to Medford, Shepherd responded, "Once Bobby called me and wanted $1,000. I took it in and laid it on his desk. Another time Randy Ledford picked up $1,000 at my pawn shop for Bobby. Another time Johnny Harrison wanted $2,000 and said that Bobby would pay me back."

"Did he pay you back?

"No."

"Why didn't you demand payment?"

"He wasn't botherin' my poker machines."

The prosecutor asked if he had ever cashed checks for Medford. "Yes. A couple of my stores cashed checks for him. At Payless a couple of checks came back NSF. I would take them to Sharon Stewart or Kay Carter and get cash."

"Did you receive a phone call on November 14, 2006 from the Buncombe County Sheriff's Department?"

"Yes. Ronnie Davis called to tell me that the Hot Dog King had been raided.

Lindsay's cross examination was brief. The most interesting new information was when he asked, "You talked about your son's drug problem. Bobby Medford's son had drug problems too."

"Right."

"And you talked about it with Bobby?"

"My son. Not his."

The next prosecution witness was Linda Clontz, a seven year veteran of the North Carolina Department of Corrections whose job involves oversight of alternative sentencing and community service and who said she had known Medford for thirty years. She identified a community service form entered in evidence as that of Jerry Pennington. She explained that it had transferred his court ordered service from Cleveland County over to

Buncombe County and that the transfer was very unusual because it also transferred responsibility for oversight from the DOC to the sheriff's department. When it first crossed her desk, she said it struck her as odd that Pennington's address was listed as Kings Mountain, and that it was highly unusual for an agency in any county to oversee community service by a nonresident. "I was uncomfortable with the arrangement, but I interviewed Mr. Pennington and followed the court order. Because I was unhappy with the order I contacted Sheriff Medford to express my discontent. I expressed my suspicion that the required hours had not been completed."

During Jayne's brief cross examination, she elicited from Clontz the information that Penland had been assigned by the court to oversee Pennington's service. The order identified Penland as "Captain."

Anna Deaton, a secretary and notary who worked with Jerry Pennington at Henderson Amusement, was next up, and indicated that she had worked for the company at both its Kings Mountain, North Carolina, and Spartanburg, South Carolina, offices. In response to Edwards' queries she said her duties included notarization and filing of records for Pennington as well as typing of his hand-written field notes and expense reports. She identified files submitted as evidence that listed all of Henderson's machines in Buncombe County, 122 locations in all.

Deaton explained a code system used by Pennington for identification of his payees. She said, "'Judge' or 'G' was Guy Penland, 'D' was Dewain Goins who was finding locations for machines, and 'R' was Randy." She said she kept careful records of all payouts to employees and to sheriff's departments. The day's proceedings were adjourned at about 4 p.m.

Judge Ellis had a plane to catch. The jury was out for the weekend.

Victoria Jayne began her cross examination on Monday, May 5, "You don't know that Pennington actually paid money to anyone?"

"No."

Jayne determined that Deaton still worked for Henderson in its Inman [greater Spartanburg] office, and didn't work much with Pennington anymore. "Sometimes in connection with Florida machines," Deaton explained, and also indicated that she had had no idea that anything illegal was going on up until the Kings Mountain office was raided on May 17, 2006.

The defense attorney pointed out that in her Grand Jury testimony Deaton had professed ignorance of what the code names or initials stood for and asked why her story had changed.

"After I appeared before the Grand Jury I was curious, so I asked Jerry," was the response.

Bidwell's cross examination was even more pointed, and he established that "Judge" had not been used until after her appearance before the 2006 Grand Jury. He asked about $1,000 in donations to "commissioners" and Deaton said that Pennington and Henderson had each donated $500 to a Buncombe County Commissioner in June, 2005.

Bidwell tried to connect the code name "Judge" to former Buncombe Capt. Tracy Bridges. "Did you know that Bridges had been a magistrate judge at one time?" he asked. But the name was unfamiliar to Deaton.

"Did Mr. Pennington provide receipts for payments to Penland, Harrison or Medford?"

"No," she replied.

Could she explain the payment to JP Racing for $10,000? "Jerry sponsored a race car," was the answer.

"And was there ever money missing?" Bidwell asked.

"Jerry said there was $9,326 missing from his safe after the 2006 raid," she replied.

"Were you ever aware of Pennington paying himself cash for placement of machines?"

"No."

Bidwell then led her through a long list of machine registrations and locations and associated initials. His effort seemed aimed at showing that the code initials were very inconsistent.

During his redirect, Edwards merely asked whether Deaton had been threatened with federal charges or given any promises concerning her testimony and she answered in the negative.

Following Deaton, Charlotte-based FBI fleet co-ordinator Patrick Kirby, Jr. took the stand briefly to identify the tag run by Penland for Pennington. North Carolina tag number MSL 3610 was assigned to a 1999 Chevy Tahoe registered to the Department of Justice.

It was, indeed, that of an undercover agent who had been investigating Henderson machines.

27: The salesman's pitch

At 10:45 a.m. on May 5 one of the government's most important witnesses took the stand. Jerry Wayne Pennington, every six foot and some inches a picture-perfect used car salesman, was at the very center of the federal case. His involvement tied together the obstruction of justice, bribery and mail fraud charges, as well as the illegal gambling and extortion under color of official right. He was good at his job, and he worked it.

Pennington's career had been in the sports betting and gambling business before he went to work for Henderson Amusement in "about 2000." He said he started placing machines in North Carolina in the late 1990s. Henderson's arrangement, he testified, was a 50-50 split with store owners, and sometimes a 40-60 split in favor of the store.

Was he aware of the new law in 2000? "Yes. You could only have three machines per location and cash payouts were illegal. They had to be registered in the sheriff's office of each county." He said Henderson operated in twelve to fifteen North Carolina counties, and that he personally registered machines, obtained stickers and took machines out to locations. He stated that he knew they were being used to give out illegal cash payments.

Pennington said the company employed a check-up person who went out once each week to split the take with store owners and to service machines. When there was a jackpot too big for the weekly receipts to cover he said he personally took cash to the store owner to pay the winnings.

In 2000, he said, the Rutherford County sheriff had phoned Henderson and given them one hour to remove all sixty of their machines then operating in that county. "We tried, but he confiscated all of them. We never got those machines back."

In response to Edwards' questions he said he had been indicted in August, 2007, and had been questioned. He had pled guilty to conspiracy to organize gambling, money laundering and bribery. He was sentenced to 63 months in prison but his sentence was postponed pending the Medford trial.

Pennington then explained that Henderson had simply imported more machines from South Carolina, in violation of the North Carolina import ban, and shuffled the paperwork to make it appear that those were actually the machines gone missing in Rutherford. He said "We had lots of machines in other counties, and we were running out of machines."

He stated that he had first had contact with Buncombe County deputies in 2002. "The first time I talked to Guy Penland, then Homer Honeycutt. At the time I came in, Mr. Honeycutt said they had plenty of machines in here and didn't want anymore. Mr. Penland said Mr. Honeycutt had no right to do that and said he'd talk to Mr. Medford. After that Johnny Harrison was in charge of registration and he registered my machines."

Asked about his relationship with Penland he replied, "I got to know him real close. We were good friends. I was in touch with him several times a week up here. At least three times per week. He introduced himself to me as Capt. Guy Penland. He told me he had been a Lieutenant and was promoted to Captain."

Under further questioning Pennington said, "He wore captain's bars and his voice mail said 'This is Captain Guy Penland." He also said he'd met Frank Orr through Penland and that his understanding was that Orr was an honorary member of the sheriff's department, but that Orr never registered machines.

How did it happen that he paid cash to Penland? Pennington said, "When I learned that he wasn't certified and didn't have a salary, we came up with a salary for him for finding locations for video poker machines."

"I think everybody knew how the machines worked. Everybody was aware that they made payouts. Everybody that was associated with the business knew that they made payouts."

Asked about Penland's business interests, Pennington said, "He had a pawn shop. We put three machines there but it didn't work out too good. They didn't make any money. We put them in his partner's name because it wouldn't have looked good to put them in his name since he worked with the sheriff's department."

Concerning the salary, he testified, "Myself and Jamie Henderson agreed to pay him $450 per week in salary plus $500 per location he came up with in Buncombe, Haywood and Henderson County. Sometimes I would go with him on sales calls and he dressed in his uniform shirt with captain's bars. Sometimes we'd go in my vehicle, sometimes in his. Later on he had a sheriff's department car. [This was actually Penland's personal Crown Victoria, which looked like a cruiser.] And although Pennington stated it this way, he contradicted himself in the next answer.

"What role did you play in obtaining that car?"

"He said the sheriff had given him the okay to get a car that looked like a sheriff's car and I located a car for him." In response to further questions he said, "It had a tag on the front that looked like law enforcement and I think it had a long antenna. I reimbursed him for all of his expenses including gas."

Pennington said he also gave Penland a free-play machine for his home, that is a video poker machine that didn't require money to play.

Did he ever give cash to Harrison? "Yes, every time we got a new location in the county I gave money to Penland for Harrison. Approximately $250 per location."

The financial arrangement changed following Harrison's retirement, when Lt. Ronnie "Butch" Davis assumed responsibility for machine registration. "I paid Davis $200 for each new location." Asked why the fee was reduced, Pennington explained that unlike Penland, Davis was a salaried officer and therefore didn't need to be paid as much. [This explanation left me with the suspicion that Davis didn't know how much Pennington had previously paid Penland and Harrison for placing machines—which, according to this testimony, amounted to $650 per location—and therefore didn't know what he might be able to demand.] Pennington testified that he paid out $200 to Davis "maybe up to twenty times" during his tenure. [June 2005 through autumn 2007.]

Pennington said he sponsored three or four teams at each golf tournament, for $400 or $450 apiece, and sometimes sponsored holes. However, he said, Henderson employees almost never actually played in the tourneys.

"Why did you keep paying if no one played?"

"I wanted to keep up good relations with the sheriff because things were doing good in the county."

"Were you ever solicited for cash in relation to the tournaments?"

"One time Chief Stewart and [District Attorney] Ron Moore were sponsoring a golf tournament and Harrison wanted more money. I gave cash directly to Medford. Another time Captain Penland said business was good and that the sheriff needed gifts. I met with the sheriff at a restaurant and he said he would prefer that I give money to him and not to anyone else."

Pressed for details, Pennington explained "Captain Penland arranged a meeting with Medford in a parking lot, close to the back of a restaurant. We talked about things. Up to then the policy was to give money to Penland, but Medford said he'd rather have nobody else involved in the money." Asked for the amount involved, Pennington said "For three months it was $2,500 per month, a couple of months it was $2,000. During the Penland era, when we rode around together, I'd give him the money, or I'd go to the lobby of the sheriff's office and tell the dispatcher I was there. Then I'd go back to the sheriff's personal office."

Penland's direct involvement ended about the time Davis took over, in part because of Medford's anger over the tag call, and Penland was evidently not as close to Davis as to Harrison. This, coupled with the direct payments to Medford, fills out the explanation for the reduced payments to Davis.

"Did Davis ever ask you to bring money to the sheriff?"

"Sometimes I was to give money to Davis, some-times directly to the sheriff. I'd walk through [secretary] Sharon Stewart's office, back to his office. I'd go around his desk and sit down. I'd take an envelope and put it on his desk, then he would slide it into a drawer. There was little or no talk and most times nothing was said. When I heard the sheriff wanted to see me, I'd know it was time to bring some money."

How many times did he go to the office? "I can't recall exactly—ten or a dozen, maybe seven or eight." And the most he ever gave at one time? "Twenty-five hundred dollars."

"Were you ever asked for a campaign contribution?" the prosecutor queried.

"Five thousand dollars, twice. And Jamie Henderson gave him $10,000 as well. We went to a Waffle House together." He explained that Penland had come to him two years before the 2006 election and suggested that campaign contributions were needed and had arranged a meeting at the Waffle House restaurant in Columbus, North Carolina. Pennington stated that these "donations" preceded the time when Medford requested that all money go to him directly.

Edwards then led Pennington through the records submitted as evidence during Anna Deaton's testimony, and Pennington identified recipients of his payroll. "J" was Johnny Harrison. "David" was a Henderson sales representative, "Marty" a technician, "Johnny" a salesman, "G" or "gy" or "Judge" was Penland, "xx" was Medford, "f" was Frank Orr, and "Chief" was George Stewart.

Asked why his code was so inconsistent, Pennington said, "I had no idea anybody would ever wind up with this. If I had, I would have been more careful." [There was laughter in the courtroom.] "But I wanted to hide his identity."

The witness then went through many of the specific entries in his accounts and identified Christmas bonuses to "Guy, $1,000; Harrison, $1,000; Medford, $1,000; James Grant, $300; and Capt. Bill Green, $300." He said Green was "a good friend. He tried to help us and got one location." Pennington said bonuses also went to Chief Deputy George Stewart and Frank Orr. "Each gift was in a gift folder with the person's initials and I gave them out personally, including the gift to Medford."

The prosecutor directed Pennington's attention to the donation of $1,000 to the "Buncombe commissioner" and the witness said it had nothing to do with the poker machines.

He also identified a $400 donation to Clerk of Court Bob Christy as being unrelated to the gambling business. "The sheriff asked that we give money to him," was Pennington's explanation.

Five months later I contacted Pennington through his attorney, J. Steven Brackett. Pennington denied having offered any testimony concerning Buncombe commissioners and declined further comment.

In further testimony, Pennington sent shock waves through Haywood County when he said that he had paid the sheriff $100 per machine per month to register machines there. "Or we could not operate," he said, and indicated that Henderson was operating 33 machines in that municipality. The Haywood sheriff, Tom Alexander, was so highly regarded that the county was about to name a law enforcement center for him. He quickly hired an attorney and was soon called to testify before a Grand Jury.

Following a long lunch break, Pennington was questioned about his arrest during a traffic stop on Labor Day, 2005, in Henderson county. The arresting officer had spotted a large quantity of cash and arrested Pennington under suspicion of illegal drug sales. At the time of the arrest he was carrying a Buncombe County Special Deputy I.D. and badge he asserted he had obtained from Penland, a photo I.D., and Bobby Medford's business card with Medford's cell phone number hand written on the back.

Had he ever called that number? "Yes."

After those I.D.s were taken from him, had he obtained other official I.D.s? "Yes, at Christmas, 2005, I received another badge from Penland, but I never filled my card out." He then identified a Lieutenant's badge and a new I.D. card that hadn't been filled out which were then entered as evidence.

Had Pennington ever asked Penland to run a license tag? "Yes, at one of our locations the employees were suspicious about a car parked nearby. They had called and asked about the car and I asked Penland to run the tag. He said it came back as an 'unregistered' vehicle and said, 'It's probably a law officer.'"

Edwards moved on to Pennington's community service. "I did no service at all," the witness stated. "The form was not truthful about hours and my charges were dismissed pursuant to 'doing service.'"

The next questions concerned Penland's help in staking out the federal courthouse. Pennington explained: "I learned about the federal criminal investigation and learned that it was being investigated in the Asheville federal courthouse. I was asked by an investigator to come by the courthouse to see if I knew anybody coming and going from the grand jury. I came and we used Captain Penland's patrol cruiser."

What explanation had he offered to Penland? "I said we were looking for video poker persons who might be testifying, and Penland had no objection." [Pennington's informant had gotten the date wrong, and he and Penland were entirely unsuccessful in their effort.]

Next Pennington testified concerning competition between video poker companies. "Penland told me it was the sheriff's rule that we couldn't move into other companies' locations. He said Medford 'wanted things to run smooth.'" In particular Pennington described his dealings with Imran Alam. "When he got involved with Henderson Amusement, around 2000, he started accumulating stores, mini-marts and service stations, and we started to help him.

"He got sort of powerful in the mini-mart business and we had machines in every store he had." The prosecution entered machine registration documents as evidence to corroborate this claim.

Was it profitable? "Yes, but he was difficult to deal
with. But we did okay. Then he decided he wanted a
bigger percentage than 40-60 and he wanted a 20-80
split. When we refused, he said he wanted to switch to
Mr. Lindsey's machines. I talked to Penland and Harrison
about it, and both of them talked to Medford. They told
me he said, 'Let it go.' Alam switched and we didn't
complain. We had lots of machines in Buncombe and we
didn't want to cause any problems." [While the
prosecutor didn't pursue this matter further at the time,
Pennington's testimony about Alam's switch to Lindsey's
machines would provide key corroboration of the other
two men's description of dealings with Medford when
they each took the stand.]

Pennington said that after Penland had run the tag
which established that an investigation was underway, he
met with Davis to inquire about the circumstances.
"Davis said, 'We didn't do it. We've been good to you.'
And he arranged a meeting between me and Medford.

"Penland and I met Medford at the Westgate Mall.
I got into the sheriff's car and we talked. He said, 'I've
never done anything wrong.' It was kind of a casual
conversation, probably in the fall of 2005.

"What I understood was, 'This is your problem.'"

Did he have any reason to think the conversation
was being recorded? "We both talked as if each of us
thought we were being recorded."

Finally, Pennington was asked how long he had
engaged in the illegal gambling business and if on any
one day he had made more than $2,000 which would
establish the crime as a federal felony.

"From the time the law went into operation in
2000, continuously until the bust." And the operation
had definitely made more than $2,000 on many days.

28: Penland penned in

In the course of his cross examination, Medford attorney Stephen Lindsay made a strong effort to pick apart minor differences between Pennington's testimony and his interviews with the FBI, but found very little traction. Every answer from the witness seemed to corroborate his testimony rather than weaken it, and Lindsay shifted tactics.

He suggested that the prosecution might have rehearsed Pennington for cross examination and the witness denied it. Finally he asked, "Did you say that Imran wanted an 80-20 split?

"Yes."

"Has that ever happened before?"

"No."

Paul Bidwell's cross would be much more extensive, for the very good reason that the relationship between Pennington and Penland had been far more intimate than that between the sheriff and the salesman. However, the outcome of the grilling seemed to leave his client in worse shape than ever which brought to mind the old adage, "When you are mired in a hole, it's a good idea to stop digging."

It was alleged that Penland had outright sold machine stickers, for $10,000, to Pennington who had been caught with a large number of them. "Were those part of the one hundred stickers you say Penland sold you?" the attorney queried.

"Yes."

"Did anyone advise you that Guy Penland had ordered one hundred stickers from the North Carolina Sheriff's Association?"

"He had one hundred stickers. I don't know where he got them," Pennington replied.

Bidwell then hammered the witness with a series of challenges about his statements to investigators. "On August 8, 2007, you did not tell investigators about the one hundred stickers."

"No."

He repeated the question, "Nor on August 22, nor on September 11. And on Dec 11, 2007, in court testimony, you made no mention of either the one hundred stickers or the $10,000."

Pennington affirmed each statement in turn.

"Why did you buy stickers you could have obtained for free [by registering the machines as required under the law]?"

"Because the machines I needed stickers for were illegal."

Bidwell then made what appeared to be a mistake and asked, "Regarding your community service. You say that Mr. Penland and Mr. Harrison cooked up a scheme to avoid community service and you just went along with it?"

"Right."

Bidwell then queried Pennington about the Grand Jury stakeout. What reason had he given Penland for the task?

"I told him we needed to stake out this procedure to see if there was anyone I might know."

Bidwell then sought and received confirmation that the Grand Jury had not, in fact, been in session on the day in question. While this made the duo seem a little incompetent, or at least ill informed, it did little to undermine the argument that Penland had participated in abuse of authority.

"Why did you deal with Guy instead of Johnny Harrison?" Bidwell asked.

Pennington explained "Johnny let Guy take over his position. When I first went to the sheriff's office to register machines, Homer Honeycutt was real rude and wouldn't register any machines. Guy said Homer didn't have authority to say that and told me he would talk to Medford. Then Guy and Johnny registered my machines."

Once again, Bidwell seemed to permit damage to his defense when he asked, "Was it helpful for your business to have a police-looking vehicle?"

"Yes. Prior to 2004 we used Guy's Lincoln Continental, or a little Dodge or an SUV. After that we used his Crown Victoria."

Then the attorney made a foray aimed at establishing some measure of innocence for his client. "Placing machines in stores was not, in itself, illegal. It was the use of the machines by the store owners that made them illegal, right?"

"Yes."

"Do you know Tracy Bridges?

"No."

"Did you know he was a former magistrate judge?"

"No."

Bidwell asserted that Bridges' name had come up during the August 8, 2007 Pennington interview by FBI agents Daley and McNeely. The effort here seemed to be to suggest that Pennington's records of payouts to "judge" were to Bridges rather than to Penland.

"During that interview, you said 'Judge may have been Guy Penland.'"

"I was real nervous. I had just been arrested, but I knew it was Penland."

What about his deputy badge? "Penland offered me an older badge, but I said I wanted a better looking one, and he ordered me a new one. I was given the badge along with my honorable deputy card and I was told it would be fine to use it as long as I didn't arrest nobody. I could use it if I was ever pulled over by the state police, as an identification."

"Did Mr. Penland ever tell you how freely badges were given out?"

"No."

"Did Mr. Penland's association with the sheriff's department have anything to do with paying him?"

"Yes."

"On some occasions did Mr. Penland wear his uniform?"

"Yes."

"Has anyone from the government promised you that there would be a motion to reduce your sentence?"

"No."

At the conclusion of Bidwell's cross, Penland looked guilty as hell.

Court was adjourned at 5:30 p.m. that Monday, and set to reconvene at 10 a.m. the next morning. The late start was scheduled to permit jurors to vote in the North Carolina primary election, May 6.

[I arrived at the federal courthouse a little late the following morning and missed the prosecution's questioning of its next witness, Alvin Ledford. Ledford is an admitted bookie and illegal gambling organizer of longstanding in the county. Lindsay was conducting his cross when I slipped into the courtroom.

I learned much later from another reporter, and then had it confirmed by Assistant U.S. Attorney Edwards during Medford's sentencing, that Ledford had testified that he had "bribed every Buncombe sheriff since the

1950s, except for Charlie Long." This bombshell never made the papers, but it represents a serious indictment of the county's Republican party. Long was the only Democrat to hold the office during that period.

Others reported that Ledford's testimony included monthly $1,000 pay-offs to Medford and an assertion that he didn't like video poker machines but had been coerced into running them by a sheriff's deputy. "I didn't like video-poker machines, they're highway robbery," he said. He said he finally accepted them after the deputy told him he'd give back $1,000 in cash he'd handed the deputy if he did. "I never got the money," he complained.]

Lindsay asked who Ledford's gambling business partners were and he identified his son, McKenzie, and grandson, Gerrin Ledford. He admitted that $38,000 had been confiscated from his farmhouse in a 2007 raid by federal officers. Then he answered a somewhat confusing question from Lindsay with a very confusing answer about Jack O'Leary giving money to Medford at a Waffle House, leaving it unclear whether he had been present at that meeting.

Judge Tim Ellis intervened in the questioning, seeking clarity. "Did you ever go with O'Leary to give money to Medford?"

"Yes. We met at the Waffle House every five or six weeks for two or three years."

Lindsay: "In 1994 you were sentenced for illegal gambling and abetting illegal gambling?"

"Yes. I served six months in the Atlanta prison." [He had been busted by Sheriff Charlie Long, and was then convicted on federal charges.]

"Were you told that if you testified in this case there would be no charges filed against you?"

"I was told there would be no charges against my family members, but not me."

Lindsay asked about an interview with Ledford conducted by FBI agents and whether those agents had mentioned Medford's name. Ledford said "no" and the attorney challenged him to read a transcript which said otherwise.

"I can't read."

"Did you tell them you had seen Medford on TV?"

"I guess."

"Didn't you know him because he had busted you one time?"

"Yes. At Golf Town."

Bidwell had no questions for Ledford.

29: Coffee, tea or cash?

The next witness was emblematic of the thoroughness of the FBI. Since 1987, Inez McGinnis had worked at a Waffle House restaurant frequented by Bobby Medford, and she identified him in court. Had she ever seen him with other people? "Yes. With the man who just passed me in the hall. At least twice." [That is, Alvin Ledford, who had exited the courtroom as McGinnis was led in.]

"Once in the evening and once in the day," she added. "In about 2004."

That was all the prosecution needed to ask.

Lindsay then questioned her about details, hoping, perhaps that her memories would be hazy. But her replies made her testimony much more believable.

"I saw him two or three times. (She gestured toward Bobby Medford.) He was always looking at his watch like he was waiting for someone. Then he went out and met people in the parking lot. Another time, someone came in and joined him. The restaurant is wide open and other people were there, but sometimes things are slow and you have time to be nosy.

"One other man had a telephone computer, one of things. [Perhaps a Blackberry?] He was busy mashing buttons."

Asked if she could identify the people in the parking lot, McGinnis said she had seen Medford go to a waiting car, but had not gained a clear view of the occupants.

Lindsay: "In November 2007 did Mr. Eric Veater from the IRS come to talk to you and another employee?"

"Yes."

"And you were showed photographs of two persons and asked if you had seen them with Medford?"

"Yes."

After Lindsay had succeeded in making the witness seem even more reliable, Bidwell homed in on her identification of Ledford.

"How did you see that other witness?"

"We were sitting on the same bench," McGinnis replied.

"Did anyone tell you to take a good look at him?"

"No."

30: The Pakistani connection

At 10:55 a.m. Imran Alam took the stand for the prosecution. Two of my informants had told me, back in 2005, that Medford's deputies had put the squeeze on at least two Pakistani convenience store owners. Neither of the owners had been willing to tell me anything about the allegations, but Alam had been busted as part of the WNC crackdown and I was eager to hear his story.

Alam said he had lived in the U.S. for twenty-two or twenty-three years, held a green card, and had been in the gas station business since 1999. He had remarkable success, perhaps abetted by a strong cash flow in the video poker racket, and at the time of the trial he owned seventeen stations. He said he first met Penland when the volunteer officer approached him about placing Henderson machines in his store near the WNC Farmer's Market. "He was in uniform," Alam recalled.

Later, dissatisfied with the financial arrangement with Henderson Amusement, Alam said he told Penland he wanted to switch companies and "Penland said I could not change, that I'd have to work things out. So I met with Pennington to discuss removing the machines."

Alam said he was unhappy with Henderson's service. "The way it works is they send someone to check out the machines and to see how much I had paid out in tickets. They are supposed to pay me for the payouts, and then we split the balance. They weren't doing what they were supposed to do."

Asked about the illegal gambling, the Pakistani owner said, "When I first had the machines I was very reluctant to make payouts, but Penland said it would be okay to pay off people I know. He helped to raise my comfort level. He said 'Just make sure you know the people.'"

After complaining to Penland and seeing no change, he said he talked to Harrison and Harrison said he would talk to the sheriff. "Harrison arranged a lunch in Candler, then he picked me up and we met Medford there. I told him, 'I'm really not happy. I really want to change and if I can't change, I'm going to take them out.' He didn't say yes and he didn't say no.

"Later, Harrison asked for $6,000. He told me to put $3,000 in each of two envelopes. I got envelopes from the bank and met Harrison at my Exxon station on Patton Avenue. He drove me to Westgate to wait for Bobby Medford. When he arrived I handed the envelopes to Harrison and he passed one through the window to the sheriff, in his car. Medford said, 'You got your envelope?' Harrison nodded and we drove away."

Alam said that Harrison had contacted Mountain Music to replace the Henderson machines. "Jim Lindsey, the owner of Mountain Music, changed out the machines."

Alam testified that he had paid money to the golf tournaments for several years and that one time Penland had expressed dissatisfaction over the amount he contributed. "Penland called Henderson and Henderson called me to tell me to write another check."

Like Pennington, Alam obtained a special deputy card. He said his was offered and issued by Ronnie "Butch" Davis, who occasionally collected money.

"Later, Johnny Harrison called me and said the sheriff needs money and that he would come to pick me up. Harrison said, 'From now on don't pay Butch Davis because the money is not getting to the sheriff.' I took a cigarette carton of Salem Lights and put $2,000 in the carton in a beer bag and took it to the sheriff in his office. Harrison was in the room when I paid him."

Why did he take Salem Lights? "Because that's what Harrison said he smoked. His girlfriend smoked Marlboro lights."

Alam said he had pled guilty to running an illegal gambling business, was sentenced to three years probation and forfeited three gas stations worth $1.7 million.

During Victoria Jayne's cross, she was able to draw out some minor discrepancies between Alam's and Pennington's version of events, though the differences were narrow. Alam denied that he had ever demanded an 80-20 split with Henderson, though he confirmed that he had obtained a better deal from Lindsey (70-30) than his 60-40 deal with Henderson. He denied that the split had been the driving issue for his switch and that Henderson's failure to reimburse him for payouts was a more critical matter.

Jayne attempted to establish inconsistencies between Alam's testimony before a Grand Jury two years earlier and his current statements, but with little success. The witness seemed plausible in his explanations of slight discrepancies in his memory. She also pressed him with the suggestion that the $6,000 cash withdrawal he made on the day he and Harrison claimed he had paid off Medford, was actually withdrawn to consummate a real estate deal, which he denied. She also tried to make a convincing case that his testimony was tainted by his need for a plea deal. Jayne scored some points in noting that Alam and his wife both held green cards and that the possibility of losing their work status and being deported was a serious threat.

Alam insisted, however, "I provided all of this information two years ago, before I was charged with anything."

Paul Bidwell's cross focused narrowly on the number of Alam's stores, and the order in which he had acquired them, together with his expansion of real estate holdings.

After a lengthy lunch break, Demetre Theodossis was sworn in and took the stand. Known as "Jimmy the Greek" to gambling insiders and more widely known for the name of his sandwich shop chain, The Hot Dog King, Theodossis said he had been in the U.S. since 1972 and became a citizen in 1979. He moved to Asheville in 1981 and started the first of four sandwich shops. "In 1993 I began to operate video gambling games. They were called Cherry Masters. I did that until 2000 when South Carolina banned video poker and I moved Pot Of Gold machines up here."

Theodossis said he had attended the operators meeting at the sheriff's office with Harrison and Medford, where he had received information about the law and been given blank registration forms. "Brenda Fraser registered my first machines. I bought them in South Carolina and put them in fifteen or sixteen locations. The split with the store owners was 50-50 or 60-40, sometimes 70-30. In the end I had sixty to sixty-five machines in Buncombe County and six machines in Henderson."

Concerning payouts, Theodossis said, "I knew they were illegal. I authorized my employees to pay out when players won. The biggest jackpot was $5,000." [So my nearly forgotten anonymous caller had been right about the amount.] He testified that he made $2,000 to $10,000 per week, per machine, and put 55 percent of his take in the bank. The rest he kept at home where federal authorities would seize it on November 14, 2006, while Theodossis vacationed in Greece.

Asked to describe what the feds had found he replied, "Some money in safe boxes. Some in other things. Some in the dog kennel. Some in the well. They confiscated $1.7 million in cash, $650,000 from my bank account, a 1998 BMW and a 2007 BMW worth $98,000." He said he had forfeited all of that and been handed a bill for $550,000 in taxes and interest. "That's without penalties. I'm not finished with the IRS yet." He had also lost three of the four Hot Dog King shops.

Theodossis said he had first been asked for a donation to Medford's golf tournament by Harrison and had delivered $5,000 to Penland in his office. "Then, after two months, Harrison wanted $500, and after that it was a $500 donation every month. Then Harrison said it wasn't a donation any more, but money for the sheriff, and it was $1,000 every month.

"At some point, Butch Davis took over and he told me it was going to continue the same way."

The prosecutor asked, "What did you get in return for all that money?"

"They didn't bother my illegal business."

"Were you concerned that you might be shut down if you didn't pay?"

"Yes."

"Did you ever receive stickers without paperwork?"

"Yes. One time Penland gave me five or six that were never registered." (Aha! A few HDK machines were among those I had discovered were missing from the sheriff's registration list obtained from Julie Kepple.)

Theodossis said Harrison would meet him at the Fairview shop for regular pay-offs and for "campaign contributions" of $2,000 to $5,000 in 2002. Then in 2006, "Butch Davis asked for a $5,000 campaign contribution."

Did he ever converse with Medford? "One time he called me and said he needed 'dough.'"

In October 2006, Theodossis was vacationing in Greece and had left his son in charge of the business. He said, "My son had my cell phone and he got a call from Butch Davis asking for more money. My son called me to get my approval. Later he called back to say he had delivered the money to the sheriff."

At this point the prosecution submitted a cell phone bill which documented calls to and from Davis and to Greece.

During Stephen Lindsay's cross examination he drew out testimony to the effect that Theodossis had never delivered money to Davis. "I never gave it to him, I always gave it to Medford directly."

"But Medford never called and asked you directly for money?"

"No."

Paul Bidwell's cross was no more helpful to the defense. He elicited the information that Theodossis had sometimes been asked for machines by store owners, and sometimes had approached them first and that he always explained the law to store owners and told them it was up to them how they ran the machines. Finally, he asked if the witness had ever contributed to other political campaigns.

"Yes. Harrison asked for $500, in cash, for Elizabeth Dole."

Following his father, Dennis Theodossis was next on the stand. The most interesting information to come out of his testimony was refutation of some of his father's hard luck tale. Not that the story of the seizure of money and vehicles was false, but that there is more to the financial story. "I run convenience stores and real estate holdings for my father's business. I am the General Manager of HDK, Incorporated. I was responsible for the video poker business when my father was away, but I had no responsibilities concerning the Buncombe County Sheriff's Department."

He then corroborated the phone calls from and to Davis and to his father in Greece concerning a pay-off. He said he took $1,000 in cash to Davis at the sheriff's office.

Again, Lindsay's cross yielded little new information. Theodossis said his home had also been raided in November, 2006, and that authorities had seized $100,000 in cash. He said he didn't play golf, knew nothing about the golf tournaments or sponsorships and had never received a call from Bobby Medford.

Dennis Theodossis was never charged with any crime. Surprisingly, neither defense attorney explored with either Theodossis whether the son's freedom from prosecution was implied or overtly made to be part of the father's plea deal.

31: Orr, what?

Frank Orr seems to have become involved with the Medford organization because he liked to play golf. A Buncombe native, he worked at Bi-Lo and Wal-Mart, and, as of the time of the trial, had known Johnny Harrison, Homer Honeycutt and Bobby Medford for "about thirty-five years." He had also known Butch Davis for "ten or fifteen years." On the witness stand he said he is a good friend of Guy Penland's and noted, "He's from West Asheville, too." Like other friends of the department, Orr carried a Special Deputy card, in his case one personally issued by the Sheriff of Nottingham.

Under Edward's questioning Orr said he helped organize the golf tournaments and that when he commenced his volunteer efforts he worked out of Harrison's and Penland's office. "When I was first there, I thought Guy was a captain because he wore a uniform shirt with a badge."

How long was he there before he realized Penland was not a deputy? "A year or so."

Orr testified that he never had anything to do with registering machines, a function handled by Harrison and Penland, then Davis. But he had worked with them collecting money for the golf tournaments and had accompanied Harrison to the Fairview Hot Dog King, though he said he never went inside.

From a list of tournament participants Orr identified several names with gambling connections, including "Papa Jack" O'Leary and Alvin Ledford. He said he'd known Ledford for thirty to forty years and that he "sold football tickets and organized other gambling." Orr recounted accompanying Harrison and Davis on multiple occasions to collect cash from Ledford as well as Jim Lindsey and Imran Alam, thus corroborating those payoffs.

Orr said he had seen Pennington and Lindsey at the sheriff's office on multiple occasions and that either Harrison or Davis usually accompanied them into Medford's private office. "They would first call Sharon Stewart or the sheriff to announce 'We have a visitor.'" He also confirmed distribution of Christmas gifts by Pennington to himself and others in the department.

Concerning the tournament money, Orr said he, Harrison and Penland had handled it. Was the money ever deposited in a financial institution? "I had occasion to put golf money into Medford's account and Ms. Bell's account at the Premier Federal Credit Union. And I've been with Harrison and Davis doing the same. We'd go up to the window and put in a deposit slip to Medford's account, or Bell's."

Had there ever been urgency about those deposits? "Yes. Sometimes they had to be made by 11 a.m."

What did he know about the use of the golf money? "In non-election years it was for the sheriff. In election years it went into his campaign fund. We kept a record of all money coming in and going out, and Harrison or Davis would note how much money was going to Medford."

Edwards showed Orr notes attributed to Davis and pointed at one line which read, "Give Tracy $6,000 cash."

Did he know who that referred to? "Captain Tracy Bridges was there for a couple of years. One time Davis gave Bridges $9,000 to buy money orders because the campaign couldn't take cash."

[The campaign's CPA, Lester Bullock, had strongly advised Medford not to take any cash donations because he thought they looked suspicious.]

Orr identified other recipients of ill-begotten cash listed in Davis' notes: Brian Medford, the sheriff's son; Lisa, a woman who "took care of the election headquarters;" $3,000 to the golf course, a prepayment for one tournament; and $2,400 for "dog."

"One of the deputies, it was Judi Bell's son, shot a family's dog. We gave Medford money to write a check for the animal hospital after the death of the dog."

"Didn't Medford tell the press that he was personally paying for the dog out of his own pocket?" the prosecutor inquired.

"Yes. But the money came from the golf tournament." Orr then affirmed that he had cashed tournament checks at George's Mini-Mart with Harrison and Penland, that he and the others had routinely endorsed checks written to Medford and that he had never discussed that practice with the sheriff. He also said he had received expense money from time to time. "One hundred or two hundred dollars at a time."

Orr explained that Davis had told him about the large amount of cash he was holding at home. Orr said he advised the Lieutenant to invest it in certificates of deposit, so as to collect interest on the money and keep it more secure. "We took $25,000 in cash to the bank, wrapped in foil, and he bought a CD," Orr said.

Did he ask where the money came from? "Yes. Davis said he'd won it, that he'd been going to Harrah's with Homer and the sheriff and Sharon Stewart and others."

Had he been present when Davis asked Theodossis for money? "Yes. Davis called Jimmy the Greek to ask for a contribution for the golf tournament. Jimmy's son came by and handed cash to Davis. He put it in his pocket."

Had there ever been an occasion when someone from the sheriff's department gave him cash and asked him to write a check to the campaign? "Yes, in 2006." He then identified photographs of three checks written on his account for $700, $500 and $2,360 respectively, as well as slips reflecting similar cash deposits to his checking account. Orr said he had received the cash from Davis and from Sharon Stewart.

Attorney Lindsay's cross examination first focused on details about the tournaments. Orr indicated he had started helping with the golf events in 2001. He defined "shotgun start" as the practice of having individual teams start on every hole at the same time and "Captain's choice" as a contest in which four players each try to make the same shot, with a winner collecting a pay-off. "The tournament was intended to let people have a good time," Orr explained.

How much profit remained at the end of the tournaments? "We guaranteed the golf course $100 per team. On non-election years we'd make $5,000 to $6,000. We'd usually comp some teams, as well."

"You had a special deputy I.D. card," Lindsay said, "Were those given out to lots of people?"

"I don't know."

"Do you recall Mr. Medford personally signing your card?"

"No."

Lindsay went on, "In May of 2005 Harrison retired and Davis took over. Did you work together?"

"Yes."

"Jerry Miller used to work there too. Was he the attorney for the sheriff?"

"Yes."

"Did Bobby borrow money from people?"

"Not from me."

"At Christmas, Jerry Pennington came to you with an envelope and said 'Merry Christmas.' Did you see Pennington give an envelope to the sheriff?"

"No. He was in there with the door closed. That was routine when people were there."

Lindsay made an effort to establish that the $2,400 cash payment labeled "dog" which Orr had identified as payment to Medford was not the same money claimed by Medford as his own when he grandstanded for the press, but he only succeeded in making the story more believable. Orr knew all the details about Bell's son who shot a family pet out of fear, which then died a slow death at a veterinary hospital, and Medford's populist posturing when he wrote a "personal" check.

Did he know Tracy Bridges? "Yes, a long time."

Did he know of Bridges' involvement with the campaign? "Davis told me he gave Bridges $9,000 to get money orders."

Did he ever have a conversation with Medford concerning the $500 and $700 he had received from Davis or the $2,360 he had received from Davis and Stewart?

"No."

Next it was Bidwell's turn to try to open some daylight between his client and Orr. He elicited the information that Orr had worked in and around the video poker registration office for five years, from four to five hours per day, four or five days each week. "We went together to do things Medford wanted done," Orr explained. "But after 2005, Penland had nothing more to do with poker. Pennington still came around after Penland was gone, but not as often." And responding to another query, Orr affirmed that after Penland was out, Pennington still had access to Davis and Medford.

In his redirect, Edwards noted that Orr had been a frequent visitor to the Buncombe County Sheriff's Department. "How often was the sheriff not in the office?"

"Sometimes."

"Was he out of town on work days?"

"Sometimes."

"Would you raise more money in election years than non-election years?"

"In good years."

Edwards referred Orr to financial records and established that profits were actually about double the amounts he had estimated in his testimony.

Never charged with any crime, and to all appearances a plain-spoken man who loves golf, Orr's testimony did more than that of any other witness to affirm the government's assertions about illegal campaign contributions and money laundering.

Of course, even if Orr was never overtly threatened with prosecution by federal investigators, that threat would have been implicit in their interviews. Like most of the witnesses at Medford's trial, Orr's testimony was presumably motivated by the desire to save his own skin. Nobody in the inner circle wanted to take Bobby down. Nobody wanted the party to end.

32: Keeping cooked books

It was past 5 p.m. on May 6 when certified public accountant Lester Bullock took the stand. A CPA in private practice for eight years, Bullock said he had been hired by the Medford campaign manager, David Brown, as campaign treasurer. He said he had been given documents from the Board of Elections by Brown, had made deposits to the campaign account and filed requisite forms as they came due. He said he had been given receipts by Tracy Bridges and Sharon Stewart as well as Brown.

At some point did he have trouble accepting cash? "Yes. We had received two cash donations of $150 each, and I learned that the law had changed, that we could not accept cash donations larger than $100. I told them to bring checks from then on.

"After I received notification about the law, I notified Tracy Bridges that donations had to be by check or money order. I met with Bridges and Medford to tell them about the law. After that, I began to get money orders." Bullock continued, "We were uncomfortable with money orders because they could be just as fraudulent as cash, they could be juried around. I called Bridges to tell him I didn't want to accept money orders."

Lindsay began his cross examination of Bullock a little after 9 a.m. on May 7. In short order he established that Bridges had been the CPA's principal contact within the campaign and that when Bullock met with Bridges and Medford he had told them that accepting money orders was legal according to the Board of Elections.

"And with his parrot," Bullock interjected with regard to his meetings with Medford, revealing his own personal allegiance to the sheriff.

The prosecution dismissed Bullock and called Charles McBennett, Jr. to the stand. He testified that he had operated gambling machines in Buncombe County from the mid-1990s through 2005 under the corporate name McBennett Amusement. He said he had registered machines with Harrison and Davis and had personally delivered cash to Medford on two occasions.

"I had to call ahead for registrations and Harrison told me I would need to do a 'favor' for Medford. He said I needed to deliver cash.

"I heard that Medford was facing back surgery, so I took him a little cross that said 'God is watching.'" He said he handed Medford $5,000 in cash along with the cross.

McBennett continued, "I wanted to grow my business. I asked Medford if it was okay to replace machines in locations where the owners were unhappy with other operators. He said, 'Yes, except for locations for Moon.'" He explained, "'Moon' is David West."

What amounts had he given Davis and Penland? "On two occasions I gave Davis $500 in cash. The year prior to that I gave Penland $5,000 for a list of competitor's locations. [That list is a public record, presumably the same one I had obtained from Julie Kepple in 2005. Penland seems to have made good use of it.] Then I tried to get locations using that list."

McBennett recounted another occasion when he had ridden with Harrison to Medford's apartment and handed Medford $3,000 and Harrison $2,000. "Medford thanked me for my help. We weren't there but ten minutes." He stated that he had also contributed to golf tournaments seven or eight times, for a total "close to $4,000."

What motivated him to pay? "I felt they could help me by registering my equipment and could help eliminate trouble with law enforcement."

McBennett also held a Special Deputy badge issued by Harrison. He said it had been taken from him by state law enforcement officers in 2006 at the time of his arrest on illegal gambling charges.

[Looking back, I note that I had mailed my first article about Medford, concerning obstruction of justice, to N.C. Attorney General Roy Cooper in July, 2003. My first story about illegal video poker operations in the county was published in July 2005 and was followed by my letter to U.S. Attorney Gretchen Shappert that October. Although both state and federal law enforcement agencies have suggested that their investigations into Medford's criminal conspiracy began in 2002, the busts, including McBennett, started in 2006.]

Lindsay's cross was, again, brief. He elicited the fact that Harrison had been close to McBennett's father, but the son countered that he had never met Harrison until he went to register machines. And Lindsay established that McBennett's father had taken the rap for illegal gambling with his son's elimination from the case being part of a plea bargain.

Did McBennett, Jr., hope his testimony would help his father who had not yet been sentenced?

"Yes."

At 9:45 a.m. Jenny Watts was sworn in and Assistant U.S. Attorney Corey Ellis commenced his questioning. A branch manager for Premier Federal Credit Union, Watts said she had worked for the company for fifteen years and knew both Medford and Bell as customers. She testified as to the accuracy of bank records submitted as evidence, and affirmed that both Medford and Bell had both signed up for direct deposit of their county paychecks starting in 2000. Watts also affirmed that Medford's account showed a total of $113,694 in cash deposits between 2002 and 2006.

At 10 a.m. the jury was dismissed for its usual 25-minute morning break, but their return was delayed due to a discussion between counsel and Judge Ellis that commenced at 10:45, concerning audio recordings submitted by the prosecution.

Tracy Bridges had become an informant for federal investigators (as would be explained in his subsequent testimony) and had agreed to wear a wire. He had recorded three conversations that prosecutors wished for the jury to hear. The defense attorneys objected.

The conversations had occurred after December 6, 2006, when Medford was no longer in office. Lindsay argued that the conversations were therefore irrelevant to the charges. He also argued that because the conversations were with Ronnie "Butch" Davis, Sharon Stewart and George Stewart, none of whom were slated to testify, that, once again, the tapes were objectionable hearsay.

Assistant U.S. Attorney Richard Edwards maintained that the fact that the sheriff had left office did not mean that the conspiracy had ended. "For example, the conspiracy to hide wrongdoing continued."

Judge Ellis responded, "Regarding Sharon and George Stewart, they are not named as co-conspirators and the recordings are therefore hearsay. I would have to find that they were part of the conspiracy.

"I don't think there is any doubt that Davis is part of the conspiracy." Davis had pleaded guilty and cooperated with the prosecution.

Edwards responded, "Miss Stewart was aware of the purchase of money orders, she knew about cash given to Judi Bell, she maintained Mr. Medford's check book and arranged cash deposits to his account. On the tape she is heard telling Bridges, 'These guys paid for their teams themselves. She talks about Jimmy the Greek being in, and she talks about the money orders and the checks. Her attempts to get her story straight with Bridges are evidence of conspiracy, for example when she is saying that golf team members bought the money orders."

The judge asked, "Why is Sharon Stewart part of the conspiracy for 801-c-3 purposes? It would be hearsay unless the speaker is part of the conspiracy.'"

Edwards argued, "Ms. Stewart was aware that cash was being used to purchase money orders, even in the name of George Stewart, and she knew that the names on those money orders were not accurate."

Judge Ellis ruled that "There is no question that Davis is part of the conspiracy, so I see no ban to the admissibility of those recordings. The Stewart tape is still a horse race. I haven't heard all the evidence."

Both Lindsay and Bidwell filed notices of objection to Ellis' admission of the Davis tapes and the jury was readmitted at 11:07 when Lindsay commenced to cross-examine the credit union manager.

Watts confirmed that Bell had signature authority on Medford's account and that both had line-of-credit accounts, that Medford had a VISA card on his account and that both had obtained other loans from the credit union. Lindsay led her through somewhat arcane differences between the way a credit union presents deposits and withdrawals as versus a bank. He stipulated and Watts confirmed that cash deposits show up as having been, in fact, cash, versus advances on loans, which are so-labeled as well.

At 11:15 a.m. the judge abruptly recessed the session, asserting that the cause had nothing to do with the current case. A few minutes later, Lindsay's cross resumed.

He observed, "There is no record as to the source of these cash deposits, correct?" Watts agreed. The deposits in question amounted to $4,000 in 2002, $26,000 in 2003, $10,000 in 2004, $3,775 in 2005, and $9,245 in 2006. Lindsay elicited the information that the credit union had no way of knowing what transpired at Harrah's other than the fact that Medford and Bell made frequent withdrawals from their accounts using an ATM located there. His effort seemed directed at bolstering the idea that the pair occasionally won cash and deposited it in their credit union accounts on subsequent days. Lindsay also suggested that it was possible in theory that the gamblers had withdrawn cash via ATMs and then deposited that money into their accounts at a later time.

During his redirect Ellis led Watts through further minutiae of Medford's and Bell's accounts, highlighting once again the large number and large amounts of cash transactions that had occurred.

Lindsay's defense for all the cash deposits Medford and Bell made into their accounts was contradicted by records from Harrah's which showed them to be regular losers. His assertion that they had withdrawn and redeposited the same funds proved equally unpersuasive.

33: Bridges (of Madison County)

At 11:35 Edwards called former Captain Tracy Bridges to the stand. Bridges testified that he was both a career law enforcement officer and a graduate of the Appalachian State University School of Law, though he never passed the bar. He started working for the Madison County Sheriff's Department at age sixteen and two years later became a jailer. When he turned twenty he became a Deputy with that agency. Later he served as a state court magistrate judge for three years.

Bridges said he had known Medford for several years through Republican Party fundraising events and that Medford offered him a job in 2005. He was brought in as a captain and was put in charge of internal affairs.

Like several other department employees, he accompanied Medford to Harrah's on multiple occasions, "With Judi Bell or Sharon Stewart. Medford was a Diamond Player, that is, the highest level player at that casino," Bridges elaborated.

Bridges explained that he had worked for Medford's election campaign in 2006, and that he was first directed to obtain forms via the internet by Chief Deputy George Stewart and the sheriff. "I called the Board of Elections and learned that the filing fee was $1,055 and that I needed to deliver a certified check. I went to the Premier Federal Credit Union as directed by Medford. George Stewart gave me $1,070 in cash and I returned $15 in change to him." At this point the prosecution submitted copies of the certified check and the credit union receipt for cash as evidence.

"One of the forms required that I write down the amount of the initial cash on hand for the election committee, so I asked Medford about that amount." Bridges continued, "Medford said, 'No way!' He was very upset. 'It's none of your business!' So Captain Lee Farnsworth asked as well and he got the same answer and I wrote down 'No cash.' on the form." [The form was also submitted as evidence.]

Had Bridges completed any other forms? "No, the sheriff hired an accountant, Lester Bullock, as campaign treasurer."

Had he ever attempted to give cash to Bullock? "Yes. Butch Davis gave me around $10,000 in cash from the golf tournament, in an envelope, and told me to take it to Bullock. He said he could not accept it, so I went back to Davis who said, 'We're going to get money orders with that money.'

"He said he had talked to the boss, which I understood to mean the sheriff.

"I took the cash to the Merrimon Avenue post office and the postal clerk giggled at me and said she couldn't take more than $3,000 unless I filled out a form. Under $3,000 she said I wouldn't have to fill out the form. So, I went back to Medford and told him the post office wouldn't sell me that many money orders. He told me to go to different post offices to keep it under the $3,000 limit. I went to several post offices and never had to show an I.D. to a clerk."

What had he done with the money orders? "I took them to Davis and he told me he had the names we were going to use. He told me the names and I wrote them on the envelope that I'd gotten from Davis. Later I wrote the names on the money orders."

Edwards handed Bridges an envelope which he identified as bearing the list he had written under Davis' dictation. "I saved it at home. Later I gave it to agents McNeely and Peters when they came to my home to interview me."

Edwards directed his attention to the name on the front of the envelope. "Would you read that and tell us whose handwriting it is?

"It says 'Butch.' That's Sharon Stewart's writing."

"And the first name on the back?"

"Larry McMahan. That's Davis' writing."

"And the other names?"

"That's my writing, taking dictation from Davis."

Copies of money orders were submitted and compared side-by-side with an image of the envelope on the court room monitors. The names matched.

"Why did you buy $500 money orders?" Edwards asked.

"Davis said to use $500 so it corresponded to the golf tournament cost."

Bridges said Davis had given him more cash in June, 2006, to buy more money orders, and had provided him with a new list of "donors." That list, in Davis' handwriting, was also submitted as evidence.

The prosecutor inquired if Bridges had attended a meeting with the sheriff, David Brown and Sharon Stewart during the campaign. "Yes. Brown was concerned about putting money orders into the campaign account during the Jim Black trial. He was worried." [Former Speaker Black, of the N.C. General Assembly, was then on trial for corruption involving campaign contributions.]

"Medford jumped on me for doing that," Bridges asserted. "He said I needed to stop doing it.

"After Brown left, Medford said 'Fuck him. We're going to continue to do it this way.' Later I bought more money orders at post offices."

To corroborate Bridges' testimony, money orders dated August, 2006, were entered into evidence. "Did you fill out these names?" Edwards asked.

"Yes, I got them from Davis."

"Your name is on one of the money orders, did you contribute to the campaign?"

"No."

"George Stewart's name is on a $500 money order, did he contribute?"

"No. The names all came from Davis."

Had Medford ever asked him for money? "Yes, he came and asked for money and told me to hold off on purchase of money orders. He asked me for cash. The highest amount was $1,000, other times $700 and $500. Medford told me not to tell Butch that I was giving him cash."

Edwards: "Did he say why?"

"No."

"Did he ever ask you to deposit cash directly into a financial institution?"

"Yes, into his account and Bell's account at the credit union. Once I got a call on my radio from Unit #1. He said I needed to immediately take cash down to the credit union and deposit it in Bell's account." Bridges added that he had kept careful notes of how much cash he turned over to Medford so he couldn't be accused of taking the money and his notes were entered into evidence.

Had Medford ever handed him a check to cash? "Yes. Once he gave me a check from Sand Hill Grocery, a store that operated video poker machines. He told me to take it to his bank and cash it and take the money back to him. I kept the receipt for cashing the check and later gave it to IRS agent Veater." This check was also submitted as evidence.

Had Sharon Stewart ever talked to him about golf or the campaign money? "Yes. She phoned me several times. She told me we were buying the money orders to put in Medford's campaign account, and that the money was coming from Democrats who didn't want their names used."

Had she told him anything about what kind of businesses the unidentified people were in? "She said they were video poker machine folks." Bridges affirmed that he had also met Jimmy the Greek "with Butch and Sharon."

Next Edwards asked, "Did you approach anyone about the events you have recounted here?"

"Yes. I went to Van Duncan who was running for sheriff. I told him I was being made to do things I didn't want to do. He advised me to contact the FBI. A month later, federal agents arrived at my house and I gave them everything I had. I agreed to wear a recording device."

The writing was on the wall by this time, October of 2006, given all the video poker busts the preceding summer. Bridges bailed out of trouble in the nick of time. He knew exactly what he was doing when he first signed on with Medford and evidently got cold feet only when sirens sounded and blue lights showed up outside the party.

At 1:35 p.m. the judge ordered the court into its regular afternoon recess and, upon returning at 2 p.m., admitted the Stewart/Bridges tapes as evidence. Lindsay objected.

Judge Ellis asked, "Mr. Lindsay, why is Stewart *not* a member of the conspiracy?"

Lindsay didn't have a ready answer and Edwards asserted, "We won't play that tape unless Stewart is called." Lindsay didn't put either Stewart on the stand, perhaps due to this warning shot from Edwards.

The prosecutor continued, "On another issue, Deputy [Robert E.] Parker's Rutherford County office was wired. He is a cooperating witness and Sheriff [Jack] Connor knew he was being taped. We have two excerpts totaling 17 minutes which show Barry Henderson in an attempt to induce Connor to cooperate and outlining how the conspiracy in Buncombe County worked."

Lindsay jumped up to object. "Once they have established that Mr. Medford was part of one conspiracy, does that make Mr. Medford responsible for all other conspiracies, anywhere?" He then argued that the video tape in question reflected a new venture, "This is a new conspiracy."

Edwards responded that the conspiracy was ongoing. "Mr. Lindsay is making an artificially false distinction."

Judge Ellis replied, "What concerns me is that it is arguably a conspiracy that this defendant is not a member of. I'm concerned that it is not worth the risk that we will have to try this case again." He then cited law to the effect that "if the conspiracy does not include the defendant, it is not admissible evidence."

Edwards argued, "Henderson was operating throughout 2000 to 2006 in many counties."

Lindsay insisted, "There is no direct connection. The conspiracy in Rutherford is a different one involving separate persons."

Ellis replied, "It is not necessary for all conspirators to know all other conspirators in order to be part of the conspiracy."

Edwards pointed out, "Anna Deaton and Jerry Pennington's expense records showed an extensive operation in multiple counties. We have focused on Buncombe, but the evidence is available and we could have gone through it. This is included in an ongoing conspiracy, headquartered in Grover, North Carolina, and Spartanburg, South Carolina, with the same people operating throughout.

"Alam was in touch with Barry Henderson as well. And we showed evidence of multiple mention of other counties where there were payoffs from Henderson Amusement."

Lindsay responded, "This whole case has been about events in Buncombe County, and Medford's power in his office. Mr. Medford had no power outside of Buncombe."

Judge Ellis said, "It arguably is the same conspiracy. A large conspiracy was ongoing in November of 2006, but it could be argued that in December they were no longer members of the conspiracy because they had been out of office sixteen days. But their leaving power does not end their participation. There is no evidence that Mr. Medford called the FBI within those sixteen days to say, 'I've got to get this off my chest.'

"To leave a conspiracy, one must do something to make an affirmative withdrawal from the conspiracy. Even if a conspirator is in jail, when the ability to commit actions is reduced or eliminated, one can continue to conspire to withhold information. Concealment and non-disclosure can constitute continued conspiracy.

"I therefore rule for the admissibility of the evidence. There is evidence that there was a continuing conspiracy. I think there is a larger conspiracy and even if the defendants were not active outside of Buncombe County, they were involved. There is no evidence that either defendant made any effort to withdraw from the conspiracy. The objection to the exhibit is overruled."

At 3 p.m. the jury returned to its box and Bridges returned to the stand. Edwards questioned him about the recording device he had worn.

"It was a recorder that looked like a cell phone and had no erase function," Bridges said.

The tapes were then played via headphones provided to all of the principal players in the trial. We in the audience could hear little or nothing. At one point the judge stopped the tape and said, "This is idle chatter."

Edwards replied, "They get back to golf and money in 57 lines." The judge let the tape roll again.

In the second tape, recorded in Davis' office on November 14, 2006, there was a lot of commotion and Davis could be heard using his cell phone and office phone, calling gambling operators and taking calls, and saying "The A.L.E. is on a roll!" [This was the day of the Hot Dog King bust.]

After the tapes ran, Lindsay engaged in a brief cross examination which did little to draw out new information or discredit Bridges' testimony.

34: The prosecution rests

Assistant U.S. Attorneys Richard Lee Edwards and Corey Ellis completed the presentation of their case on May 8, with two final witnesses.

Former Rutherford County Deputy John Parker had taken the stand briefly the previous afternoon to confirm that he had been involved in Henderson's attempt to bribe that county's sheriff, had been arrested and was now cooperating with authorities. His morning testimony was to identify the video tape from a camera which had been hidden in his office.

Once again the principals in the case had the advantage of headphones, and the audio was very indistinct for the audience. The gist of the exchange was that Barry Henderson tried to convince Sheriff Connor to accept bribes in exchange for granting permission for Henderson Amusement to run machines in his county. The argument included a description of Henderson's mutually profitable relationship with Medford. Connor, who was then working with the FBI, played along, drawing as much information as possible out of the machine operator.

One bombshell that dropped from the video tape was Henderson's claim that "Up at Haywood County, I give him $100 every month for each machine."

This was the first public notice that Haywood's highly respected sheriff was on the take. Soon that lawman had obtained counsel and before long would find himself summoned by a Grand Jury.

The final prosecution witness was Jim Lindsey, a 77-year-old retired gambling operator and former Buncombe County deputy under Sheriff Harry Clay in the 1970s. He said he had known Medford for some 30 years and that while his tenure had overlapped Medford's, he had not worked with him directly.

In response to questions from Corey Ellis, Lindsey said he had gotten into the gambling business in the 1980s and had worked at it until turning over Mountain Music to his son in 1995. He testified that he had continued to help out his son. "If there were complaints about some locations, I'd talk to Johnny Harrison to try to get it straightened out. "

He said, "I helped Medford when he first ran for office in 1994, and every time he ran I helped financially. I gave him money. And I was in the golf games." Lindsey said he had paid $1,000 for each of the 2005 tournaments. Asked why he donated in non-election years, he replied, "Johnny Harrison said Medford needed money for the election when he ran again."

Lindsey said that his son was reluctant to pay off the sheriff. "A lot of video poker people were doing it. Mark wouldn't, so I did it for him."

He testified, "When we started in 2000, we only redeemed in merchandise." He added that some locations that ran Mountain Music machines ran them legally, others illegally, and he admitted to having serious concerns about law enforcement.

Asked about his relationship with Imran Alam, he replied, "Alam approached my son to put machines in his stores, but Johnny Harrison called me and said the sheriff wouldn't let that happen. He said the sheriff needed to talk to me and we met at the restaurant across from the sheriff's office.

"The sheriff said we had a good chance of getting our machines in there, but he needed five or six thousand dollars. I told him I didn't have it."

Lindsey said he withdrew $2,000 from his bank account. "I went to the sheriff's office and gave it to Bobby. Then another time I gave another $2,000 to Bobby. The third time, I was working up in Haw Creek and he called me. I went to Groce Methodist Church and met Bobby in the parking lot and gave him another $2,000. It was about lunch time, in early 2006, probably in March. I took my truck and Bobby was in his car. He pulled up and I got out of my truck and got into his car."

He said that they never discussed money during these exchanges and that he had always delivered cash in fifty and hundred dollar bills. Then he identified his cell phone billing records which included calls to and from Medford's number.

Next Lindsey was shown a money order with his name on it. Had he ever donated money to Medford's campaign via money order? "No."

Had he ever given Medford money for a vacation? "Yes. He called me and told me he was taking his grandchildren on vacation and wanted to borrow some money. I gave him $1,500. He just drove up and I gave it to him. He never paid me back, but he said, 'I'll take care of you.'"

Attorney Lindsay then conducted one of his longer cross examinations. He asked, "When you first started contributing you wrote business checks for the golf tournaments. If he'd asked for a personal check, would you have been willing to pay that way?"

"Yes."

"Is it correct that you were Assistant Chief Deputy under Harry Clay and Johnny Harrison worked there as well?"

"Yes."

"When did you last see Harrison?"

"We've been friends for years. The last time I talked to him was when he was in jail. I went down to take him some medicine and clothes."

"You gave Mountain Music to your sons in 1995, but you kept some involvement, is that right?"

"Yes. My younger son, Mark, is up here. My older son is in Wilmington. I helped Mark."

Lindsay asked, "Were you interviewed by federal agents?"

"Yes. Three times, here at the courthouse."

"When you talked, did you know that you or your children were the target of an investigation?"

"Yes. I came with my attorney, from Waynesville."

"Did you tell the agents about giving money to Bobby?"

"Yes."

"Did you talk about the meeting at the church?"

"Yes. Well, I'm not sure which meeting."

Lindsay handed Lindsey a transcript. "Does that refresh your memory. At the first meeting, did you talk about giving money to Medford?"

"No."

"Have you been charged with a crime?"

"Yes."

"Have your children been charged?"

"No."

"Have you entered into a plea agreement?"

"Yes. But I don't know what they're going to do. I have not yet entered a plea in front of a judge."

"What are you charged with?"

"Running a gambling operation."

"Are you facing prison time?"

"I really don't know."

"Is it true that in exchange for your cooperation they have agreed not to prosecute your family?"

"Yes."

Bidwell's cross was perfunctory, and largely

focused on why Lindsey paid to sponsor golf teams but never played. He also established that Lindsey's business name had appeared on a golf cart at least once.

In his redirect, Ellis simply asked Lindsey to explain what he understood the rules to be concerning his plea bargain.

Lindsey said, "If I tell the truth, I might get consideration in sentencing. If I don't tell the truth, I can be prosecuted and they can go after my whole family."

After a short recess, the prosecution introduced one final item, a finding of fact concerning United Parcel Service, which the judge read to the jury. "UPS qualifies as a commercial interstate carrier."

35: Looking for daylight

At 11 a.m. on May 8, Attorney Stephen Lindsay called the first witness for the defense, Buncombe County Sheriff Van Duncan. The physical appearances of the former and current chief law enforcement officer for this jurisdiction are strikingly different, and the difference is much more than the disparity of age. Whereas Medford is stooped and wears the haggard visage of a heavy smoker, making him look curled up and somewhat defensive, Duncan looks robustly healthy, with a rosy complexion and an open facial expression that suggests absolute frankness and honesty.

Duncan said he had been elected sheriff on November 7, 2006, sworn in December 4, and had then taken custody of the office.

Did he see Tracy Bridges at Starbucks in October, 2006? "Yes. He asked to speak to me."

Lindsay: "What about?"

Duncan began to answer "Bridges said ..." but Judge Ellis intervened.

He barked, "Subject matter."

Duncan started again, and again the judge interrupted, "Subject matter. You can only say, 'This is what I spoke about yesterday. You can't say what someone else said." He called the attorneys to the bench for a conference that lasted several minutes.

Lindsay started again, "When you met with Bridges, did he tell you he held any position with the Medford campaign?"

"He said he was treasurer of the campaign. I told him if he felt he was going to get into trouble he should go to the FBI."

Lindsay asked, "What was your job at the time?"

"I was an instructor at the academy."

"Did you have any authority or jurisdiction?"

"No."

The prosecution declined to cross.

Lindsay's next witness was Julie Kepple, staff attorney for the Buncombe County Sheriff's Department from 2002 to 2006, and later employed as an Assistant District Attorney under Ron Moore. She said she had worked out of a home office as well as in the sheriff's department and at the county jail.

Did she have access to Medford? "Yes, I was not limited."

Was there any area of the sheriff's department from which she was restricted? "Yes, the property room."

Did she feel free to go into offices to talk to people? "Yes."

Had she worked with the internal affairs officer? "Yes, at first with Pat Hefner, toward the end with Tracy Bridges."

Asked about her involvement with video poker registration, she said, "In 2003 we received a request for public records from a newspaper editor. Sheriff Medford told me to ask Brenda Fraser. Although she was not then in charge of those records, she had set up the computer records. She told me to go to Johnny Harrison." Kepple said she had gone to Harrison's office to look for the records after making the determination that they were, in fact, public records.

"As I looked through the records, I realized that they hadn't been kept very well, so I contacted the owners to update the records."

Asked to describe the process, Kepple explained, "I went through and tallied the current records. I had Harrison contact the owners, and worked with Penland and Harrison." She affirmed that Harrison had been in charge of the records before and after she worked on them, and that she had recommended an audit to ask owners where their machines were currently located. She said she had no idea whether Harrison complied with her suggestion, that she had updated Medford on the condition of the records and that the sheriff had not resisted release of the records.

Kepple said that after she had updated the records, "I showed the file to the editor of the newspaper who had requested the information."

Had she ever had occasion to meet any video poker operators? "I attended one golf tournament," she replied.

Penland's attorney, Paul Bidwell, then questioned Kepple.

"Was it possible for a person off the street to come in and request to view the video poker registration records?"

"Yes."

"How many records were there?"

"Probably in excess of one thousand records."

The prosecutors again waived cross examination.

Medford attorney Victoria Jayne called Jerry Wayne Miller as the next defense witness. He said he was currently a Buncombe County reserve deputy and the Attorney Advocate for the Guardian ad Litem and had been the Assistant U.S. Attorney for WNC from January 1980 through September 2004. "In October 2004 I was brought in to the Buncombe County Sheriff's Department as a Major. For the first five months I went to all the schools and represented the sheriff at community meetings. I was his community relations officer. I also had limited legal duties and did a legal update for other officers."

Miller said he had frequent contact with Medford and his secretaries, first Sharon Stewart, later Rhonda House, as well as Chief Deputy George Stewart.

Had he had any dealings with the video poker registration office? "Yes. In late summer and early fall of 2005 I had conversations about video poker. A close friend of mine was concerned that allegations would be made about illegal activities." [I couldn't help but notice that this followed the July publication of my story alleging illegalities in the video poker trade.] But Miller was unwilling to identify his source other than to say it was a powerful Democrat who "warned me for my protection."

Miller added, "Medford said he didn't want me to be in the way when the bomb went off. He cursed extensively and was very upset."

What action had he taken as a result of the warning? "I looked into ways the sheriff could eliminate video poker in Buncombe. I called the Sheriff's Association and learned that apparently, under the regulations, he could choose to eliminate machines in the county on his own initiative. I told Medford that.

"I also learned that in other counties there was a law suit against a sheriff who had banned the machines by a machine owner, and the suit had not yet been resolved.

"Then I learned that the state lottery legislation would phase out the video poker machines."

Miller identified Butch Davis and Guy Penland as holding responsibility for machine registration during his tenure at the department, but said he had never discussed the matter with either of them. Nor had he had any contact with Tracy Bridges.

Asked about golf tournaments in general, Miller said he had played in many of them, but only two of the Medford events. He also said he had contributed to Medford's 2006 campaign with a personal check.

Bidwell then asked Miller a few questions about the tournaments and elicited the fact that he had known Medford for about thirty years.

Had he changed his party affiliation? "Yes. Medford said he may have wanted me to serve out his term if he was reelected in 2006, and his replacement would be appointed by the Republican Party county committee. To facilitate that, I registered as a Republican."

When he investigated ending video poker in Buncombe who in the department had known about it? "Medford and Penland."

Had he encountered any interference with his research? "No."

Assistant U.S. Attorney Corey Ellis conducted the cross examination and started by asking how much Miller had paid to play in the Medford tournament and where he thought the money would go.

"The fee was $175, and I assumed some charity would receive the money."

"After you announced that the sheriff could unilaterally remove video poker machines in the county, were any removed?"

"No."

Evincing a lack of pretrial preparation, Jayne's redirect was brief. "Did you ever observe any charitable work on the part of the sheriff?"

"No. Though I do remember an old couple who were out of heating oil who came to the office to seek assistance."

Lindsay then called up Rhonda House. House said she currently worked for Carver Realty and Uppercut

Hair Design and had been a Buncombe resident since 1994. She had been a teller and then a loan officer at Premier Federal Credit Union from 1998 through 2005 and got to know Medford and Bell during that tenure. She affirmed that both had accounts at that financial institution and that Bell had had signature authority on Medford's checking account. "Judi would come in," House said, "I rarely saw the sheriff. He had a personal loan, a signature loan that permitted advances on his credit card.

"When I left the credit union in January, 2005, I called Sharon Stewart looking for work and filled out an application. In June or July I had an interview with Sharon and the sheriff and I was hired as secretary to the sheriff."

Lindsay asked, "When people came to see the sheriff, did they go by your desk?"

"Yes."

"Were you involved in the reelection effort?"

"Yes, I helped put signs together and went to meetings at the headquarters."

"Who served on the committee?"

House replied, "There was no formal list." In response to questions she said Tracy Bridges had been there "at first" and that Lester Bullock had taken over as treasurer.

Had she ever given Bullock money? "No. Sharon handled the money, I guess."

She then denied ever meeting Jerry Pennington, Demetre Theodossis or Imran Alam. "I've never heard that name."

After the election was over had she seen Bridges? "Yes. Tracy told me about the meeting with Davis where he was wired. He came by my house later that night. He said I was his personal banker and told me Medford was in trouble and that they were watching me."

Asked about the presence of paper shredders in the

sheriff's office, House said, "There was a small one in my office and a big one in records. The big shredder is not movable."

House said she had returned to work after the election, up until December first, and that she had not shredded any documents. "I saw Bill Morrissey shredding documents after the election, but I don't know what they were. Tracy told me not to shred any documents and I told him, 'There's nothing to shred.'" She said she hadn't seen Sharon Stewart removing documents during that period and that she had never seen any cash in the office.

Bidwell then asked House if she knew Butch Davis and she said she had seen him on a daily basis because the coffee machine had been in her office and he was in there drinking coffee every morning.

Asked if she knew anything about Bridges going to the Greenville Sheriff's Department, House replied, "No." She also stated that to her knowledge, all phone calls to the sheriff came through two lines she answered at her desk.

Edwards did the cross examination, and it quickly seemed that the defense had made a misstep in putting House on the stand. He asked if House had accompanied visitors into the sheriff's personal office. "No, the door was closed." She said "weird people went into his office" and "meetings weren't always in his office. He often went to Butch Davis' office."

Next he asked who had maintained the special deputy records. "Maria Buckner and Sharon Stewart."

"Do you have any knowledge why paperwork was missing when the new sheriff took office?"

"No."

"Did you ever go to Harrah's with Medford?"

"Yes."

"Did you see him play?"

"No, I was playing myself."

"On frequent occasions, when he was not in his office, did he go to Harrah's during work hours?"

"Yes."

"During 2006, how many days was he not in his office?"

"Quite a few."

"Who would do leave forms?"

"I don't know."

"Did Medford claim unused leave upon retirement?"

"Yes."

"Were you familiar with the Medford and Bell accounts at the credit union and how they handled their paychecks?"

"Yes. They had direct deposit."

A series of questions made it clear she knew that they often deposited cash and that the sheriff "often teetered on the edge of overdrawn." She said that sheriff's department employees were occasionally sent to withdraw cash. "Every now and then, they'd take cash to him."

Lindsay conducted a brief redirect to ascertain that House knew when the county instituted its direct deposit policy and asking where the "weird people" she had mentioned came from.

"The weird people came in off the street," she replied.

And with that vital fact established, the court recessed for lunch.

36: Weighing the evidence

When the principals returned at 1:45 p.m., Lindsay announced that his next witness would be former Chief Deputy George Stewart, but first he and Bidwell made a series of motions under Rule 29. This rule is routinely invoked in the course of a federal criminal trial. It permits the defense to assert that the government has not made its case and requires the judge to decide whether or not sufficient testimony and evidence has been presented to afford the jury a basis for determining guilt beyond a reasonable doubt.

Lindsay challenged the prosecution's evidence on Count 1, which involved interstate commerce, and cited case law to support his argument that the gambling activity was not an interstate conspiracy. He challenged Counts 2-7, which involved transport of stickers by UPS, by asserting that use of the stickers was voluntary rather than official, and that there was no evidence that Medford ordered them. And he challenged Counts 10 and 11, arguing that Medford had not been shown to be part of a conspiracy.

Bidwell offered similar arguments. Count 1 also included extortion and he said no evidence had been offered that Penland had extorted anyone. Per Count 2, he noted that more stickers were ordered than were ever used and that fully one quarter had been used in the first month of registration. On Counts 3-7, Bidwell argued that there had been no evidence presented of intent to use UPS to commit mail fraud. For Count 8 he argued that no evidence had been presented connecting Penland to the money orders and money laundering. And on Count 10 he questioned the evidence that Penland had participated in a conspiracy to obstruct local law.

In response, Edwards argued that Count 1 involved extortion under official right, that is, using the power of the office of the sheriff to coerce and that Henderson Amusement, Inc. is a South Carolina company. "Mr. Bidwell argued that his client extorted no one, but he did conspire with others who had official positions. What's more, he held himself out to be a deputy."

Judge Ellis observed, "Conspiracy to commit extortion does not require an actual threat."

Edwards added, "It need not be an explicit *quid pro quo*, but it has to be motivated by the official position, either something that might be done or not done.

"On Count 2, we would argue that in this conspiracy to defraud the people of Buncombe County, mailing took place to further the scheme. As a *de facto* matter the stickers were considered important and valuable even if they were not official, and those stickers were mailed. The mailing scheme continued beyond the last mailing of stickers, at least another year."

The judge noted, "Mr. Lindsay said that Medford had not ordered stickers."

"Perhaps not," Edwards replied, "But Medford held a meeting about registration and the stickers and to explain the law. That qualifies as aiding and abetting because Medford must have known the stickers came from somewhere."

Judge Ellis: "He knew the purpose of the stickers, and how they would be used. What basis is there for inferring that he knew about allowing registration of illegal machines or of machines that would be operated illegally? The affidavits were false according to Pennington, but he didn't necessarily make that information clear to Penland or others."

Edwards argued that Medford had been tied to the money laundering, had concealed the source of funds, had engaged in illegal activity that included not just money orders, but checks as well, from on or about October 1, 2000 through December 3, 2006. "Although we couldn't connect Penland to the money orders—that happened later—he is connected to the illegal cashing checks, so it's important not to overlook the checks."

The judge said he had heard enough and retired to chambers to consider the Rule 29 arguments. He returned a little after 3 p.m. and explained his reasoning and order.

"The court must take evidence in a light most favorable to the government as to whether there has been enough evidence for the jury to reach a conclusion beyond a reasonable doubt. This is not to say that they will or must find the defendants guilty, just that there is enough evidence.

"Count 1 alleges a conspiracy to obtain money through extortion under color of official right. There is ample evidence that the object was to obtain property under color of official right and that these actions affected commerce.

"Extortion conjures up images of threat, but really, that is in the mind of the payer. The government is only required to show that the payment to which a government official was not entitled was made because of the position."

"Count 2 and 3 through 7: There is ample evidence of a conspiracy to commit mail fraud. The fraud is on the citizens of Buncombe County—depriving them of honest service. The mailing itself is not the fraud, it is the use of mail as part of that scheme, aiding and abetting that fraud.

"Count 8: Money laundering, at its heart, is that one takes money from an illegal activity and tries to disguise its source. It describes financial transactions involving criminal activity, transactions conducted knowing that it came from unlawful activity and done to disguise the proceeds. The court has heard ample evidence that money laundering occurred.

"Count 9 of this indictment does not involve these defendants. [This charge, "giving false statements" was against Ronnie "Butch" Davis, a codefendant in the case.]

"Count 10 is conspiracy to obstruct enforcement of criminal law in the State of North Carolina. There has been ample evidence that they did conspire, to do illegal things, and that the conspiracy extended past thirty days and exceeded $2,000 in any single day."

"Count 11 is of a conspiracy to conduct an illegal gambling business. There has been ample evidence that the conspiracy involved five or more persons, that it continued operating in excess of thirty days, and exceeded $2,000 in any given day."

Having determined and ruled that the trial would continue, Judge Ellis told the defense attorneys that their written challenges to his ruling were due by 5 p.m. Friday (the following day). He ordered both defense and prosecution lawyers to deliver their suggestions for jury instructions by the end of the day on Monday. Ellis then called in the jury and adjourned the trial until Monday, May 12, citing urgent court business that required his attention in his home district in Eastern Virginia.

37: In his own words

The trial seemed to wake up slowly on Monday. At 9:10 a.m. Judge Ellis inquired about upcoming defense witnesses. George Stewart would not appear, an accountant might be called. Shawn Ledford was on the short list, as were Sondra McKinney and FBI Agent Rick Schwein. A suggestion was advanced that Tracy Bridges had violated his bond agreement over the weekend and the judge ordered a court officer to look into the charge.

At 9:40 a.m. the jury was brought in and Lindsay immediately called for a bench conference. While the attorneys and judge huddled, I noticed that Guy Penland leaned in from his end of the table and said two words to Bobby Medford, the first apparent contact between the co-defendants in the course of the trial. Medford did not reply.

Five minutes later, Medford took the stand in his own defense. He grimaced and squinted throughout his testimony, looking uncomfortable and belligerent at the same time. Lindsay led him through an iteration of his job and responsibilities and used a building plan of the three story Buncombe County Sheriff's Office to help the witness explain the complicated nature of his management position there. He said he employed 325 to 330 people, was responsible for the jail, civil process, court security, patrol, detectives, a senior citizens' program and school resource officers.

Medford explained, "I entered law enforcement at age 20 and worked at the Buncombe County Sheriff's Department under Harry Clay. I was a patrolman for four and a half years then I made Sergeant. John Harrison was there too, as a patrolman, then a detective.

"I left to do bounty hunting. I was a bounty hunter for a couple of years, then I went back to law enforcement at the Asheville Police Department. I was a patrolman for twelve years, then I was promoted to detective.

"That's where I met Guy Penland's wife. She was a meter maid and then moved on to patrol. Sometime around then, I met Guy.

"I returned to the sheriff's department under Buck Lyda for almost four years, as a detective. Then when Charlie Long beat Lyda, I left and took a job as police chief in Rutledge, Georgia. I didn't like Georgia, so I worked my one year contract and came home.

"I ran against Long in 1994 and won."

Lindsay asked him about his experience as an administrator and Medford said he had "very little. I went to the Sheriff's Association school in Raleigh for a few days."

"Did you create departments at the sheriff's office?" Lindsay asked.

"Some. Others were there already. I selected people to run the department based on their education."

His top priority? "Crimes. Pat Hefner was in charge of the detective division."

Had his income changed when he was elected? "Yes, I was making $65,000 a year. I never made more than $25,000 before. I put in at least sixty hours per week in the early years."

Did the general public have access to him? "Yes. They could talk to me any time they wanted to. Not many made appointments. I would get a call from out front, from my secretary. If they left a message, I called everybody back during the same day if I could."

Who were his ranking officers? "Second in command was [Chief Deputy] George Stewart. Third was Major Bill Stafford."

He said that Sharon Stewart had been his secretary for nine years or better, "We changed then. She became a receptionist and ran things in that section. She was over all the secretaries and records and helped with the Reassurance Program [for seniors]. Most people coming in, she would do what she could for them.

"Later, Rhonda House became my secretary. Sharon had some medical problems with her ears, and couldn't do the phone, so we brought in Rhonda."

He described the Reassurance Program, "We called 300 elderly people every morning to see if they were all right. It was run by two part time employees."

Lindsay then led Medford through a recitation of changes in the video poker law in 2000. He repeated the details offered by earlier witnesses, but pointed out that, "Multiple law enforcement agencies had responsibility for enforcement. To make an arrest, you'd have to see someone paid off or play the machines and get a pay-off."

Medford said he thought the guidance offered by the law was vague and asserted that he had called the Attorney General and the head of the Sheriff's Association for advice. "The Attorney General had a different concept of the new law than Eddie Caldwell. One said you had to have the machines be taxed, while the other said, 'No.' It was different every time you called them." [This was evidently in reference to the clear stipulation in the law that in order to register a machine with a sheriff, the owner had to affirm that the machine had been registered as a business asset with the county tax office.]

Medford said, "Brenda Fraser and Miles Goforth were the first deputies in charge of registration."

Why Fraser? "She was pretty good with a computer. She had been a school resource officer and had worked with the victim assistance program. Goforth had been a detective and later in internal affairs. I assigned him because he had the time."

Was there some plan for using a computer for registrations? "Yes. It started out on a computer. Fraser and Goforth went to a class put on by the Sheriff's Association."

Lindsay asked, "Did you ever personally order stickers?"

"No. Fraser said she had to order stickers. I never had anyone ask for permission to order them."

Had he ever seen a sticker? "I never seen one, except on a machine."

He testified that Harrison and Penland were later in charge of registration, "Until Harrison retired. Then I appointed Davis based on the recommendation of George Stewart."

Asked next about Penland's work with the department, Medford said, "He wanted to be a deputy but I never hired him. I let him work for free since I needed help and had no funding for the registration. The legislature kept promising money but they never delivered."

Lindsay encouraged Medford to explain more about Penland's history. "When he came to talk to me about doing the job, I told him he couldn't be a deputy because he had no high school diploma or law enforcement training. He brought his paperwork back with his G.E.D. and then went to B.L.E.T. [Basic Law Enforcement Training].

"I didn't think he'd get through B.L.E.T., but he went through and passed and came back again. He wanted a job, but I had nothing open.

"To get your certification, you have to be working in law enforcement within one year of B.L.E.T., and if you have your certification you can work as an auxiliary officer. I let Penland volunteer. Then he got a D.U.I. charge and was convicted and they pulled his certification so he could no longer be employed as an officer, but he continued to volunteer."

Lindsay asked if Medford had ever authorized Penland to have a hand-held law enforcement radio and he said, "No."

Did others in the video poker unit have hand-held radios? "Yes."

Lindsay then asked about badges and Medford said they were only available for full-time employees and that volunteers did not have badges. He said he had never authorized Penland to hold a badge as a volunteer, "Only when he had certification."

Medford insisted he had never seen Penland wear a badge, but, "He had an embroidered shirt with the emblem of a badge." He said that others in the department also wore such embroidered shirts.

Lindsay: "Mr. Medford, did you ever give out badges to people in the community?"

"Probably six times," he replied. "They were my badges, I paid for them. I gave a badge to Jeff Hewitt's son. [Hewitt was a deputy who had been gunned down in the line of duty.] I gave one to the son of Highway Patrol Officer Anthony Cogdill [also killed in the line of duty]. I gave one to the actor, James Garner, who was filming a movie here. I had to because I had given one to Jack Lemon, and Garner got mad at me. [Garner and Lemon filmed part of "My Fellow Americans" in Asheville in 1995.] And I gave one to a lady at the court house who retired after 45 years."

Did Penland every have authority to give badges to anyone? "No," Medford insisted.

"What about Special Deputy cards," Lindsay asked, "Did you give them away?"

"Yes. Whoever was in the office could issue them."

Lindsay continued, "Who got them between 1994 and 2006?"

"We didn't keep a list."

Were volunteers authorized to give out special deputy cards? "No."

Did Penland hold any rank at the Buncombe County Sheriff's Department? "No. I saw him once in captain's bars and I told him he couldn't wear them."

Was he concerned that Penland was wearing the bars? "No. Everybody knew he was just volunteering."

Was he aware that Penland was telling people in the community that he was a Captain? "No."

Lindsay pointed out, "The golf tournament flyer said 'Capt. Penland.' Did you authorize that or the business cards he ordered from the county?"

"No, and I never authorized him to get business cards."

Had he ever given Pennington his contact number? "No."

Lindsay then returned to Penland's car and its police radio. "Who issued radios?"

"Any ranking officer could issue a radio," Medford replied.

"Were you ever consulted about buying a vehicle for Penland?"

"He had a Town Car," Medford said. "That's all I ever saw him drive."

"Were you ever aware that Penland was receiving payment from Henderson Amusement?"

"No."

And had he ever met Jerry Pennington?

"I met him a couple of times. I called him when I learned that he was getting Guy to sign video poker statements. I called the video poker office and had Pennington come to my office. I think it was the same day.

"I told him I didn't appreciate him getting Penland to sign off on registrations and Pennington apologized. I told him Penland could not sign and that he was not an employee."

Were there any other occasions when he had contact with Pennington? "One other time that I called him in and we had an argument about something. Right now I can't recall what it was. He had done something that he wasn't supposed to do. I can't recall."

At this point the court went into recess until 1:30 p.m., for lunch. When Judge Ellis returned at 1:48, the prosecution raised an objection to photos Lindsay wanted to submit as evidence and Ellis sustained the objection. He ruled that the photos of Medford's modest apartment "were of little probative value and were unfairly prejudicial." At 1:55 the jury returned to its box and Medford's testimony continued.

Lindsay: "What medications do you take?"

"Dilantin for seizures and Oxycontin for back pain."

Lindsay: "Concerning Jerry Pennington, were you aware of his community service in Buncombe County?"

"Not until I got a call from Linda Clontz. I talked to Harrison and told him to get information about it. I was never consulted by Harrison or Penland concerning Pennington."

Was he aware of Pennington's traffic stop in Henderson County? "No, not until I heard it in court."

Was he aware that Penland accompanied Pennington to surveil the Grand Jury? "No."

Had Pennington ever given him cash or a check? "No."

Had he ever received money from Henderson Amusement? "No."

Had he ever met James Henderson? "No."

Next Lindsay discussed Kepple. "Did the Buncombe County Sheriff's Department have an attorney working for the office?"

"Yes. We had three different attorneys over twelve years, involved in the Detective Division, civil process and training."

Had there been a County Attorney at the time? "Yes, but we never used him. Julie Kepple, a former District Attorney, was hired in finance, and then we used her abilities and her knowledge to handle legal matters."

"Was there a time when she was asked by a news agency about video poker," Lindsay inquired.

"I asked her to go get things ready for them, to make sure everything was in order. She said there were a couple of pieces of paper she couldn't find, but she got it in order." Medford testified that he had never restricted Kepple in any way.

What about Jerry Miller, the former U.S. Attorney? "He called and said he was about to retire and was looking for work. I told him to come on in. I gave him a few months to do whatever he wanted to do. If I had ran and won [in 2006], he'd have replaced me."

This testimony confirmed rumors that had circulated during the 2006 election cycle, as well as Miller's statement to the court. It offers a particularly clear view of the power politics at work in North Carolina's elected-sheriff system. Medford wasn't running for office that year because he felt called to public service or intended to work for the people of Buncombe. He hoped to be a place-holder for the Republican party which, under our law, would have had the right to appoint his replacement when he stepped down. And he may also have hoped that such a scheme would have helped keep the lid on investigation of his corrupt administration.

Lindsay asked, "Did you and Miller discuss video poker?"

"Yes. Miller conveyed a message from someone in the Democratic Party about an investigation. I asked Miller to look into what he could do to get rid of the machines. The lottery had already been instituted in North Carolina and it seemed video poker would be phased out. Miller stayed several months, then left the department. Later he came back."

Medford then said he had once arrested Alvin Ledford for "gambling tickets," and that he had "been to the Waffle House by the airport eleven or so times." But asked if he had ever received cash from Ledford he replied, "Alvin Ledford wouldn't give me anything."

Had he known Charles McBennett, Jr.? "No. I knew his father. He wanted help with his son who was doing drugs." Had he ever received money from either McBennett? "No."

Lindsay then returned to video poker rules. Medford said that the law mandated a maximum of three machines at any one location and added, "I didn't let anybody move. I didn't want any problems."

Medford claimed that two locations had been shut down during the first year and a half [of the 2000 law] because, "We got a call. There were problems." He said one location was in Candler and the other in Arden. Also, he said a location on Smoky Park Highway had been operating four machines and he'd told them to remove one.

Did he know Jim Lindsey? "Yes. We served together at the Asheville Police Department. He was president of a coin-machine company and he was complaining about other businesses wanting to move in on his business." Medford added, "I told Harrison and Davis not to bring video representatives back to my office. A year later there was an issue about 'Islam' something."

"Imran Alam?" Lindsay suggested.

"That's who I mean."

"Did you ever have a conversation with Lindsey about Imran Alam?"

"No." Medford went on to state that his video poker office handled all issues about the machines, that he had never received money from Alam, and had never heard anything about a change of machines at Alam's stores. "I did not know who Alam was." He also denied ever having a discussion with Harrison about Alam but admitted having a conversation with Lindsey about moving machines to Alam's stores. Lindsay, not surprisingly, didn't pursue the discrepancy.

Was there ever a time he went to a parking lot to meet Harrison and Alam? "No." Had he been handed an envelope by Harrison, through a window? "No."

"Do you know Demetre Theodossis?"

"Yes. I met him twice, in the sheriff's office. But until the other day, here, I didn't even know he spoke English. I was led to believe that he didn't speak English." But, he said, Theodossis had never been in his private office and he had never met him in the video poker office. He did admit to having eaten at a Hot Dog King, "Years ago."

Medford then denied ever receiving money from Theodossis or calling him for money.

"Did you ever campaign for Elizabeth Dole?"

"No."

"How long have you known Jackie Shepherd?"

"Eighteen to twenty years. We met in the sheriff's office, we both worked for Buck Lyda." Later, he said, he had worked for Shepherd. "I collected money from laundry machines, counted it, put it in a bank bag. I also set fuel prices. I'd see how much gas was at the nearest competitors and set our price one cent lower."

Had Shepherd helped with his election? "He gave us a car. Gave us some money. He had a couple of functions for us to raise money. He bought me three suits. He was part of my transition team." Medford explained that the transition team interviewed personnel at the department to decide who would be let go and who would be kept on. He confirmed that the two had a falling out at one point, which was later resolved.

"Did you ever borrow money from Shepherd?"

"Yes. I'd call him. I borrowed money, probably twice, and I paid him back." He then identified three personal checks in the amounts of $500, $600 and $900 as repayment of loans. Medford said he thought Shepherd had bought the Cherokee Trading Post in 2004, and had no idea whether video poker machines were in operation there.

Did he recall an occasion when Penland called in a tag? "Yes. It was late 2004 or early 2005. Rick Schwein of the FBI called me." He explained that he had an officer, Cody Muse, "on loan" to the FBI to work on homeland security, and that Schwein had been his contact there. "He wanted to know if Guy Penland worked for me. He said he had run a tag number on an agent in Charlotte. He didn't want me to do anything. He said at some time Penland might be charged, but he said not to do anything with it. I found out that Mr. Pennington had been going to Penland, because most people knew that he was being investigated for gambling."

Lindsay asked, "You say that it was common knowledge that Pennington was being investigated. Who told you?"

"Johnny Harrison told me that there was an investigation into Pennington."

"Did you take any steps?"

"I told Butch Davis that Penland couldn't work in the video poker office and told communications that any tag he called in should be referred as 'not on file.'

"About twenty percent of tags come back 'not on file' so it was a good thing to tell him. Rick Schwein told me not to tell Penland what was up."

Had he had any further conversation with Schwein concerning Penland? "I called him back a couple of months later to ask if Penland was going to be arrested. He said it was still under investigation. I discussed it with Chief Stewart and Butch Davis."

Lindsay then explored Medford's experience with the golf tournaments. "How did they come about?"

"We started in 1998, trying to raise money. George Stewart and Butch Davis started it. At first it was once a year, then became twice a year the second year after the election. They put it on for me. I don't play golf."

What did he do with the money in non-election years? "It was my money. I gave it away."

He said that he had nothing to do with recruiting players and that while he knew Frank Orr and Johnny Harrison were also involved, he had no knowledge of Penland's role. Medford also denied knowing how much the players were charged or who collected the money.

Had he ever discussed money with Harrison? "He gave me money after the tournaments. The most I ever gave away was $1,440." He indicated that he had only a general awareness of the expenses involved, paying the golf course for use of the facility and carts and purchasing trophies.

Had he ever attended the tournaments, given that he didn't play golf. "I went to say hello to people. I'd stay for 15 or 20 minutes. I welcomed them and let someone else do the speech."

Did he know how much was left over after expenses were covered? "About $2,500, within $100 either way, according to Harrison. I gave the money to people, people who needed it."

When had he started that practice? "The first year in office, and second, I gave away about $18,000. Then the Eblen Foundation stepped in. I helped people with oil, food, clothes, children's clothes. In 2002 and 2003 I gave away cash."

"Was the money from off-year golf tournaments always used for gifts?" Lindsay asked.

"Yes. Sharon or George handled the money. We put the money into the election account in election years."

Had he planned to run for reelection in 2006? "No. I was hurtin' and tired and didn't want to fool with that anymore. I decided not to run in 2005 but they wanted me to. I told them that if I ran and won, I wouldn't stay four years. I said I would go to three functions and that was it.

"Ron Honeycutt, Sharon and George Stewart and David Brown ran it for me. He's a friend who has always helped me in elections. Rhonda House and Pat Hutchins helped too. Lester Bullock was the accountant, David Brown preceded him as accountant."

Following a twenty minute recess, Judge Ellis returned at 3:50 p.m. and told Lindsay, "I have received information that your investigator has misinformed someone. Let your investigator know that it is a felony to misinform a witness in a federal case. He said he was a federal agent." Ellis exited again and returned ten minutes later to call Lindsay and Jayne to the bench.

Assistant U.S. Attorney Edwards was not present, and Ellis complained to fellow attorney Corey Ellis who explained that Edwards was finishing the prosecution's jury instructions and would be back shortly. He returned at 4:10 and the judge scolded him.

Lindsay continued his direct.

"Who is Tracy Bridges?"

"He worked at the Buncombe County Sheriff's Department for Bob Long until he could take the Bar exam. Tracy had finished B.L.E.T. and he became the chief magistrate in Madison County. He said he'd gone to law school and needed to pass the bar. Maybe late in 2004, he would come up every other week and ask if I could hire him at the Buncombe County Sheriff's Department. Later, when Jerry Silver went back up north, I gave Tracy a job because Julie Kepple was expecting a child."

Did Bridges have anything to do with the campaign? "Very little, I thought. He did pay the filing fee in 2006. He had to have a certified check or money order. George went to get it with money from me. George, Pat Hefner, Tracy, there were four or five of us involved." He indicated that he had been reimbursed by the Committee to Re-elect Bobby Medford, by check, on May 3, 2006.

Lindsay showed him a $1,000 check written to Bridges by the campaign on May 12 and Medford said he had no idea what that was for.

Was he aware that golf tournament checks were being cashed at George's Mini Mart? "No." And had he authorized that practice? "No."

Had he met with Lester Bullock in his office? "Yes. He said that almost everything that went in was by money order."

Lindsay said, "Go back to an earlier meeting when Bullock said the campaign couldn't take cash. Who was there?"

"Bullock, Sharon, Tracy, myself."

"Did you know cash deposits were being made before that point?"

"No. I asked Bridges if cash deposits had been made and he said that Bullock refused them. I told Bridges to go to the Board of Elections and find out the rules.

"Later, I got a call from David Brown who came to see me. He had a folder with a bunch of money orders and some reports he showed me. Everything that went into that account was money orders. I was mad."

Judge Ellis intervened in the questioning. "Why? Were money orders legal?"

"Yes."

"Then why were you mad?"

"I just wanted to know why people who were usually giving me personal checks were giving me money orders. So I knew they were cashing checks and buying money orders."

Ellis pressed him further. "What were you upset about? Money orders were legal."

Medford had no answer and Lindsay jumped in. "Did Mr. Brown tell you that he was concerned about the money orders that were paid to the campaign?"

"Yes. Brown said it was illegal to use cash to buy money orders."

Ellis intervened again, "Did you know where the cash had come from?"

"No."

Lindsay: "Those forms had already been filed at the Board of Elections. What did you think would happen?"

"I thought if it came out, the election was over."

"What did you do about it?"

"David Brown handled it. Later, Bullock called Sharon and said there were more money orders. I told Bridges that I thought he was just trying to get me into trouble. He asked me if he needed to start looking for another job. I told him 'Not just yet.'"

Judge Ellis asked, "Why didn't you fire him?"

"He would have sued me."

Lindsay asked, "Was Bridges ever assigned to internal affairs?"

"He worked out of the internal affairs office, but he never had an assignment in internal affairs from me. Maybe from George."

"Why were you concerned about being sued?"

"There was a sergeant in the highway patrol whose son had an affair with Tracy Bridges. He was being paid off by Tracy Bridges, out of pocket. I thought he would claim that was the reason for firing him."

Lindsay then discussed banking and Medford described his accounts at the credit union, said he and Judi Bell had signature permission on each other's accounts and that Bell balanced his check book and paid all of his bills. He said that for the last few months in office he had direct deposit of his paycheck and that Brian, his son, also had his pay deposited directly into Medford's account. "Before that, I used to cash his checks."

Lindsay: "Do you gamble at Harrah's?"

"Deputies weren't allowed to gamble in Buncombe County. They were fired after one warning. I started going to Harrah's several years ago. Once every other payday. I went several times and took people from the office. My brother worked for the county and he went. My son went with me one time. Most of it was in the last year."

How much money was he spending? "Considerably more than in the early years."

What level players card did he hold? "The highest." He explained that benefits included the chance to win trips to other casinos and that he'd won trips to Reno and Mississippi. He said that Butch Davis had accompanied him to Reno for three or four days.

Lindsay asked where Medford obtained cash for Harrah's. "I'd cash a check at Ingles. Three or four times at George's Mini Mart. At Jack Shepherd's place, his gas station or at Payless grocery." He said he occasionally used his debit card at Harrah's and that "Judi didn't usually have money. I took the money. When we won, we'd spend the money, after."

Had he deposited winnings in their accounts? "Yes." Had he ever enlisted employees to make deposits? "Probably."

"Your income tripled when you became sheriff, and then there were raises," Lindsay said. "Did the increase in your income change your personal life in any way?"

"No."

Lindsay then showed the jury pictures of Medford's apartment building and Medford said the rent had been $250 per month, later $350. Lindsay offered interior pictures as well.

Judge Ellis: "I don't see the relevance. You are wasting time."

Lindsay moved ahead quickly to offer a photo of Medford's personal auto, purchased in 2003 and paid off by 2006.

"You signed two North Carolina Sheriff's Association letters asking to make video poker illegal in the state?"

"Yes." Medford replied. And. with that, Lindsay turned over his witness to Penland's attorney.

Attorney Paul Bidwell was in the awkward position of attempting to establish his client's innocence separate from Medford's, which meant claiming on the one hand that nothing illegal had gone down. But, oh, if it had, it was Bobby and Butch and Johnny—not Guy. So he went back to the beginning.

Bidwell: "How closely did you supervise Brenda Fraser?"

"I didn't have time to supervise her."

How closely had he supervised Johnny Harrison? "It was the same. I didn't have time."

And Butch Davis? Same answer.

Did he know about Guy Penland's work with the video poker office? "I found out from Butch that Guy Penland was signing registrations and I told Penland I wanted to see him. I met Mr. Penland very quickly and told him he was taking advantage, that he couldn't do it anymore." He testified that Davis had told him, in 2005, that Penland had signed "many registrations."

Bidwell asked, "What else did Davis tell you about Penland?"

"He said Pennington and Penland were riding

around together. I thought it wouldn't look right for Penland to ride around with Pennington."

Judge Ellis, "Why? Was it because the machines were being operated illegally?"

Bidwell jumped in, "Did you know that some machines were being played illegally?"

Medford: "Yes."

Ellis: "How did you know?"

Medford: "Because I ate at a truck stop and saw that nobody was playing the machines when I was there. So I knew they were running them illegally."

Ellis: "Did you ask Penland why he was riding with Pennington?"

Medford: "No."

Ellis: "Wouldn't that have been useful to know?"

Medford: "No."

Bidwell asked, "Was it common knowledge that Pennington was under investigation?"

Medford: "Butch Davis told me."

Bidwell briefly turned to the license tag calls and elicited Medford's assertion that some "not on file" reports were due to data problems in the computer system in Raleigh. He also affirmed that Van Gill, an FBI agent, had played golf in at least one of his tournaments. At that point, the attorney had no further questions.

38: Caught in the crossfire

Assistant U.S. Attorney Corey Ellis handled the cross-examination of the former sheriff. "In non-election years, you said the money you collected from the golf tournaments was yours to give away, for the sheriff's office to give away, is that right?"

"Yes. I was sheriff."

"You also testified that the most you cleared on any golf tournament was $2,500?"

"Or possibly $3,000," Medford replied.

Ellis then referred to campaign records previously entered as evidence. "In spring of 2002, your campaign filing showed $11,680 gained from the golf tournament. And in fall of that year, $9,270."

Medford replied, "It was always $2,200 to $2,800 in the early years."

"Can you explain why it was $20,000 in 2002, but in other years it was less?"

"No."

"Is it a coincidence that three of four of the golf organizers were involved in video poker registrations?"

"I can't say."

Ellis then went over the names of the golf organizers and Medford confirmed them. "Harrison was one of those responsible for the golf tournaments?"

"Yes. and Davis, Stewart and Orr."

"And Penland?" the prosecutor asked.

Medford indicated he hadn't known of Penland's involvement and Ellis showed him a flyer for the May 2005 event which listed "Captain Guy Penland" as a contact. Medford asserted he hadn't seen the flyer, nor others from September of that year or 2006.

Ellis went on, "You had back surgery in late August, 2005, performed by Dr. Maxwell?"

"Yes."

How many days of work had he missed afterward? "Eight weeks. Then when I came back, I worked four or five hours per day."

Ellis pounced, "Bank records show that you made withdrawals from your account from Harrah's casino in Cherokee, but you were not at work. On September 24, 2005, you spent thirty-one minutes in front of a machine."

Medford indicated that he supposed he had done so, and Ellis listed a few other dates and times from the casino records. Then he moved to 2006. "You gambled over $50,000 in 2006, is that correct?"

"Yes," Medford replied.

"And on your 2006 tax return you claimed gambling losses of $35,645?"

"Yes."

"In order to claim losses, you have to show that you won as much as you lost, isn't that correct?"

"I guess so."

"You often made cash withdrawals while you were at Harrah's. Didn't you often take you account down to nothing, or nearly nothing?"

Medford hesitated and Ellis directed his attention to a bank statement dated April 19, 2003 which recorded a withdrawal via casino draft of $22.50 which reduced the balance to zero.

Medford said, "That was about the time my income tax refund check came back and I usually received about $9,000 as a refund."

Ellis referred to Exhibit #111, a bank statement that recorded cash deposits to Medford's Premier account. "Where did the cash come from?"

"I used my VISA card to get cash from an ATM to deposit in my account. Also, I could get money from anyone I wanted to."

"Who is that 'anyone?'" Ellis queried.

"My sister. My brother."

"In 2003, you deposited $26,630 in cash over the course of one year?"

Medford said he had received a $40,000 cash settlement from the county for a work-related injury, though that didn't appear to explain the cash deposits spread out over the course of the year. Ellis asked, "What did you do with the rest of the money?" and Medford had no answer, but said that he had also cashed in a 401K.

"When did you cash in the 401K?"

"2004." But he said he hadn't received cash, that it had gone directly into his account. Then Medford said "I won $12,500 the next year, and a couple of times I won $4,000."

"Are you testifying that you won $12,500 in 2005?"

"Yes."

Ellis referred to a tax return, "You reported that you lost money gambling that year. Are you saying that the winnings account for your cash deposits?"

"Yes."

The prosecutor then showed Medford documentation of a payday loan for $350 he had obtained in September 2004. "How did that work?"

"You called them, and they put it in your account," he replied.

"Your account balance was negative when you took out that loan?"

"Yes."

"Did you have an addiction to gaming?"

"No. It was just some place to go and take things off my mind."

"Did it become an addiction?"

"No."

"In 2006, when you lost $60,000, it was not an addiction?"

"No."

"Was it a responsible thing to do, to gamble when you had a negative balance?"

"No. But I knew I had cash coming in."

"You knew you had cash coming in. From where?"

"I had a VISA card."

Ellis moved on. "Judi Bell made many more cash deposits than you did in some years?"

"Yes."

"Did you give cash to Ms. Bell?"

"Yes."

"Ms. Bell's cash deposits exceeded $50,000 over five years."

"Maybe."

At this point the jury was excused for the day and the prosecutor told the judge he anticipated another hour and a half of questioning for the defendant.

When Medford took the stand on May 13, Ellis returned to the golf tournaments.

"Mr. Medford, you have testified that you were entitled to the proceeds of your golf tournaments, and that the money was given away at your sole discretion."

"Yes."

"You testified that thousands of dollars were given away to individuals over the years. Can we expect to hear from some of those individuals in this trial?"

"I don't know."

"There was no golf tournament in the spring of 2007. Is the fact that you were sheriff the reason for the golf tournaments?"

"Yes."

"So the money was provided because you were sheriff?"

"Yes."

"Did your income decrease after you were sheriff?"

"I get three retirements."

Ellis shifted course, "Now, concerning Mr. Penland. What was your policy concerning who could hand out badges?"

"The finance office and personnel."

"Was that the same policy concerning special deputies?"

"No."

"What were your policies concerning volunteers?"

"They worked at their own discretion. If they did something wrong, we didn't let them come back."

"You called Mr. Pennington into your office, why was that?"

"It was because I was upset that Penland had signed up his machines."

"So Guy Penland violated your policy?"

"Yes. I told him he couldn't register machines."

"Guy Penland was wearing a shirt with a sheriff's department insignia. Did you make him stop wearing that shirt?"

"No."

"Did you restrict his access to the sheriff's office?"

"No."

Ellis asked, "There was a second time you called Pennington into your office, about the automobile Penland purchased. Why did you confront him if you didn't know he was involved in that purchase?"

"I don't know."

"How far apart in time were the two confrontations?"

"I don't know."

"On July 10, 2002, you signed a special deputy

card for Jerry Pennington. That was the same day that Mr. Pennington was pulled over in Henderson County [when the Henderson deputy confiscated Pennington's previous special deputy card]." Ellis then referred to the card entered as evidence, "Is that your signature?"

"Yes."

"Mr. Pennington had a criminal history, but you said you did a criminal background check before issuing special deputy cards. Why did he pass that check?"

"I don't know."

"You spoke to Ms. Clontz concerning Pennington's community service. Did you tell Ms. Clontz that Guy Penland was a 'good old boy'?"

"I could have. I don't remember."

"You said that Johnny Harrison advised you that Pennington was a crook."

"Yes."

"You also hired Jerry Miller who researched machines for you. He discussed with you your power to remove machines in Buncombe County. Is that right?"

"Yes."

"But you didn't ban anyone. How do you explain your failure to act?"

"Two counties had tried to ban them and lost in court. We were waiting to see what happened."

"You said you have had no contact with Alvin Ledford other than the one time you arrested him?"

"Yes."

"Do you know Jack O'Leary?"

"Yes. He was an old time gambler from way back."

"Do you recall seeing O'Leary at the golf tournament in April of 2006?"

"No."

"Do you recall the total profit from that tournament?"

"About $2,500 to $3,000."

Ellis showed Medford notes recorded by Butch Davis listing "$7,500 to Bobby" and "$3,000 to Tracy."

Medford had no explanation.

Ellis returned to 2002. "Your campaign filings with the Board of Elections showed over $20,000 from the golf tournaments. But you had a problem in 2006, because you were unable to get cash into the campaign account. That was a problem, wasn't it?"

Medford: "I don't know where the cash came from."

"In 2006, it didn't concern you at all that you couldn't get that money into your campaign account?"

Medford sounded exasperated. "In 2006, I was only going to do three appearances. I did not know how much cash they had, what they had. No. It didn't concern me."

"You said you had met Demetre Theodossis on two occasions at the Buncombe County Sheriff's Office?"

"Yes.

Ellis referred to phone records and said, "On October 24, 2006 there was a call placed from the sheriff's office to Mr. Theodossis' number, and then a call from that number to Greece, and a subsequent call to the sheriff's office. Do you deny getting any cash from Theodossis on or about October 24, 2006?"

"Yes." Then, in a seeming non sequitur, Medford added, "I didn't know he could speak English."

Ellis referred to a bank deposit slip, "You deposited $500 in cash to your account on October 25."

"Yes."

Ellis then referred to a check drawn on the same account, "You wrote a check to your campaign for $500 on October 25 as well?"

"Yes."

"You deny that you received money from Theodossis?"

"Yes."

"You heard Dennis Theodossis testify that he took cash to you. You then deposited cash to your account and wrote a check to your campaign. Is that a coincidence?"

"Yes."

"Who did you get the $500 from?"

"I guess it was in the bank."

Ellis pressed ahead. "Was it your practice to withdraw money from your account to deposit in your account?"

Medford offered no answer.

The prosecutor showed Medford registration forms for machines at George's Mini Mart and then a $2,100 check he had cashed at the store in 2003. Could he identify the check?

"Yes. It's mine."

"Were you aware that golf tournament checks were being cashed at the Mini Mart?"

"No sir."

"How did you learn that it was a good place to cash checks?"

"I buy gas there."

"Why didn't you go to your credit union, " Ellis asked.

"It was closed. You can't get cash out at night."

"When you cashed checks there, were you aware that they had video poker machines?"

"Yes. I guess I was."

"In November 2006, McBennett put machines in George's Mini Mart. But you had made a rule about moving machines, is that right?"

"I said that nobody gets into anybody else's business."

"You said there would be no changes?"

"Yes."

"You, as sheriff, were subject to the laws of the state of North Carolina, but within those laws you had discretion to tell people where to put machines?"

"Yes. But I didn't want to get sued."

"Mr. Miller had informed you that you had the power to move machines in 2005?"

"I don't remember."

Ellis then pulled up tournament accounting notes from Davis, written in 2005 and directed Medford's attention to an entry that read "$2,400—dog."

"Do you recall when your girlfriend's son, a deputy, killed a dog while on duty?"

"Yes."

"You said you'd pay the vet bill yourself."

"Yes."

"You deposited $2,400 in cash into your account," Ellis said, referring to a bank statement.

"Yes. I know it didn't come from the golf tournament. Others contributed. Pat Hefner. George Stewart. Randy Bradford."

"Why did you deposit it to your account?"

"Because I needed to write a check."

"You made statements to the media that you had used your own funds, but they were not your own funds?"

"No. Six or seven others paid in."

Ellis then had Medford identify his tax return for 2006. "You reported charitable donations which added up to $45,000 plus."

Medford examined the paperwork for several minutes, flipping back and forth between the pages.

"On the fifth page," Ellis offered.

Medford turned the pages again. "I don't believe I stated $45,000."

Ellis said, "There on the fifth page, do you see the $45,000 in charitable donations?"

"Yes."

"Is the $2,400 part of that?"

"I don't think that is right."

"Is your tax return in error?"

"Yes. Apparently it is. Nobody would ever let you get away with that."

"In 2006 your reported income was $215,000. That was significantly more than you had ever reported in the past."

"I only made $125,000. That had to be my 401K."

"Would you agree that getting a $45,000 deduction benefited you considerably?"

Medford didn't respond.

"On your 1040, on line seven, is your salary correct?"

Medford spent some time reading, then replied, "The $45,000 is not known to me. It must be a typographical error."

"On the second page, line nine, it states that you paid $9,722 in taxes."

"Yes."

"On line ten it lists mortgage interest, but you say you rented for 15 years."

"I borrowed money against my parent's house and let my sister-in-law live there."

"On line fifteen, it says gifts to charity totaled $45,000, and your total itemized deductions, at line twenty-eight, are $97,000."

"No, that's not right. I have sent my taxes to the same lady for several years. I'd have to ask her."

Ellis asked, "In 2006, these numbers significantly benefited you from a tax standpoint, didn't they?"

"These numbers do."

"You were sheriff of this county for twelve years. Did you ever submit paperwork for leave from work?"

"For eight weeks, after surgery. Then when I came back I only worked a few hours a day."

"Did you continue to get a regular salary during that time?"

"I was paid per year, not hourly."

"Did you ever request leave time?"

"No."

"When you separated from the county you collected $12,000 for unused vacation in 2006. But during 2006, you spent 160 work days at Harrah's. When you went to the casino during the the work week, you never submitted for leave. Is that right?"

"I didn't have to. I worked seven days a week, twenty-four hours a day. So I was always working."

"When you traveled to Biloxi and Reno, you never claimed leave?"

"I don't recall."

"Who would know?"

"Rhonda House."

"Here is a deposit slip for $11,292. What does that represent?"

"That was for unused leave."

"Why didn't you take leave when you spent 160 work days at Harrah's?"

"I was always on call."

"So you didn't consider that to be vacation when you were sitting at Harrah's?"

"No. I didn't take vacation away from Asheville. Harrah's is only fifty minutes away. I have always had the maximum amount of hours available."

"Can you explain why you didn't take leave?"

"I don't know what I took."

"Who prepared your tax return?"

"Her name is on there. I can't recall the name. She lives in Madison County."

"Is it Sandra Robinson?"

"No."

"There is no name of a preparer on the return is there?"

"No."

Ellis moved on to Medford's spotty credit history. "You have had three revolving credit accounts closed for failure to pay, is that correct?"

"Yes."

"You had an MBNA credit account charged off as bad debt, and more than one account of that nature."

Medford replied, "People were trying to collect things I'd never heard of."

"Did you submit information to the credit card company that it was in error?"

"Yes."

"Concerning Jim Lindsey—you had known him since 1966, and you have known Harrison since the same period, is that correct?"

"Yes."

"And Lindsey wanted to move some machines?"

"He was trying to take over another guy's business," Medford replied.

"You determined that it was okay?"

"I didn't let anyone move machines."

Ellis showed Medford a cell phone bill that recorded a phone call from his number to Mountain Music on April 14, 2005. Medford said, "I don't remember that particular number." He was then shown a counter check signed by Imran Alam for $6,000, dated April 20.

"Mr. Lindsey wanted to discuss moving some machines and you called him," Ellis said.

"I probably did. I don't remember."

"Did you discuss with Mr. Lindsey his desire to move machines?"

"No. That's when Mr. Lindsey was mad at me because I wouldn't let him move his machines."

Ellis offered a registration form that showed that Lindsey had placed machines at Alam's store on April 11. "That was against your rule, wasn't it?"

"Yes. People were never supposed to change machines, never. If he did it, he did it on his own."

"Weren't you angry that Mr. Harrison brought the problems back to you?"

"Yes."

"Did Mr. Lindsey come to your office within a few days of the phone call you made?"

"I don't recall."

"Do you recall yesterday's testimony that Harrison brought Lindsey to your office?"

"No. I met him in the hall, not in my office. I told him what the rules were."

Ellis: "So you *did* talk about placing machines in Alam's store?"

"Yes."

"And then he did that?"

Medford insisted, "Not by any authority from me."

"Did you receive money from Lindsey?"

"Jim never gave me any money. He wouldn't have the nerve."

Judge Ellis spoke up. "What about Alam?"

"No."

The judge continued, "Why didn't you talk to Lindsey about machines in your office?"

"After the new law went into effect, I didn't want any changes. It would only cause problems."

The judge persisted. "Was there any other reason you didn't want video poker operators in your office?"

"I was very busy. People wanted my attention. I didn't need the distraction."

After the morning recess the prosecutor turned to Medford's career in office. "Did you get better at it, the longer you did it?"

"Yes."

"Did the office involve political obligations?"

"Yes. But I wasn't much of a politician."

"Did Jackie Shepherd ever provide you with a speech coach?"

"No."

"Did he buy you suits?"

"Yes. I had one on yesterday."

"You were reelected several times?"

"Yes."

"You got to know political people?"

"Yes."

"Did you have to learn much when you took office?"

"No sir. I've been in law enforcement all my life."

"Your job involved investigation obligations?"

"Yes.

"Did you assist in investigations?"

"Yes."

"It involved administration as well?"

"Yes."

"And you testified that you had 325 employees?"

"Yes."

"With all of those obligations, how could you justify all that time at the casino?"

"I had cancer, surgery and arthritis. I wanted to get out and see what the world was like."

At 11:03 a.m., Lindsay began his redirect. He first established that the sheriff's department phone number on the Theodossis bills was generic: that any outgoing call from any extension in the department appeared the same. "Did you hear testimony that Harrison called the Hot Dog King?"

"Yes," Medford agreed.

Lindsay turned to submission of leave time. "Did you work hourly or yearly?"

"Yearly."

"How many hours did you work?"

"Sixty hours per week at first. Never less than eight hours per day."

"Did you ever receive overtime pay?"

"No."

"What hours were you on call?" Lindsay asked.

"All of 'em," Medford replied.

Turning to campaign finance, Lindsay asked who had prepared Medford's campaign reports. "David Brown and Mr. Bullock."

"Were you required to sign those reports?"

"No."

Had he prepared his own tax return for 2006? "No." Concerning the $45,000 mistake, would he have to file an amendment? "I'm sure I will have to now."

Who had balanced his personal accounts? "Judi Bell. I seldom wrote checks."

Before the current case, had he ever seen the notes from the golf tournament? "No."

Had he ever registered machines? "No. Fraser, Harrison and Davis had registered machines."

Had he ever authorized Harrison or Davis to transfer registrations? "No."

Lindsay then referred to a photo of a special deputy I.D. Did Medford recognize the signature?"

"No."

Did that signature resemble that of a signature stamp in your office? "Yes."

"If Mr. Harrison wanted to change machines out he could have done it without you knowing. Is that correct?"

"Yes."

"Where did you get Lindsey's phone number?"

"From my pager, I think."

Lindsay then compared Medford's rubber-stamp signature to that on Pennington's I.D. and even at some distance from the screens, the difference was clear.

39: Not adding up

At 11:17 a.m., Lindsay called his next witness, Eric Lioy, a Charlotte-based forensic CPA employed by the firm of Grant, Thornton, which he said had fifty offices across the U.S. Lioy was a witness-for-hire, and the immediate impression he gave was that of a witness-for-hire—the engineer your lawyer would employ to explain why your brakes had failed or the psychiatrist lined up to bolster an insanity defense. It was hard for me to believe him, even before he spoke.

Yet, on the other side of the scale, he testified that he was a certified fraud examiner with all manner of professional credentials and a stellar work history with major corporate connections.

Lindsay followed Lioy's recitation of bona fides with, "I tender Mr. Lioy as an expert witness.

"What types of information do you evaluate?"

Lioy replied, "I first come to understand the allegations in a case, then I begin to examine records. I was asked to understand the allegations in this case and then examine bank statements, loan documents, others' background statements and interviews."

What were the allegations as he understood them? "That Mr. Medford accepted large sums of money as kickbacks or bribes as sheriff."

What had he considered concerning Medford's income? "Tax returns, W-2s and bank statements. Mr. Medford and Judi Bell had a close personal relationship."

Judge Ellis interposed, "You were *advised* that they had a close personal relationship?"

Lioy: "There were transactions between them."

Lindsay: "You were asked to look at both accounts?"

Lioy: "I looked at bank statements from Premier Federal Credit Union, loans to both of them and tax returns.

Lindsay: "In these things you were looking at, you were looking for sources of legitimate income?"

Lioy: "Yes."

Lindsay and Lioy then introduced a chart detailing Medford's known income based on his tax returns from 2003 through 2007. The numbers ran from $88,000 in 2003 to $180,000 in 2006 with a drop to $88,000 in 2007, after he left office. In summary, the accountant said Medford's gross income for five years was $487,000 plus $122,000 in pension payments and $4,158 in tax refunds and incidental income.

"I looked at his lifestyle spending and expenditures," Lioy explained. "I looked to see if he was spending more than he was making, to look for another source of income.

"I considered statements from casinos. I did a background check on his assets. I noted that Mr. Medford lived in an apartment, owned an inherited home and no other real estate. I saw that he owned a 2003 Chevrolet and carried $23,000 in debt."

Lioy said that he had looked at records of Medford's and Bell's gambling with the understanding that the documents he examined were obtained by the government.

Judge Ellis spoke up: "He got those documents from Harrah's from the defense."

Lioy: "Yes. I looked at the winnings and losses at Harrah's Cherokee, from Mississippi and from Nevada."

Lindsay asked, "Did you conduct interviews?"

"Yes. I spoke with an accountant at Harrah's Cherokee casino."

"Why was gambling of interest?"

"It is important because any large expenditure could reflect kickbacks." Lioy then offered a yearly breakdown of income and losses. He noted that in 2002, Medford's salary was $81,000 and his reported losses, $941. In 2003 he made $89,000 and lost $1,500.

Judge Ellis asked, "Wouldn't it have been more accurate to do post-tax income?"

Lioy answered in several different directions, but failed to provide a coherent response, then continued to note income and gambling receipts of: $91,000 and $1,500 won (2004); $97,000 and $1,800 (2005); $180,000 and $72,000 (2006); and $83,000 and $45,000 in 2007. The total, Lioy said, was $622,000 income and $122,000 in losses.

In similar fashion Lioy reported Bell's income and gambling results as: $38,000 and $3,800 winnings (2004); $38,000 and $8,800 lost (2005); $43,000 and $12,000 lost in 2006. Bell's totals for three years ran to $119,000 in income and losses of $17,000.

Lindsay inquired, "In making your valuation, do you consider cash transactions?"

"Yes, but it is hard to understand the source of cash. It is fungible. Cash can be replaced. Two twenty dollar bills can replace each other with equal value. You can get cash out of an ATM, write a check to cash or a check to a supermarket. The source of a cash deposit is impossible to determine from bank statements. Cash can go in through a deposit at a branch bank or via an ATM machine.

"When you look for possible sources, you look for evidence related to allegations in a case, at money coming out and going in over a period of time. You look at the timing between a known cash payment and a deposit."

Lindsay: "What did you observe about the manner in which Medford and Bell removed cash from their accounts?"

"There were lots of ATM transactions and checks to grocery stores in rounded amounts which appeared to be cashed checks."

As Lindsay's questioning continued, Lioy said he had considered the total of cash deposits into Medford's and Bell's accounts and tried to understand where the money was coming from. "I would never rely exclusively on cash deposits to evaluate an account."

Lindsay: "If you took $1,000 out and then deposited it again every day, you would show deposits of $100,000 in one hundred days?"

Lioy: "Yes."

Asked about the flow of transactions, Lioy said, "I could see a pattern of money being withdrawn before they traveled to Harrah's and deposited after. I understood the frequency of their gambling daily at Harrah's Cherokee. There were not huge losses on given days, but it was very frequent."

Lindsay asked, "What do you know about the player I.D. cards at Harrah's?"

"It allows the casino to track your playing," Lioy responded. "If you don't insert your card, your winnings and losses are not recorded."

Finally Lindsay asked Lioy to explain IRS form W2G.

"It reports gambling income. Casinos must issue the form for winnings over $600."

Assistant U.S. Attorney Edwards handled the cross. "The W2G is not issued as a patron exits a casino, it is just a snapshot, isn't that right?"

Lioy: "Yes."

"And a W2G is not generated at Harrah's until $1,200 or more is won?"

"Yes, but if I want money, a payout, above that level, the machine freezes. If I play it down to nothing again, the winning does show on the casino records."

"How do you know that?"

"I talked to Sihanouke, the casino manager. I talked to him for fifteen minutes and did some other research."

Edwards elicited testimony to the effect that winnings had to be reported on IRS form 1040 and that one is allowed to deduct losses up to the level of gross winnings. "If Mr. Medford reported $36,645 income from W2Gs, he could lose more than that, but not claim the loss. Is that right?"

"Yes."

"According to their tax returns, Bell and Medford's losses were always equal to their winnings as reported, so at best they broke even?"

"Yes."

"But from Harrah's records," Edwards continued, "They lost more than they reported?"

"Yes."

"In 2004, you report that Mr. Medford won $1,516, but on his tax return he reported losses of $6,450, so the information Medford gave to the IRS was wrong according to your investigation."

"Yes."

"In 2004, you report that Ms. Bell had a net profit of $3,511 from gambling, but on her tax return she reported gambling losses of $3,750."

"Yes."

"So that is not the truth according to Harrah's records?"

"No."

Edwards continued, "And there is the possibility that the records you were looking at, at Harrah's, are only what shows up when a player's card is used?"

"I would not know."

"If they chose not to use their players' cards, there would be no record. You would not know if they were there?"

"Yes."

"So if somebody has a player's card and chooses not to use it, they could avoid reporting?"

"Yes."

"There is a hierarchy of player's cards, which track what you spend. The more money you spend, the more incentives you get. What level was Medford at?"

"I don't know," Lioy replied.

"Have you heard that they have a seven star level?"

"No."

"Once you are at the highest level, there wouldn't be much incentive to use the card, would there?"

"No."

"Did Mr. Medford have a net loss on his card?"

"Yes."

"Did Ms. Bell have a net loss?"

"Yes."

"What were those losses?"

"From 2003 to 2006, Mr. Medford had a net loss of $73,600 on his card."

Edwards said, "The Harrah's card tracks the amount of money put in play?"

"Yes. It is called 'coin play'."

"Did you see that from 2003 to 2006 Mr. Medford put more than $815,000 cash into play according to Harrah's reports?"

"No. I didn't report that or consider it, only that it was a large amount."

"What stakes machines did he play?"

"The dollar machines."

"Mr. Medford played machines on 225 different days from 2003 to 2006. Did you notice which days of the week he played?"

"No."

"Ms. Bell showed a net loss from 2003 to 2006 of $50,309. Is that right?"

"Yes."

"And she put in play over $600,000 in that time period?"

"Yes."

"In the long run, casinos generally make a profit, isn't that right?"

"Yes."

"From the tracked record, they both lost. So playing without cards, they would also lose over time?"

Lioy replied, "Generally the casino wins."

"In order to prepare documents for this trial, you interviewed Medford, Bell and Sihanouke. Did you interview anyone else?"

"I spoke briefly with the tax preparer for Mr. Medford."

"You are a member of the Association of Certified Fraud Examiners?" Edwards asked.

"Yes. I'm a member of the Charlotte chapter."

"You subscribe to their principles and rules?"

"Yes."

"That organization publishes a magazine and Web site for information, and Joseph Wells is the founder of the organization?"

"Yes."

"Are you familiar with his work?"

"Yes. I have found it useful."

"According to Wells' principles, doesn't a fraud examiner write up a report?"

"Yes, generally."

"Why didn't you do that here?"

"I decided it was not necessary because the primary investigation was done by the government."

"Were you told not to do it?"

"Mr. Lindsay said it was not required to have a report."

"What's your understanding about whether such a report would be filed by the government?"

Lioy offered a complicated answer that failed to answer.

Edwards continued: "You talked about how hard it is to track cash. Would you look at this three page document that shows frequent cash deposits into Bell's and Medford's accounts. Can you explain them?"

"When cash comes in it is hard to know where it comes from. I saw some instances of cash withdrawals at Harrah's then later cash deposits. But I couldn't find that for many of the deposits. With all the days they spent at Harrah's it would be inevitable that some dates would correlate with cash deposits."

"You didn't interview anyone other than Medford, Bell and Sihanouke?"

"No."

"Wouldn't it have been useful to talk to the people who made the cash deposits?"

"I made no effort to talk to anyone else."

Edwards showed Lioy witness statements from the FBI and said, "You recall that at least one person said he made cash deposits. Would you agree that it would be a good thing to talk to people who made these deposits?"

"Yes."

"You noted Medford's frequent ATM withdrawals?"

"Yes, at Harrah's."

"You noted Bell's frequent check cashing at Harrah's?"

"Yes. It was something over fifty checks."

"It was something over $25,000 in $500 checks?"
"Yes."

Following a lengthy lunch break, Edwards continued his questioning and asked Lioy to look over Bell's check record.

"Checks to casinos total $34,000, but you reported $25,000 in checks to Cherokee," Edwards observed.

"I don't recall seeing checks to casinos other than Cherokee."

"Wouldn't checks to other casinos be important if you wanted to account for gambling costs?"

Lioy balked.

Judge Ellis asked, "Wouldn't it be important?"

"Yes."

Edwards asked, "Why haven't they been included in the costs you reported?"

Lioy mumbled and stuttered but made no clear response.

"You analyzed Bell's account. Did you notice that Bell would write checks to Harrah's when she didn't have sufficient funds?"

"She never bounced a check at Harrah's."

Edwards offered images of several checks written by Bell, and corresponding bank statements which showed insufficient balances. "Yet there was always cash deposited just in time to cover Bell's checks?"

"Yes."

"In 2006, Bell showed a larger than ordinary income which included cashing in unused leave hours; then, on December 12, she cashed out $46,000 from her retirement plan. Economically, wouldn't it have made more sense to cash out three weeks later, when she was in a lower tax bracket?"

"Yes."

"Did you analyze Mr. Medford's account from December 2006 into January 2007?"

"Yes. There was a $28,111 check deposited on December 18 and $11,000 deposit on December 22. That was his Buncombe County vacation pay."

Edwards: "With $40,000 in deposits in December, his checking balance was down to $100 by the end of January?"

"Yes. And $246 in savings."

"By February first, his savings account was down to $25. Is that correct?"

"Yes."

"And his checking was overdrawn?"

"Yes. But later in the month the direct deposit of his retirement check had put the account back in the black."

"Did you check to see whether the pattern of frequent cash deposits to their accounts continued or decreased after December?"

"I don't recall, specifically, whether it decreased."

"It decreased dramatically, did it not?"

"I don't recall."

Edwards went over records of the two accounts and Lioy confirmed few cash deposits in either account throughout 2007.

"But they continued to gamble," Edwards noted, observing also that Medford had refinanced his car that year. He went on, "Before lunch you testified that some cash could have come from casino winnings. But the cash deposits dropped off in 2007, could that suggest that the cash was from some other source?"

"Yes."

"In your analysis you show Medford's 2006 income as $180,000 without deducting the $45,000 in charitable contributions or taxes or other expenses. Doesn't that have the effect of showing a great difference between income and losses?"

"Yes."

Edwards handed Lioy a copy of an article from the Association of Fraud Examiners written by Joseph Wells. "The article is titled, 'Follow the Greenback Road," would you read it to yourself?"

After giving Lioy time to read the article, Edwards directed him to one paragraph and asked him to read it aloud.

"Gambling winnings can often be negated by showing that they were not reported."

"How much time did you spend analyzing these records?"

"About forty hours, plus forty to sixty from others in my firm."

At 3:45 p.m., Lindsay stepped up to redirect.

"Mr. Lioy, you used the phrase 'put in play,' does that mean 'put in the machine'?"

"No. Put in play can go up very high without high actual losses."

"Does put in play have anything to do with actual losses?"

"No."

"You reported losses in 2006 of $72,000. Do you recall his winnings?"

"$30,000."

"Was he playing with their money?"

"Yes, with his winnings."

"What if you don't use your card and trigger a win that requires a W2G?"

"It won't pay out until you fill out a form for an attendant."

"Mr. Lioy, was this a big investigation?"

"I've done larger investigations."

"Would you be required to follow up if you interviewed other people?"

"Yes."

"When were you retained?"

"At the end of February or the beginning of March."

"Since that time, have you had other matters you have been working on as well?"

"Yes."

"Did you have sufficient time to analyze this case?"

"No."

"If you saw checks cashed at Harrah's or withdrawals by card at other locations, you can document outgoing funds?"

"Yes."

"If that money was deposited back into the account, how would it show up?"

"As a cash deposit."

"What kind of records does a gambler have to maintain?"

"You have to maintain reasonable records if you want to write off your losses."

"What figures did you use in your analysis?"

"I used net figures from Harrah's documents."

"Regarding Medford's bank account in 2007, what was your understanding about his income?"

"He was no longer sheriff, so there was a change in income."

40: The defense rests

At 3:02, Lindsay called FBI agent Michael Kniffen to the stand who testified that he had been assigned to investigate Medford and had questioned witnesses together with IRS agent Eric Veater. He said he had interviewed Jim Lindsey at the Hobby Shop in Asheville.

"Did you tell him you were investigating Medford and that you were looking at illegal gambling money?"

"To the best of my knowledge, I talked about money orders."

"Did you tell him it was a violation of federal law to tell you lies?"

"I don't recall."

"Did he say anything at all about paying $2,000 cash to Mr. Medford?"

"No."

"Did he say anything about other cash?"

"No."

"How long was that interview?"

"I don't recall. I include the time at the top of my memorandum of contact."

Lindsay directed Kniffen's attention to the memo and he said, "It was thirteen minutes long, on October 24, 2007."

"Did you attempt to cover everything in the case in thirteen minutes?"

"No."

The prosecution had no questions for Kniffen and he stepped down. There was a short delay because the next defense witness didn't appear and Judge Ellis was clearly annoyed. Attorney Victoria Jayne left the courtroom to round up the witness and finally reappeared at 3:12 p.m. with Jerry Biddix in tow.

Biddix was a 63-year-old, lifelong Woodfin resident, was married to a Henderson County native, had been self-employed for many years and had known Medford a long time. "I have a picture of us in third grade," he said. They had maintained close contact through the years, though less during the time he was sheriff.

"Do you have an opinion about his truthfulness?"

"Yes. He is very truthful."

"Has your opinion ever changed?"

"No."

The prosecution had no questions.

At 3:16, Reverend Bob Carter was called. He said he had lived in the area since 1987 and was currently pastor at the Missionary Baptist Church in Swannanoa. "I was chaplain, on the chaplain corps, for the Buncombe County Sheriff's Department for eight years. I met Sheriff Medford in 1998. I tried to be up there a couple of days a week for an hour or so."

Under Lindsay's questioning, he said he had maintained steady contact with Medford during that time, including outside contact at a funeral and offering counseling of one inmate. "I conducted a funeral for his sister-in-law."

"Have you developed an opinion as to his truthfulness?"

"Yes. He's always been true to me, as far as I know."

No questions from the prosecutors.

At 3:21, Charles David Hazelett took the stand. He said he was a retired Asheville Police Department officer, having spent 26 years on the force. He said he met Medford in 1980 when he was an investigator, and that they had worked together for five or six years.

"Have you maintained contact?"

"Since I retired in April, 2006, I have been to see him. I've known him for 28 years."

"In the years you have known him, have you developed an opinion about his character or truthfulness?"

"Yes. He is truthful."

"Has anything changed your opinion?"

"No."

Lindsay told the court he had no more witnesses.

Following a thirty minute recess, at 4:07 p.m., Penland attorney Paul Bidwell called the first of four witnesses, Reverend Rex Collins.

Collins testified that he had been a chaplain for sixty years and had known Penland for eight. "He and my brother had a business on Merrimon Avenue. I knew his wife, Nancy, and have had some social contact over the years."

"Have you formed an opinion as to whether Mr. Penland is a law abiding person?"

"Yes. He is law abiding."

Assistant U.S. Attorney Ellis asked Collins, "Are you aware that Mr. Penland has a D.U.I. conviction?"

"Yes."

"Does that change your opinion about him being law abiding?"

"No."

It was 4:12 when Judy Jones took the stand. She told Bidwell she had been a lifelong resident of Buncombe County, "Except for ten years in Alaska and eight in Fort Lauderdale." She had retired from a bank job in Florida, and said she had known Penland since 2000. "I was referred to him through the Council on Aging. My father was in a nursing home and having problems and I was referred to Mr. Penland." She said it was her understanding that he was a retired deputy.

"I continued to have contact with him over the years, perhaps once a week. We had lunch or dinner once in a while."

Had she observed Penland in interaction with other people? "Yes. A lot of people would come up to talk to him."

Had she ever traveled with him? "Yes, to buy tires for my motor home, and to buy a motor home. I have traveled with him thirty or forty times in the last seven years."

Did they have friends or acquaintances in common? "Yes."

"Do you have an opinion whether Guy Penland is a law abiding citizen?"

"Yes."

"What is that opinion?"

"He is a law abiding person."

"Do you find him to be an intelligent person?"

"Yes, about things like tires for a motor home. He took me to Greenwood, South Carolina last April or May to buy tires. Everywhere we went, people knew him and would interact with him."

At 4:21, Penland inadvertently bolstered the government's case by calling Cynthia Roberts to testify.

Roberts said she was the manager of City Transmission Service, a business she owned with her father, Tony Roberts. She said she had known Penland as a family friend for about seventeen years. "He did business with us. I saw him working out at the mall, at the Jewel Box, maybe twenty years ago."

Roberts said she knew who Bobby Medford was, but had never met him, although her father "knew him from thirty years back."

Had there ever been financial contributions from her business to Medford? "Yes. We contributed to his campaigns. We sponsored teams at golf tournaments. We didn't play golf, but my uncle and his friends would play."

Were any of those teams involved in the video poker industry? "No."

Roberts said she would learn of upcoming tournaments when Penland or Harrison dropped off a flyer.

Had they ever *not* sponsored golf? "Probably."

Had she ever felt pressured to sponsor it? "No."

Had she formed an opinion as to whether Mr. Penland is a law abiding person? "To the best of my knowledge, he is a law abiding person."

Bidwell's mistake came to light when Corey Ellis cross-examined Roberts. He asked, "When investigators came to you, you gave them records of over one dozen checks written to political campaigns, is that correct?"

"Yes."

"Did you think that those moneys were going to his election campaign?"

"Yes sir."

Ellis showed her a check written in 2004. "Do you know if there was an election in 2004?"

"No."

"How many money orders did you supply to Medford's campaign?"

"None. We always wrote checks."

"Can you explain how a money order from Tony Roberts went to Medford's campaign?"

"No, I cannot."

Bidwell next called FBI Special Agent Michael Dean McNeely to the stand.

"Did you interview Tracy Bridges?"

"Yes, at Tracy's apartment."

"Who was with you?"

"Agents Daly and Veater."

"How long was that interview?

"We interviewed him from around 8 or 8:30 in the morning until afternoon. 4:30 or 5 p.m."

"Did Tracy Bridges make any statement to you about someone named Jerry who delivered money to Lieutenant Davis?"

"Yes. He described a tall, white male with a beard who delivered money to Davis."

With that, McNeely was dismissed and the jury was sent out for a brief recess while Judge Tim Ellis interviewed Penland who had declined to testify in his own behalf.

Penland said that he was 77 years old and able to write but not read too well, though he had completed his GED at age 66.

"Are you taking any drug that affects your ability to see, hear or understand things?"

"No."

"How do you feel today?"

"Nervous and scared."

"Have you discussed your right to testify with Mr. Bidwell?"

"Yes."

"Are you generally satisfied with his counsel?"

"Yes."

Satisfied that Penland had knowingly rejected his right to speak, Ellis recalled the jury at 4:43 and offered them instruction on the closing arguments they would hear the next day.

"That completes the taking of evidence," he told the jurors. "I want to remind you that closing arguments are not evidence. Counsel is entitled to tell you what the evidence was, but you are the judges." He then dismissed the jury.

Judge Ellis next inquired how long closing arguments would take.

Speaking for the prosecution, Corey Ellis said "Less than an hour and a half."

Judge Ellis: "Mr. Lindsay, can you do yours in an hour?"

"I think so."

"Mr. Bidwell?"

"I think under an hour," Bidwell replied.

"So the closing arguments will take three and a half hours. My instructions to the jury will take a while. I may take one or one and a half hours.

"We will begin at 11 a.m. tomorrow," he told the jurors, and excused them at 4:48 p.m.

Turning to counsel, Judge Ellis said, "We must finish with the exhibits [which would be sent into the jury room during deliberation] this afternoon. Show each other your exhibits and agree. You will not receive my jury instructions until 9 a.m. tomorrow.

"I will give the jurors two verdict forms with all of the charges listed. I do not give jurors the indictments, because jurors too often mistake an indictment for evidence. I don't know what electronic evidence arrangement there is for deliberation."

Assistant U.S. Attorney Edwards explained that electronic evidence would only be available in the court room, and the judge ruled, "If the jury wants to consider electronic evidence, they will reconvene here to listen. It will not be public, and they will have to be instructed in how to turn it on and off because no one else will be permitted to be present."

Lindsay then requested that "Medford be allowed to see Bell, now that evidence and testimony is over."

The judge said he would consider the matter and ended the session at 5 p.m.

41: The decanter of insanity?

Having received Judge Ellis' proposed jury instructions at 9 a.m. on May 13, both sides were ready with minor objections when he entered the court room an hour later. The objections amounted to relatively simple changes of wording and were resolved in short order.

When agreement had been reached, Ellis said, "Once there have been closing arguments and my instructions have been given to the jury, I will dismiss the alternative juror who must nonetheless remain available and silent concerning the case. When the jurors have reached a verdict, the deputy will ask if a verdict has been reached, and if so, will deliver the form to me. I will read the form to look for formal errors, that is, a failure to mark the form accurately. Then the deputy clerk will read it aloud."

At that point, the judge declared a ten minute recess, to reconvene at 11 a.m.

At 11:08 the jury was in and the judge returned at 11:10.

Assistant U.S. Attorney Ellis rose to deliver the government's closing argument. [Although I have done my best to accurately reflect his and others' concluding comments, the delivery was fast enough that my note-taking couldn't quite keep up. So my rendition is necessarily choppier than the various attorneys' often eloquent oration.]

Ellis said, "Johnny Harrison was placed in charge of video poker registration by Bobby Medford. You have read the evidence and read the plea agreements. There are consequences for failing to tell the truth.

"Harrison said he cashed checks at Bi-Lo and George's Deli, starting in 2002. Medford cashed his own checks there starting in 2003. Remember there was one check in the amount of $2,100 that year.

"There's a pattern here of strange behavior at the very best."

"Jerry Pennington was charged with numerous gambling charges and made a plea agreement for community service.

"Judge Bridges, in Superior Court in Cleveland County signed an order to move that service to Buncombe County under the direction of Guy Penland.

"Judge Bridges thought Penland was a Captain. Somehow, the Buncombe County Sheriff's Department engineered this fraud on the court.

"Recall that Linda Clontz called Medford concerning Pennington's service record. That conversation took place in 2003. Recall that Ms. Clontz told you, 'He placated me," about fraud in his department.

"There was the tag run in May 2005 by Penland.

"It is insulting to your intelligence and common sense to claim that Penland was not working for the county sheriff.

"You heard that Pennington paid Penland $10,000 for one hundred stickers and that Pennington had a badge and Medford's card with his pager number hand written on the back. He surveilled a grand jury with Penland and Penland transported Pennington around to meet people.

"You learned that money in excess of $150,000 went from Henderson Amusement to the Buncombe County Sheriff's Department.

"Jackie Shepherd said he helped Medford get into office because Charlie Long threatened his gambling business.

"You heard from Alvin Ledford, a career gambler and close friend of Papa Jack O'Leary. It was kind of funny that he was forced to put video poker machines in a gambling establishment, against his will. And you heard that he met with Medford at the Waffle House.

"You heard from a waitress at that Waffle House who confirmed their meeting. What's her motivation to tell you anything other than the truth?

"You heard that when Alam wanted to switch machines he was subject to direct extortion. He wrote a $200 check for a golf tournament and Medford wanted and got another $500. There was his $1,000 check on the same date as issuance of a special deputy card for Alam. And there was the $6,000 that bought him the right to switch machines. That deal was confirmed by Jim Lindsey.

"It took Lindsey three installments to pay his $6,000.

"You heard that Medford had rules about moving machines, but those rules were bent for $12,000.

"Demetre Theodossis and Dennis Theodossis corroborated each other's testimony, together with corroborating phone and bank records. How could they possibly have contrived those records?

"You heard that Ron Honeycutt was on Medford's campaign committee and ran machines in his business, as well.

"All of the witnesses you heard here, including Tracy Bridges, were chosen by Mr. Medford and his associates.

"You saw hand written notes from Bridges that corroborated his money order purchases.

"You heard from Frank Orr about more money laundering and cashing of checks.

"You saw a video of John Parker, in Rutherford County, with Henderson talking about payments to Medford.

"You learned that the use of an interstate carrier, UPS, in the course of a conspiracy constitutes mail fraud.

"Mr. Medford aided and abetted the conspiracy by employing his associates, by letting them work at the department, by providing them with an office.

"The argument that the witnesses in this case conspired to come up with this story is laughable. One would have to drink from the decanter of insanity to believe that argument.

"You heard about $2,400 paid for a dog. Mr. Medford sat there and testified that the money came from other sources and it was just a coincidence that Davis' note mentions a dog associated with the same amount.

"You heard that Mr. Medford took out loans for cash in order to deposit it in his account. Does that comport with your common sense? His statements about where the cash came from are not credible.

"You also recall that Mr. Lioy was not able to answer questions about where the money in Medford's account came from.

"The truth is hard to keep out. All of these circumstances point to no other conclusion than that the defendants are guilty of extortion under the color of law, that they prostituted the office of sheriff.

"Considering all of the evidence you have heard here, I believe you will conclude beyond a reasonable doubt that these two men are guilty."

When Ellis finished, Judge Ellis excused the jury for a lunch break.

Defense attorney Stephen Lindsay began his closing argument by extolling his client's bona fides.

"Bobby Medford is a man who was born here. He is a man of the people. He was elected three times as sheriff of this county. He is a man who would see anyone, he would answer every phone call, he would go out in the middle of the night.

"I won't focus on why you shouldn't accept their case, but I want to spend this hour talking about why Mr. Bobby Medford is innocent.

"We need to back out and look at a larger context."

Lindsay paused, then said, "On May 15, 2005 Mr. Penland received a call from Pennington to run a tag." He continued, "But Mr. Medford received a call from Rick Schwein who told him to do nothing.

"He removed Penland from video poker registrations and moved him to another position. He kept him in the dark about the investigation.

"Has Mr. Medford ever had a single write-up? Has there ever been any suspicious behavior? Has he ever been anything other than a good, hard-working, decent law enforcement officer?

"There is a bigger picture here than just the small office in charge of video poker. There were 325 employees working in a very large department." Lindsay went on to describe the duties and functions of the sheriff's office.

"Video poker registration was not high on the list of his responsibilities. And the 2000 law mandated registration but it did not impose additional enforcement responsibilities on the sheriff.

"Recall the training that was put on when the new law went into effect. Mr. Medford did not attend that training. Fraser and Goforth attended that training and reported, briefly, to Medford about what they learned.

"There is no evidence that any sticker was ordered by Bobby Medford or delivered to Bobby Medford.

"Recall that there was no budget for that department. The General Assembly never came through with funds.

"When Julie Kepple stepped in to organize the records, she was not restricted in her work. And when an editor wanted to see the records, Bobby Medford co-operated." [This was the moment during the trial when I came closest to shouting "Liar! Liar!" Medford had stonewalled me until I filed a formal request under the state's open records law, and then delayed cooperation until Kepple cleaned things up, as she had testified earlier in the trial.]

Lindsay continued, "Then he asked Jerry Miller to investigate the matter, and Miller told Medford he could get them out.

"Bobby Medford was an investigator for years. When the FBI told him to do nothing to jeopardize their investigation, he cooperated. He knew Penland was involved with Pennington.

"How would someone act if he was part of that whole thing? You've been told that extortion increased after 2005. Does that make sense? Would he increase his demands, or slink back into the darkness?

"We are told that as the investigation was going on, he was going to parking lots, churches, restaurants and having people come to his office to make pay-offs.

"You saw records of his bank account that showed that he began receiving direct deposit of his paycheck six months before he left office. If you were guilty, would you continue to make cash deposits?"

Lindsay then moved to undermine the credibility of the government's witnesses.

"Recall that Mr. Medford's name was nowhere on Anna Deaton's records. It was just ex-ex-ex-ex or sometimes ex-ex-ex. Pennington was the only person who knew the names represented by his codes.

"But you heard that Pennington lied to Linda Clontz. He lied to police officers, to a judge, and on affidavits he said he knew were false. And that's when he had a lot to gain financially. Now he is facing imprisonment.

"Consider Imran Alam. According to Pennington, most stores were paid 50/50 or 60/40, but Alam was greedy. He wanted an 80/20 split. Alam thinks he could be deported to Pakistan, and he's building a multi-million dollar home here in Asheville. He has a lot to lose.

"Look at the $6,000 counter check he says he cashed. It appears not to be signed. Was it cashed?

"And he said he put $3,000 in each of two envelopes Why would it be necessary for Alam and Medford to meet face-to-face? There was no need to meet.

"You heard testimony from Mr. Ledford, including the fact that the rest of his family was not charged with any crime. They all go free.

"And the waitress from the Waffle House said she had seen Medford meet with people in the parking lot, but she couldn't identify them.

"You heard from Jim Lindsey whose son had a gambling business. He pled guilty as long as the government did not charge his son.

"You heard from Charles McBennett, Jr., who wanted to help his father who could possibly go to prison. There is pressure on the son to save the father.

"When Mr. Theodossis first talked to authorities, he said nothing about paying money to the sheriff. His story changed.

"You heard from Jackie Shepherd that he loaned money to Mr. Medford. And you saw checks written by Medford to pay him back."

Now Lindsay made a foray into obfuscating the transaction concerning the dog, adding up checks written at widely different dates. "You heard about $2,400 next to the word 'dog' on a note pad, but you heard Mr. Medford testify that when he borrowed money, he always paid it back. Recall a check from Medford to his campaign for $1,700. In fact if you look at all of the checks from Mr. Medford to his campaign, you will see that they total $2,500."

To conclude, Lindsay painted a sad portrait of his client. "Mr. Medford spent six hours on the witness stand. He tried to give you information about his life and this case.

"He told you he gambled and gambled a lot. He mentioned his illness and not wanting to run for reelection. It is no coincidence that he began to go to Harrah's a lot, and to other places to gamble. He was looking for relief.

"You heard that Tracy Bridges kept a lot of records, but when he got into trouble, he didn't go first to the FBI. He went to Van Duncan, who had no authority.

"Mr. Medford is an old, sick, tired man who did not want his job and did the best he could as long as he was there. He was kept in the dark by others so they could use his name.

"Bobby Medford is an innocent man."

Stephen Lindsay sounded so utterly sincere at the end, that, absent two weeks of testimony and several years of reporting, I might have wanted to believe him.

When Paul Bidwell rose to deliver his closing argument, he draped himself in populism. "Your job here is to stand as a power check against the awesome power of government. The government is good at accusation, but they can get it wrong.

"Guy Penland is a gentle old man. I am not here claiming that he is gullible, though he may be. I will show you that when the government is going after big fish, it will change the lives of people like Guy Penland.

"He is guilty of trusting friends and he was interested in making a little money on the side. He is guilty of associating with Pennington, Harrison, Davis and Medford. Mr. Penland and Mr. Medford are being tried together, but they are separate people.

"The government has argued that registrations were for sale, that stickers were ordered and not used appropriately. But those stickers are not legally mandated.

"The government says you should be shocked, horrified and disgusted that Guy Penland helped Pennington find locations. Mr. Penland did not get his money under color of official capacity. He was a volunteer. The evidence shows that Guy Penland was paid because he knows people outside of the sheriff's department. Pennington had access to people through Guy Penland. There were no more cold calls.

"Jerry Pennington is a consummate salesman and his sales pitch continued here in the courtroom.

"Pennington called my client one day and said, 'Someone is following my girlfriend. Can you check the tag?' On another occasion he said, 'Someone is scaring my employees.' The tags came back 'Not on file.'

"Guy Penland did that as a friend, not as part of Pennington's business.

"Was Guy Penland used? Of course he was.

"You were told that Penland used his authority to get Pennington out of community service. Guy Penland had nothing to do with getting his name on Pennington's community service. And there is no evidence that serving out seventy-five hours of community service would have had any effect on Pennington's ability to organize gambling.

"Pennington got Penland to help watch who was going in and out during Grand Jury hearings, but he got the day wrong. They didn't use the information to change anything Pennington was doing.

"Pennington said he paid $10,000 for one hundred stickers and Pennington had stickers in his car when he was stopped on July 10, 2002. The government offered documents from Pennington, but you saw that he forgot to put the $10,000 expense for one hundred stickers on his books.

"You heard from Harrison that when stickers were given out without registration papers, he made sure he got registration papers from the machine owners. He said that Guy Penland was signing registrations at one time, but that when he was told not to, Guy Penland stopped.

"You heard that Imran Alam only leased stores until he got video poker machines at which time he began to buy locations. Alam wanted to sponsor a golf team with less money than he was asked for and wrote a check for $200. That's why Guy Penland was upset and asked for more money.

"You heard from Mr. McBennett, an admitted drug addict, who said he came in and paid for a list of machine locations that included locations without machines. There is no evidence that my client charged money for a list he obtained from the sheriff's department.

"Now consider the raids. Demetre Theodossis, Butch Davis and others. It sounds terrible, but there is no evidence that Guy Penland got money he wasn't entitled to.

"Consider the golf tournaments. In politics, if you want something done you support a candidate for your own self interest. We all know that. Who was in charge of those tournaments? Butch Davis, Johnny Harrison, George Stewart and Frank Orr. Maybe there were violations of election reporting laws, but they don't amount to conspiracy or extortion.

"Recall the innumerable bad things that happened that were not charged in this case. You may find that things were done wrong, but that these men are not guilty.

"There is no evidence that Guy used any official capacity. Yes, he wore those shirts and captain's bars, but there is no evidence that he used that to gain money.

"Recall that not every machine that came into the county was illegal, and not every use was illegal.

"There has to be specific evidence that Guy Penland knew the machines were being used illegally. Pennington said Guy thought the machines were being used legally, then, later, that some of the machines *may* be used illegally.

"There is a problem with the first charge. The sheriff's department treated all machines the same. There is no evidence that Guy Penland did anything different for Pennington.

"On charge number two, the government failed to prove that it had anything to do with Guy Penland.

"On the mail fraud charges, numbers three through seven, there is no evidence that Guy Penland ordered stickers.

"There is evidence that Guy did get money from Pennington, but there is no evidence that it was illegal for him to have secondary employment.

"As for the charge of money laundering, there is no evidence that Guy Penland had anything to do with obtaining money orders.

"You heard about a badge. That badge was a gift between friends.

"What you have seen here is an example of the awesome power of government to make accusations against the innocent. You have seen the government attempt to use shock and awe to overwhelm the truth in this case."

Bidwell suggested that the government witnesses had every reason to offer helpful testimony. "Maybe you're on trial," he said, "how will your testimony affect your sentence?"

"I believe that if you look carefully at the evidence presented in this case, you will see that Guy Penland is an innocent man."

Following a short recess, and before the jury returned to its box, Assistant U.S. Attorney Edwards addressed Judge Ellis. "I want to correct Mr. Bidwell's statement about the indictment of witnesses in this trial. There was an improper statement from Mr. Bidwell. He said, 'Maybe you're on trial,' and suggested to the jury that the witnesses in this case were also on trial concerning their testimony. That is not the case."

Ellis responded: "It is perfectly appropriate that people testify hoping to get government cooperation, but it is ultimately up to me as to whether and how much benefit there will be to the witness during sentencing." Ellis indicated that he would make that clear to the jurors as part of his instructions. "And I will tell the jury that it appropriate for counsel to meet with and interview witnesses preparatory to their testimony."

When the jury returned, Edwards commenced his closing arguments.

"The purpose of my argument is rebuttal, to address issues raised by the defendants in their closing.

"Mr. Bidwell talked about what a nice guy Mr. Penland is, and what a shame it is that he was included here. The shame is what Penland did. No one in the government made him do what he did.

"It is up to the judge and judge alone to tell you the elements of the law. If the law were what Mr. Bidwell said it was, then Mr. Penland is not guilty. But he is charged with 'conspiring under color of law.' What they agreed to do was that people were extorted because of the official position of *at least one* member of the conspiracy.

"There was an agreement, and Guy Penland knew what was going on. Holding himself out as a captain was wrong, but it is not necessary for him to be found guilty of conspiring with others who held office.

"If the conspiracy affected interstate commerce, even if only a little bit, the law is applicable.

"Mr. Bidwell said that on Count One and Count

Two, there wasn't any evidence that Penland knew the machines were run illegally, that, in fact, some machines were run legally.

"This recalls a case a few years ago in which an Assistant Secretary of the Air Force was found guilty of accepting bribes when he decided to award a contract for construction of super tankers. It is not illegal to build super tankers, but is against the law to pay or accept bribes that affect federal contracts. It doesn't matter if some machines were run legally, what matters is the question of whether bribes were paid.

"Concerning conspiracy to commit mail fraud, there is no need for Penland to be an officer or to order stickers himself if he was part of the conspiracy.

"There was a scheme to defraud the citizens of Buncombe County of their right to the honest services of a public official. Mr. Medford was a public official who deprived the citizens of his services. Mr. Penland was a member of the scheme and the mailings themselves do not have to be illegal. Just the use of the mail in furtherance of illegal activity.

"Mr. Bidwell said that the stickers were not mandated by law, but people on the ground thought they were legal, that they were required.

"Mr. Lindsay said that Mr. Medford didn't order the stickers and didn't receive the stickers, but aiding and abetting a crime is knowing that it is happening and trying to make it succeed. Mr. Medford knew about the stickers, that they were issued by his office. He knew that they had to be ordered and shipped from somewhere.

"Mr. Bidwell said that Mr. Penland had nothing to do with the money orders, but the conspiracy for money laundering encompasses not just the money orders, but the cashing of checks.

"Mr. Penland knowingly joined in the conspiracy, this was an agreement that he knew about and entered. money laundering law is to make sure that crime does not pay. Sometimes cash cannot be used due to pesky voting laws. You can't put in over $100 in cash. Mr. Penland knew there was a scheme to launder the money for the campaign.

"As for the conspiracy to conduct illegal gambling which involved over five people, in this case there were at least hundreds of people involved. And there was a conspiracy to obstruct state and local law enforcement by a state official. Mr. Medford was the one running the conspiracy.

"There were approximately 350 machines in Buncombe County when the law went into effect and Medford's office ordered 1,350 stickers.

"Mr. Bidwell suggested that Mr. Penland didn't know what he was doing when he sold a list of names for $5,000, when he solicited golf contributions and so forth. But Mr. Penland didn't have to receive specific money to be guilty, he just had to be part of the conspiracy and to receive money due to his position in the conspiracy.

"As for Mr. Bidwell's suggestion that we are using 'shock and awe' to convince you of his client's guilt, we are not appealing to your emotions. We want you to have the facts and the law and let you decide."

Edwards then moved on to Medford's defense.

"Mr. Lindsay made his argument about two phone calls made in May of 2005. He said that Imran Alam switched machine operators in April of 2005, a month before the phone calls and payments. But the timing doesn't show that the payment and switch were not connected, rather it suggests that Alam was satisfied with the outcome.

"Mr. Lindsay also asked, 'If Medford knew about the federal investigation, would he continue to violate the law?'

"Think back. Mr. Medford was told that the investigation was in Cleveland County, not Buncombe.

"Mr. Lindsay suggested that his client must be

innocent because he obeyed a request from the FBI, but you heard that Medford was spitting mad and that Guy Penland finally admitted he had run a tag.

"You heard that Mr. Medford was making a lot of money breaking the law. And what was his reaction to learning of the investigation going on? He beat a path to Harrah's. What we see here is arrogance, power, greed and, I would submit, addiction. His idea of 'seeing the world' was sitting on a stool at Harrah's, staring at a machine.

"Some Pennington or Deaton records are missing, but the records that are there consistently show G, GY, ex-ex-ex-ex and ex-ex-ex. The records are kind of loosey-goosey. Mr. Lindsay said Pennington could have attached the name of any sheriff to those exes. But all the other names on that list are Buncombe people.

"The tape confirms the identity of those people when Mr. Henderson was talking to the sheriff in Rutherford County.

"Note that gambling at Harrah's is not a crime, but we wanted to show where the money was going.

"And we showed that the criminal activity ended when Mr. Medford left office, which makes sense because nobody bribes an ex-sheriff.

"All of the rights we enjoy are due to the rule of law. Mr. Medford prostituted himself and his office, and it is only right that he be found guilty for his criminal activities."

42: And so, to the jury

Following Edwards' closing, Judge Ellis delivered instructions to the jurors. He said that in order to be found guilty, the defendant had to knowingly and willfully commit a crime. "That is, know what he was doing, and then, knowingly commit the crime anyway." He said that a good motive was not a defense, except insofar as to determine the intent or state of mind of the defendant. "Intent is not a sufficient defense, however. You can only consider statements and evidence in determining guilt or innocence.

"Your instruction package will include the charges in this case, a short version of the indictment.

"In Count One, the defendants are charged with criminal conspiracy, an agreement or mutual understanding between two or more people that they and perhaps others will violate the law. It is not necessary that there be a written contract or express oral agreement. It is not necessary that all of the people named were involved in all of the acts.

"The defendants must have known the purpose, but it is not necessary that they be a part of the conspiracy at the beginning, nor participate in everything. It is not necessary that a conspirator be a major player.

"To be guilty, there must be at least one overt act by one member of the conspiracy.

"The government need not prove that the members of a conspiracy were successful in their scheme, only that they conspired to break the law.

"The evidence must establish that the conspiracy was knowingly formed and that two or more participants were knowing members.

"In Count Two, the defendants are charged with conspiracy to commit mail fraud. The fraud in this case is to take money to which the defendants are not entitled and the conspiracy is that two or more persons entered into a scheme to obtain money through color of office. The scheme is the intent to defraud, cause financial loss and deprive the public of its right to honest services.

"It is the obligation of a public servant to provide honest services. It is not necessary to prove that the scheme was successful.

"Each use of the mail or United Parcel Service may be deemed a separate violation. There is no need to prove that any item actually travelled out of state in order to be guilty of use of an interstate carrier." Ellis further explained that it is not necessary that the item mailed is itself illegal, if it is used to further a conspiracy.

"Counts Three through Seven are individual mail fraud counts which state that on or about five specific dates, the defendants knowingly received items shipped from the North Carolina Sheriff's Association in Raleigh. Under the law, it is a crime to use the mail or an interstate carrier in a scheme to defraud."

Ellis went on to say, "The essential elements of mail fraud are, one, that the defendants knowingly devised and participated in the fraud; two, that they did so knowingly and with intent; three, that a mail system was used; and four, that they did some act in furtherance of the conspiracy. If an official acts for his own benefit, it doesn't matter what particular effect it has. Aiding and abetting counts as well."

"Count Eight is conspiracy to launder money. That involves a financial transaction designed to disguise the proceeds of some form of unlawful activity and conspiracy to do the same. It involves: one, that two or more people knowingly entered into a conspiracy for money laundering with intent to disguise unlawful activity; two, that the defendant knowingly became a member of the conspiracy; three, that the defendant knew it was illegal; and four, that the defendant knew there was an attempt to disguise the source of funds.

"Proof of action is not necessary as long as the defendant was part of the conspiracy. The laundering occurs when there is an investment or transfer from an original source into legitimate form to disguise the source."

"Count Ten involves conspiracy to obstruct enforcement to facilitate illegal gambling. In order to establish guilt: one, two or more people must have knowingly participated; two, the defendants must have knowingly become members of the scheme; three, one of the conspirators must have held an official office; and four, one or more of the conspirators owned or operated an illegal gambling business.

"The illegal gambling business must have included at least five persons and continued for at least thirty days and involved at least $2,000 on any one day.

"Count Eleven is conspiracy to conduct an illegal gambling business. To establish guilt: 1. Two or more persons must conspire for the purpose of gambling; 2. they must knowingly participate in the scheme; 3. One person must have committed an act in furtherance of the scheme; 4. Five or more persons must have participated; and 5. The gambling activity must have include at least five persons and continued for at least thirty days."

In conclusion the judge pointed out that "Your verdict must be unanimous, but you must each decide for yourself based on the evidence presented. You may change your mind. Do not sacrifice your considered opinion for the reason of arriving at agreement."

At 5:57 p.m. Ellis called counsel forward for a bench conference. Shortly thereafter, he excused the alternative juror, admonishing him to remain mum about the proceedings until the end of the trial. The jurors then repaired to the jury room and quickly announced that they preferred to begin deliberation the following morning. Ellis said the trial would resume the next morning.

The jury commenced its work at 9 a.m. Wednesday, May 14 and reached a verdict in less than two hours. Just after 11 a.m., Judge Ellis returned to the bench and explained that he would ask the foreperson whether a verdict had been reached, then read the verdict to determine whether the forms had been filled out accurately. He would then have the deputy clerk publish the verdict by reading it aloud to the court. "If the verdict is guilty, I will instruct the jury to step out while I consider a waiver of forfeiture hearing."

At 11:15 the jury returned and the clerk inquired as to whether they had reached a verdict.

"Yes, mam, we have." The jury had found both defendants guilty on all counts and the judge polled the jurors individually to ascertain that all were in agreement.

In the gallery Guy Penland's daughter was audibly sobbing.

Ellis sent the jurors out while he discussed the forfeiture hearing. "Defense counsel has the right to ask for a jury trial on the matter of forfeiture," he said, and called for a fifteen minute recess while the attorneys considered that move. When the judge returned, Lindsay requested that the jurors deliberate on forfeiture and there was discussion of the details.

The jury was recalled. Judge Ellis told the jurors that according to the indictment, certain sums of money were be forfeited in the case of a guilty verdict. He said the sums included: First, all property involved in the violation of the law; and second, all property received as proceeds of the violation if that first property was unavailable.

He stipulated that the total dollar amount received from the crimes was $287,776 according to evidence presented during the trial. "Your findings of guilt are binding on you. You may not revisit your decision. What you must decide is if the property of the defendants represents the proceeds of the crime.

Edwards presented the government case. "You have already found the defendants guilty beyond a reasonable doubt. Now you will use a lower standard, that is, whether the preponderance of the evidence suggests that the defendants profited from their crimes. The reason for stipulating forfeiture is to ensure that crime does not pay."

He went on to list the sums paid to defendants in the case by: Pennington, $152,000; Shepherd, $1,000; McBennett, $10,000; Alam, $7,000; Ledford, $26,000; Demetre Theodossis, $800; Dennis Theodossis, $500; and Lindsey, $7,500. Edwards said that the golf tournaments from 2003 through 2006 netted at least $80,000 and argued that the resulting $287,000+ total was a conservative estimate of defendants' receipts. The figure, he said, was calculated by the Grand Jury which indicted the four conspirators.

"Under the law, it is not the jury's duty to divvy up the gains among the conspirators. You need to find out how much the conspiracy netted and decide if by a preponderance of evidence that through the criminal activity of these defendants they profited."

Stephen Lindsay then rose to challenge the figures. "Did you believe Jerry Pennington? Is it possible that he double-dipped, recording payments that were never actually made? Was Charles McBennett telling the truth about his payments? Was Alvin Ledford? Did he give all he said he gave? What about Mr. Theodossis, did he actually give all he said he did? How about Jim Lindsey?

"Recall also that there were a number of legitimate people playing in those golf tournaments. Do their fees count as part of criminal activity?

"Finally, it becomes a matter of mathematics. You have to ask whether these numbers really add up."

Paul Bidwell chose to make the point that the proceeds, if any, had not been found. "The purpose of this proceeding, as Mr. Edwards said, is to ensure that crime does not pay. But it is likely that all of the money involved in this matter is gone. There were no raids and no seizures of cash.

"And you will need to cull out duplicate payments, for instance those of Mr. Lindsey, which seem to appear twice in these figures."

Edward then rebutted, saying, "The question is not 'is the money out there?' or if we can collect it. Collecting it is our problem.

"What you need to worry about is gross proceeds. The $287,776 figure the government seeks is well within the conservative estimate we have made.

Judge Ellis then instructed the jury that they were to determine if the amount received by the defendants directly or indirectly amounted to $287,776. "You found them guilty. One item on the verdict sheet asks if you find that amount to be accurate. If you answer 'yes,' you mark 'alleged.' If answer 'no,' you go to the second page and fill in the amount you think is correct. You are to determine the gross proceeds. You do not determine who received what.

"Concerning the burden of proof, all of my previous instructions apply except the burden. In this case a preponderance of evidence is sufficient. That is, it it more likely so than not. You do not have to decide this matter beyond a reasonable doubt."

The jury was sent out to deliberate and a recess was called at 12:15 p.m.

Following the recess, the judge explained to Medford and Penland that he would next order a pre-sentence report and that they were to cooperate fully with the probation officers who solicited information from them, though they could have counsel present. He said the sentencing would occur not sooner than four to six weeks from the conclusion of the trial.

Edwards then argued that the pair should be incarcerated pending sentencing, given that the risk of flight was likely to be greater now that they faced certain imprisonment.

Lindsay argued that they should be permitted to continue as before, with GPS monitoring ankle bracelets. "There have been no violations during this time."

Bidwell reiterated that argument.

Ellis opined, "The question is whether now that they have been convicted of ten counts they are at risk of flight. There could also be a continued danger to the community, but that was true before and they were released with the GPS monitoring. Now the landscape has changed. There is near certainty that the defendants will be incarcerated and there is an increased incentive to flee. However, I deem that likelihood to be remote and so I will rule that the current monitoring is sufficient."

Lindsay asked if Medford would be free to return to his apartment, rather than continue to stay with his sister and brother-in-law. The judge said, "There is one problem with that," and called for a bench conference with counsel.

One could only infer that Medford's girlfriend, Judi Bell, was either the subject of an ongoing in-vestigation or likely to be called in some related case as a witness.

No public decision was issued concerning Medford's residence.

At 12:45 p.m. the jury announced that it had reached a verdict. They agreed with the amount stipulated by the government and the judge ordered that the forfeiture be added to the record.

Judge Ellis then thanked the jury for their service, stressing that jury service was one of the cornerstones of liberty in our nation. He told them they were free to discuss the case with anyone they chose, but cautioned them that circumspection was likely to be the wiser course. He particularly admonished them about discussing what had gone on in the jury room. "You owe a duty to each other to keep confidential what went on during deliberation."

He then addressed all present. "I would like to express my view that all parties were fully and effectively represented here. I appreciate the cooperation of counsel. This is obviously a case of great significance to this community. These defendants deprived the community of their honest services.

"I would add that this doesn't indicate that there are not other, good, decent sheriff's office employees. There are lots of good deputies out there doing their jobs honestly."

"The court stands adjourned."

43: The sentencing

Former Buncombe County Sheriff Bobby Lee Medford was sentenced to fifteen years in prison on Monday, Oct. 6, 2008, his incarceration to be followed by three years supervised probation. The sentence included eight fifteen-year sentences and two five-year sentences, to be served concurrently. Judge Tim Ellis noted, "There is no parole in the Federal prison system, but if he behaves himself, he may only serve eighty-five percent of that sentence." After some quick figuring, Ellis indicated that Medford would definitely be behind bars for twelve and a half years.

Defense attorneys Jayne and Lindsay then argued that Medford should be permitted to undergo minor surgery scheduled for Oct. 13, followed by a ten day convalescence before reporting for incarceration. Ellis said he would consider the procedure, evaluating the ability of the federal system to undertake the treatment, and weighing the reputation of Medford's doctor, Dr. Maxwell. Ellis noted, "There was testimony [during the trial] about Dr. Maxwell's over-prescription of oxycontin. That concerns me."

Assistant U.S. Attorney Richard Edwards, added, "We have concerns about Dr. Maxwell as well. In pretrial interviews with Dr. Maxwell and his wife, we learned that Bobby Medford sent Capt. Tracy Bridges down to Henderson County twice to take care of a traffic ticket issued to Mrs. Maxwell. The prosecution considered including ticket fixing in our case, but decided it was relatively minor when weighed against the other issues we were addressing."

This mention recalled to mind the taped bragging of Medford confederate Homer Honeycutt to a police officer, "I fix more tickets than you write!"

Lindsay countered that Mrs. Maxwell had been out of town when Bridges made his forays, and was in a treatment facility "out west." Lindsay said that Maxwell's attorney told him that the traffic charges were dropped when the Henderson court was informed that she had voluntarily entered treatment.

In the end, the judge ruled that Medford would be permitted to undergo the scheduled procedure and convalesce for two weeks before being remanded to federal prison on October 28, 2008.

Other prison sentences included:

Guy Penland—five years

Johnny Harrison—two and a half years

Butch Davis—three years

Jerry Pennington—63 months, reduced to 30

Tracy Bridges—30 months, reduced to six months community confinement

Jackie Shepherd—two years probation and just over $1 million in forfeiture

Imran Alam—21 months, reduced to five months community confinement

Demetre Theodossis—one month, $4.1 million forfeiture of back taxes and gaming receipts

Charles McBennett, Sr.—two years

Jim Lindsey—five months

Irwin Keith Comer—two years probation

Kerry Lee Comer—two years probation

Joseph Wayne Vinesett—two years probation

Afterword

Considering that a one-time possession of cocaine can net a twenty-five year mandatory minimum, the punishment meted out for Medford's crimes seems somewhat mild. This was a powerful public official who aided and abetted crimes worth hundreds of millions of dollars, conspired to obstruct justice, reduced respect for the law, and stole directly from taxpayers..

Beyond that, the crimes he committed and permitted led directly to the impoverishment of families of untold numbers of addicted gamblers. Uncountable lives were wrecked, including those of spouses and children. The schemes punished store owners who refused to run illegal gaming and thereby lost business to their crooked competitors. Add to that the inmates who died or suffered abuse under his administration of the county's detention center. Anyone who imagines that the costs were only borne by a handful of operators who made pay-offs is missing the bigger story.

Federal sentencing guidelines as calculated by Ellis indicated thirty years as a minimum for Medford's conviction on each of eight charges. Ellis said he ruled for the downward variance based on the ex-sheriff's clean criminal history and record of service, perhaps abetted by consideration for his age and poor health.

This sidesteps the reality that Medford was only prosecuted for a portion of his probable criminal conduct and that the gambling racket exposed in court is by no means a comprehensive account of all of the various gaming enterprises that were presumably protected under his administration. Numerous other violations were mentioned in passing during the trial including payroll fraud, misuse of county vehicles, traffic ticket fixing and alleged prescription drug abuse.

An official criminal history only includes convictions, but surely reputation counts for something. Only a fool or a friend could suggest that the trial covered all of his crimes in a chain of county-wide, even regional, corruption that extends backward sixty or more years.

In addition, there are the outstanding questions about Medford's evidence locker: $217,000, hundreds of guns, and drugs from more than 1,300 cases—all gone missing. Perhaps North Carolina will still move forward on those matters, since they are state-level crimes.

I'm not holding my breath.

What emerges even more clearly for me, in my engagement with this matter is what a large debt we owe to any reporters who take on public corruption stories. I don't say this by way of self-aggrandizement, but to tell you that from my personal experience it is a largely thankless pursuit. Reporting pays poorly (less than two-thirds the state's median income, and this for experienced professionals), it is arguably dangerous, definitely tedious and resists any attempt to confine it to regular work hours. Most publishers don't want to foot the bills or take any chances on legal repercussions, as I learned first-hand. Many editors don't want to spend hours on hard stories. Perhaps most advertisers prefer to park their images and names beside happier news, and it may well be that most readers don't give a damn.

For my part, investigating Medford's department was extracurricular. I was the managing editor, then senior writer for *Mountain Xpress*, and covered the matters related in this book in my spare time. The book itself was written in the year after I left the paper, and all of the time I spent in court was my own.

I was never paid for the investigations while employed by *Mountain Xpress*, insofar as I also did all of the other work expected of me—editing, beat reporting, garden columns and editing, book and theater reviews as well as feature stories—and produced as much published work as any two other writers at the paper. Then I had to wrestle editors to the mat to get a little of my "weekend hobby" investigative material into print.

I don't mean to suggest that the paper had any obligation to indulge my proclivities. They had every right to decide what constitutes meaningful content for their readers and advertisers. But it sure as hell seems like *somebody* owed it to the community to expose our crooked sheriff and the racket that ate some poor folks alive, created unfair competition for store owners who eschewed gambling, and abetted untold other criminal activity in the region.

Who, for instance, owns those missing guns today? And who have they gunned down?

The consistent failure of journalism to get to the heart of corruption and official lies yields up debacles like the war in Iraq and the sub-prime mortgage meltdown as surely as it enables a sheriff engaged in widespread criminal activity to head up a law enforcement office for many years after such behavior comes to light. Had Asheville's daily paper and sole TV station been willing to explore and expose Medford's corruption when Brian Sarzynski and I wrote about it in 2002, Medford's criminal career could have been substantially shortened.

We worked for an "alternative" paper that wasn't accorded much respect in official circles, even when we were right. (And I would challenge anyone to point out when we were ever wrong.)

Weeks before my first major story went to press in 2003, I contacted WLOS TV 13, in Asheville, and offered a producer the chance to break the story simultaneously. She declined, saying that they couldn't participate in the release unless they were part of the investigation from the beginning.

I said, "Fair enough. But there will be other stories. How much advance notice should I give you, how much time do you need?"

"On a story this big? I could put a reporter on it for half a day."

I had just spent ten months investigating obstruction of justice by the sheriff and either the D.A. or the SBI and the TV station thought it might be worth half a day?

Nuff said.

But the media is merely the "fourth estate" and its power is only that of shining a strong light. Elected and appointed government officials were well aware of the broad outline of Medford's criminal behavior for many years, not to mention that of his predecessors in the Buncombe County Sheriff's Department. I personally and repeatedly conveyed information about Medford's criminal actions to: N.C. Attorney General Roy Cooper and District Attorney Ron Moore (beginning in 2002); the Buncombe County Board of Commissioners (beginning in 2004); Ron Kaylor of Alcohol Law Enforcement, U.S. Attorney Gretchen Shappert and Asheville Police Chief Bill Hogan (beginning in 2005). At least dozens of Buncombe County deputies were personally exposed to Medford's corruption.

Brian Sarzynski had reported on questionable conduct in Medford's department even before we exposed his obstruction of justice in October 2002. Why was Medford permitted to continue his criminal career for so long?

Furthermore, I believe that Bobby Medford's generous treatment by the court reflects more of the bias toward wealth that I reported in connection with Marvis Davidson's death and possible settlement. The fact that Medford was permitted to stay out of prison long enough to have minor surgery to adjust a pain relief device may be humane, but is entirely predicated on his having enjoyed excellent insurance coverage in the first place. A poor, uninsured defendant wouldn't ever have been fitted with that appliance. With luck, he'd have been on pain medication and the bottle of pills might have accompanied him to prison. (Though not necessarily—if, for example, a "Bobby Medford" was running the place the way Medford ran the Buncombe jail.)

At least, at long last, despite the media failures and a well-placed syndicate of cronies, Bobby Lee Medford finally faced his day(s) in court. He may well spend the rest of his life in prison. Perhaps there is some justice after all.

Appendix A : Case Summary

1:07-cr-00122-TSE USA v. Medford et al
Date filed: 12/11/2007
Date of last filing: 08/04/2008

Bobby Lee Medford (1)
Office: Asheville   Filed: 12/11/2007
County: Buncombe   Terminated: Reopened:
Other Court Case: None

Count: 1   Citation: 18:1951.F   Offense Level: 4
INTERFERENCE WITH COMMERCE BY THREAT OR VIOLENCE
Count: 1s   Citation: 18:1951.F   Offense Level: 4
INTERFERENCE WITH COMMERCE BY THREAT OR VIOLENCE
Count: 2   Citation: 18:1349.F   Offense Level: 4
ATTEMPT AND CONSPIRACY TO COMMIT MAIL FRAUD
Count: 2s   Citation: 18:1349.F   Offense Level: 4
ATTEMPT AND CONSPIRACY TO COMMIT MAIL FRAUD
Count: 3s-7s Citation: 18:1341.F   Offense Level: 4
FRAUDS AND SWINDLES
Count: 8   Citation: 18:1956-9999.F   Offense Level: 4
MONEY LAUNDERING - FEDERAL STATUTES, OTHER
Count: 8s   Citation: 18:1956-4999.F   Offense Level: 4
MONEY LAUNDERING - FRAUD, OTHER
Count: 10   Citation: 18:1511.F   Offense Level: 4
INTIMIDATION OF WITNESSES, JURORS, ETC.
Count: 10s   Citation: 18:1511.F   Offense Level: 4
INTIMIDATION OF WITNESSES, JURORS, ETC.
Count: 11s   Citation: 18:371.F   Offense Level: 4
CONSPIRACY TO DEFRAUD THE UNITED STATES
Def Custody Status: Released

Defendant: Bobby Lee Medford represented by M. Victoria Jayne(Designation CJA Appointment)

Defendant: Bobby Lee Medford represented by Stephen P. Lindsay(Designation CJA Appointment)

•••

John David Harrison (2)
Office: Asheville   Filed: 12/11/2007
County: Buncombe   Terminated: Reopened:

Other Court Case: None

Count: 1   Citation: 18:1951.F   Offense Level: 4
INTERFERENCE WITH COMMERCE BY THREAT OR VIOLENCE
Count: 1s   Citation: 18:1951.F   Offense Level: 4
INTERFERENCE WITH COMMERCE BY THREAT OR VIOLENCE
Count: 2   Citation: 18:1349.F   Offense Level: 4
ATTEMPT AND CONSPIRACY TO COMMIT MAIL FRAUD
Count: 2s   Citation: 18:1349.F   Offense Level: 4
ATTEMPT AND CONSPIRACY TO COMMIT MAIL FRAUD
Count: 3   Citation: 18:1341.F   Offense Level: 4
FRAUDS AND SWINDLES
Count: 6   Citation: 18:1341.F   Offense Level: 4
FRAUDS AND SWINDLES
Count: 3s-7s Citation: 18:1341.F   Offense Level: 4
FRAUDS AND SWINDLES
Count: 8   Citation: 18:1956-9999.F   Offense Level: 4
MONEY LAUNDERING - FEDERAL STATUTES, OTHER
Count: 8s   Citation: 18:1956-4999.F   Offense Level: 4
MONEY LAUNDERING - FRAUD, OTHER
Count: 10   Citation: 18:1511.F   Offense Level: 4
INTIMIDATION OF WITNESSES, JURORS, ETC.
Count: 10s   Citation: 18:1511.F   Offense Level: 4
INTIMIDATION OF WITNESSES, JURORS, ETC.
Count: 11s   Citation: 18:371.F   Offense Level: 4
CONSPIRACY TO DEFRAUD THE UNITED STATES
Def Custody Status: Released

Defendant: John David Harrison   represented by William
Drummond McDowall, Jr(Designation Retained)

•••

Ronnie Eugene Davis (3)
Office: Asheville   Filed: 12/11/2007
County: Buncombe   Terminated: Reopened:
Other Court Case: None

Count: 1   Citation: 18:1951.F   Offense Level: 4
INTERFERENCE WITH COMMERCE BY THREAT OR VIOLENCE
Count: 1s   Citation: 18:1951.F   Offense Level: 4
INTERFERENCE WITH COMMERCE BY THREAT OR VIOLENCE
Count: 2   Citation: 18:1349.F   Offense Level: 4
ATTEMPT AND CONSPIRACY TO COMMIT MAIL FRAUD
Count: 2s   Citation: 18:1349.F   Offense Level: 4

ATTEMPT AND CONSPIRACY TO COMMIT MAIL FRAUD
Count: 7   Citation: 18:1341.F   Offense Level: 4
FRAUDS AND SWINDLES
Count: 3s-7s Citation: 18:1341.F   Offense Level: 4
FRAUDS AND SWINDLES
Count: 8   Citation: 18:1956-9999.F   Offense Level: 4
MONEY LAUNDERING - FEDERAL STATUTES, OTHER
Count: 8s   Citation: 18:1956-4999.F   Offense Level: 4
MONEY LAUNDERING - FRAUD, OTHER
Count: 9   Citation: 18:1001.F   Offense Level: 4
STATEMENTS OR ENTRIES GENERALLY
Count: 9s   Citation: 18:1001.F   Offense Level: 4
STATEMENTS OR ENTRIES GENERALLY
Count: 10   Citation: 18:1511.F   Offense Level: 4
INTIMIDATION OF WITNESSES, JURORS, ETC.
Count: 10s   Citation: 18:1511.F   Offense Level: 4
INTIMIDATION OF WITNESSES, JURORS, ETC.
Count: 11s   Citation: 18:371.F   Offense Level: 4
CONSPIRACY TO DEFRAUD THE UNITED STATES
Def Custody Status: Released

Defendant: Ronnie Eugene Davis   represented by Charles R. Brewer
Defendant: Ronnie Eugene Davis   represented by Albert M. Neal, Jr.(Designation Retained)

•••

Guy Kenneth Penland (4)
Office: Asheville   Filed: 12/11/2007
County: Buncombe   Terminated: Reopened:
Other Court Case: None

Count: 1   Citation: 18:1951.F   Offense Level: 4
INTERFERENCE WITH COMMERCE BY THREAT OR VIOLENCE
Count: 1s   Citation: 18:1951.F   Offense Level: 4
INTERFERENCE WITH COMMERCE BY THREAT OR VIOLENCE
Count: 2   Citation: 18:1349.F   Offense Level: 4
ATTEMPT AND CONSPIRACY TO COMMIT MAIL FRAUD
Count: 2s   Citation: 18:1349.F   Offense Level: 4
ATTEMPT AND CONSPIRACY TO COMMIT MAIL FRAUD
Count: 4-5   Citation: 18:1341.F   Offense Level: 4
FRAUDS AND SWINDLES
Count: 3s-7s Citation: 18:1341.F   Offense Level: 4
FRAUDS AND SWINDLES

Count: 8   Citation: 18:1956-9999.F   Offense Level: 4
MONEY LAUNDERING - FEDERAL STATUTES, OTHER
Count: 8s   Citation: 18:1956-4999.F   Offense Level: 4
MONEY LAUNDERING - FRAUD, OTHER
Count: 9   Citation: 18:1001.F   Offense Level: 4
  STATEMENTS OR ENTRIES GENERALLY
Count: 9s   Citation: 18:1001.F   Offense Level: 4
  STATEMENTS OR ENTRIES GENERALLY
Count: 10   Citation: 18:1511.F   Offense Level: 4
INTIMIDATION OF WITNESSES, JURORS, ETC.
Count: 10s   Citation: 18:1511.F   Offense Level: 4
INTIMIDATION OF WITNESSES, JURORS, ETC.
Count: 11s   Citation: 18:371.F   Offense Level: 4
CONSPIRACY TO DEFRAUD THE UNITED STATES
Def Custody Status: Released

Defendant: Guy Kenneth Penland   represented by Paul Louis
Bidwell(Designation Retained)

Appendix B : The Jurors
A
#8
Employed for twelve years in quality control in chemical plant.
Spouse a teaching assistant in Burke County.
#16
Employed for sixteen years as civil engineer—a NC Department of
Transportation inspector. Spouse an optometrists' assistant.
#25
Employed for seventeen years as cafeteria manager at public school.
Spouse in maintenance work. Lives 150 miles away.
#28
Employed for two-and-one-half years as carpenter. Spouse an
instructor in Henderson County (tapped as Foreperson).
#30
Retired—golfing, fishing, hunting. (Has never played golf in a
tournament for a political campaign.)
#31
Employed for one-and-one-half years as carpenter. Once won $60 on
a video poker machine. (Note: That is an illegal pay-out.)
#39
Employed for eight years as mechanic, previously installed
insulation. Spouse has degree in computer services.
#48
Retired school principal from Shelby. Spouse teacher in county
schools.
#51
Home-maker, former administrative assistant to vice president of a
company. Spouse a physician employed by State of North Carolina.
#53
Employed for eighteen years as sales representative for a refractory
company.
#55
Employed for six years as a project manager for a construction
company.
#58
Employed for thirty-four years by Kimberly-Clark, now retired.
Alternates
#13
Employed for nine years in maintenance department of company.
Has English degree.
#20
Employed for thirty-five years at Union Camp and International
Paper, now retired.

Index

About the author

Cecil Bothwell was elected to Asheville's City Council in 2009. He is an investigative reporter and biographer based in Asheville, North Carolina. He has received national awards from the Association of Alternative Newsweeklies and the Society of Professional Journalists for investigative reporting, criticism and humorous commentary. He is former news editor of *Asheville City Paper*, former managing editor of Asheville's *Mountain Xpress* and founding editor of the Warren Wilson College environmental journal *Heartstone*, he served for several years as a member of the national editorial board of the Association of Alternative Newsweeklies and currently serves on the boards of two international educational nonprofit organizations working in Latin America. His weekly radio and print journal, *Duck Soup: Essays on the Submerging Culture*, remained in syndication for ten years.

He blogs at: http://cecilbothwell.com

Made in United States
North Haven, CT
25 September 2022

24562865R00183